CW00688585

Hands-On Serverless Applications with Go

Build real-world, production-ready applications
with AWS Lambda

Mohamed Labouardy

BIRMINGHAM - MUMBAI

Hands-On Serverless Applications with Go

Copyright © 2018 Packt Publishing

All rights reserved. No part of this book may be reproduced, stored in a retrieval system, or transmitted in any form or by any means, without the prior written permission of the publisher, except in the case of brief quotations embedded in critical articles or reviews.

Every effort has been made in the preparation of this book to ensure the accuracy of the information presented. However, the information contained in this book is sold without warranty, either express or implied. Neither the author, nor Packt Publishing or its dealers and distributors, will be held liable for any damages caused or alleged to have been caused directly or indirectly by this book.

Packt Publishing has endeavored to provide trademark information about all of the companies and products mentioned in this book by the appropriate use of capitals. However, Packt Publishing cannot guarantee the accuracy of this information.

Commissioning Editor: Richa Tripathi
Acquisition Editor: Denim Pinto
Content Development Editor: Pooja Parvatkar
Technical Editor: Subhalaxmi Nadar
Copy Editor: Safis Editing
Project Coordinator: Ulhas Kambali
Proofreader: Safis Editing
Indexer: Priyanka Dhadkee
Graphics: Tom Scaria
Production Coordinator: Deepika Naik

First published: August 2018

Production reference: 1280818

Published by Packt Publishing Ltd.
Livery Place
35 Livery Street
Birmingham
B3 2PB, UK.

ISBN 978-1-78913-461-2

www.packtpub.com

mapt.io

Mapt is an online digital library that gives you full access to over 5,000 books and videos, as well as industry leading tools to help you plan your personal development and advance your career. For more information, please visit our website.

Why subscribe?

- Spend less time learning and more time coding with practical eBooks and Videos from over 4,000 industry professionals
- Improve your learning with Skill Plans built especially for you
- Get a free eBook or video every month
- Mapt is fully searchable
- Copy and paste, print, and bookmark content

PacktPub.com

Did you know that Packt offers eBook versions of every book published, with PDF and ePub files available? You can upgrade to the eBook version at www.PacktPub.com and as a print book customer, you are entitled to a discount on the eBook copy. Get in touch with us at service@packtpub.com for more details.

At www.PacktPub.com, you can also read a collection of free technical articles, sign up for a range of free newsletters, and receive exclusive discounts and offers on Packt books and eBooks.

Contributors

About the author

Mohamed Labouardy is a software engineer/DevOps engineer and AWS Solution Architect. He is also a certified Scrum Master.

He is interested in serverless architecture, containers, distributed systems, Go, chaos engineering, and machine learning. He is a contributor to numerous open source projects such as DialogFlow, Jenkins, Docker, Nexus, and Telegraf. He has authored some open source projects related to DevOps as well.

He currently works at Foxintelligence as a lead DevOps engineer. He is also a technical content writer at several platforms and is a regular speaker at multiple international events and conferences, such as Nexus User Conference and AllDayDevOps.

You can find him on Twitter at `@mlabouardy`.

> I would like to thank everyone at Packt Publishing who has contributed to the realization of this book. I would also like to thank all my friends for their support and motivation. Special thanks to Rania Zyane for encouraging me to embrace this opportunity. Finally, I want to thank my parents for their love, good advice, and continuous support.

About the reviewers

Arpit Aggarwal is a programmer with over 7 years of industry experience in software analysis, design, effort estimation, development, troubleshooting, testing, and supporting web applications. He is among the top contributors of StackOverflow with more than 9,000 reputation and more than 100 badges in multiple areas such as Java, Scala, Go, Spring, Spring-MVC, GiT, Angular, Unit Testing, Web Services, and Docker, and has written many technical articles for Java Code Geeks, System Code Geeks, Web Code Geeks, and DZone.

Radomír Sohlich received the master's degree in Applied Informatics from Faculty of Applied Informatics at Tomas Bata University in Zlín. After that, he got a job in a start-up company as a software developer and worked on various projects, usually based on the Java platform. Currently, he continues a software developer career as a contractor for a large international company.

In 2015, he fell in love with Go and kept exploring the endless power and possibilities of the language. He is passionate about learning new approaches and technology and feels the same about sharing the knowledge with others.

Packt is searching for authors like you

If you're interested in becoming an author for Packt, please visit `authors.packtpub.com` and apply today. We have worked with thousands of developers and tech professionals, just like you, to help them share their insight with the global tech community. You can make a general application, apply for a specific hot topic that we are recruiting an author for, or submit your own idea.

Table of Contents

Preface

Serverless architecture is popular in the tech community due to AWS Lambda. Go is simple to learn, straightforward to work with, and easy to read for other developers, and now it's been heralded as a supported language for AWS Lambda. This book is your optimal guide to designing a serverless Go application and deploying it to Lambda.

This book starts with a quick introduction to the world of serverless architecture and its benefits, then delves into AWS Lambda through practical examples. You'll then learn how to design and build a production-ready application in Go using AWS serverless services with zero upfront infrastructure investment. The book will help you learn how to scale up serverless applications and handle distributed serverless systems in production. Then you will also learn to log and test your application.

Along the way, you'll also discover how to set up a CI/CD pipeline to automate the deployment process of your Lambda functions. Moreover, you will learn to troubleshoot and monitor your applications in near real time with services such as AWS CloudWatch and X-Ray. The book will also teach you how to scale up serverless applications and secure the access with AWS Cognito.

By the end of this book, you will have mastered designing, building, and deploying Go-based Lambda applications to production.

Who this book is for

This book is for Gophers who would like to learn about serverless architectures. Go programming knowledge is assumed. DevOps and solution architects who are interested in building serverless applications in Go will also benefit from this book.

What this book covers

Chapter 1, *Go Serverless*, gives a foundational explanation of what serverless is, how it works, whats its features are, why AWS Lambda pioneered serverless compute offerings, and why you should use Go for building serverless applications.

Chapter 2, *Getting Started with AWS Lambda*, supplies guidelines for setting up an AWS environment alongside the Go runtime and development environment.

Chapter 3, *Developing a Serverless Function with Lambda,* describes how to write your first Go-based Lambda function from scratch and how to invoke it manually from the console.

Chapter 4, *Setting Up API Endpoints with API Gateway,* illustrates how to trigger your Lambda function in response to incoming HTTP requests with API Gateway and build a unified event-driven RESTful API backed with serverless functions.

Chapter 5, *Managing Data Persistence with DynamoDB,* shows how to resolve Lambda functions stateless issue by using a DynamoDB datastore to manage data.

Chapter 6, *Deploying Your Serverless Application,* presents advanced AWS CLI commands and options that you can use while building serverless functions in AWS Lambda to save time. It also shows how to create and maintain multiple versions and releases of Lambda functions.

Chapter 7, *Implementing a CI/CD Pipeline,* shows how to set up a Continuous Integration and Continuous Deployment pipeline to automate the deployment process of Lambda functions from end to end.

Chapter 8, *Scaling Up Your Application,* covers how autoscaling works, how Lambda can handle traffic demands during peak service usage with no capacity planning or scheduled scaling, and how you can throttle and limit the number of executions using concurrency reservation.

Chapter 9, *Building the Frontend with S3,* illustrates how to build a single-page application with a REST backend backed by serverless functions.

Chapter 10, *Testing Your Serverless Application,* shows how test the serverless application locally using the AWS Serverless Application Model. It also covers Go unit testing and performance testing with third-party tools and shows how Lambda can be used to perform test harness.

Chapter 11, *Monitoring and Troubleshooting,* goes a step further in order to show you how to set up function-level monitoring with CloudWatch and how to debug and troubleshoot Lambda functions with AWS X-Ray to profile the application for abnormal behavior detection.

Chapter 12, *Securing Your Serverless Application,* is dedicated to the best practices and recommendations to follow in AWS Lambda to make your application resilient and secure according to the AWS Well-Architected Framework.

Chapter 13, *Designing Cost-Effective Applications,* covers also some tips for optimizing and reducing your serverless application billing and how to track the Lambda cost and usage with real-time alerts, before this becomes an issue.

Chapter 14, *Infrastructure as Code*, introduces tools such as Terraform and SAM to help you design and deploy your N-Tier serverless application in automated way, in order to avoid human errors and repeatable tasks.

To get the most out of this book

This book is written for anyone who work under Linux, Mac OS X, or Windows. You will need Go installed and an AWS account. You will also need Git in order to clone the repository with the source code provided with this book. Similarly, you are expected to have a basic knowledge of Go, the Bash command line, and some web programming skills. All prerequisites are described in the Chapter 2, *Getting Started with AWS Lambda*, with instructions to make sure you can follow this book with ease.

Last, keep in mind that this book is not intended to replace online resources, but rather aims to complement them. So you will obviously need internet access to complete your reading experience at some points, through provided links.

Download the example code files

You can download the example code files for this book from your account at www.packtpub.com. If you purchased this book elsewhere, you can visit www.packtpub.com/support and register to have the files emailed directly to you.

You can download the code files by following these steps:

1. Log in or register at www.packtpub.com.
2. Select the **SUPPORT** tab.
3. Click on **Code Downloads & Errata**.
4. Enter the name of the book in the **Search** box and follow the onscreen instructions.

Once the file is downloaded, please make sure that you unzip or extract the folder using the latest version of:

- WinRAR/7-Zip for Windows
- Zipeg/iZip/UnRarX for Mac
- 7-Zip/PeaZip for Linux

The code bundle for the book is also hosted on GitHub at https://github.com/PacktPublishing/Hands-On-Serverless-Applications-with-Go. In case there's an update to the code, it will be updated on the existing GitHub repository.

We also have other code bundles from our rich catalog of books and videos available at https://github.com/PacktPublishing/. Check them out!

Download the color images

We also provide a PDF file that has color images of the screenshots/diagrams used in this book. You can download it here: http://www.packtpub.com/sites/default/files/downloads/HandsOnServerlessApplicationswithGo_ColorImages.pdf.

Conventions used

In this book, you will find a number of text styles that distinguish between different kinds of information. Here are some examples of these styles and an explanation of their meaning.

Code words in text are shown as follows: "Within the workspace, create a main.go file using vim with the following content."

A block of code is set as follows:

```
package main
import "fmt"

func main(){
   fmt.Println("Welcome to 'Hands-On serverless Applications with Go'")
}
```

Any command-line input or output is written as follows:

```
pip install awscli
```

Bold: Indicates a new term, an important word, or words that you see onscreen. For example, words in menus or dialog boxes appear in the text like this. Here is an example: "On the **Source** page, select **GitHub** as the source provider."

 Warnings or important notes appear like this.

Tips and tricks appear like this.

Get in touch

Feedback from our readers is always welcome.

General feedback: Email feedback@packtpub.com and mention the book title in the subject of your message. If you have questions about any aspect of this book, please email us at questions@packtpub.com.

Errata: Although we have taken every care to ensure the accuracy of our content, mistakes do happen. If you have found a mistake in this book, we would be grateful if you would report this to us. Please visit www.packtpub.com/submit-errata, selecting your book, clicking on the Errata Submission Form link, and entering the details.

Piracy: If you come across any illegal copies of our works in any form on the Internet, we would be grateful if you would provide us with the location address or website name. Please contact us at copyright@packtpub.com with a link to the material.

If you are interested in becoming an author: If there is a topic that you have expertise in and you are interested in either writing or contributing to a book, please visit authors.packtpub.com.

Reviews

Please leave a review. Once you have read and used this book, why not leave a review on the site that you purchased it from? Potential readers can then see and use your unbiased opinion to make purchase decisions, we at Packt can understand what you think about our products, and our authors can see your feedback on their book. Thank you!

For more information about Packt, please visit packtpub.com.

1
Go Serverless

This chapter will give you a foundational understanding of what **serverless architecture** is, how it works, and what its features are. You'll learn how **AWS Lambda** is on a par with big players such as Google Cloud Functions and Microsoft Azure Functions. Then, you will discover AWS Lambda's different execution environments and its Go support. Moreover, we'll discuss the advantages of using Go as your programming language for building serverless applications.

The following topics will be covered in this chapter:

- Cloud-computing models—understanding what they are and what they can be used for.
- Pros and cons of serverless architecture.
- Why Go is a great fit for AWS Lambda.

The serverless paradigm

Cloud-based applications can be built on low-level infrastructure pieces or can use higher-level services that provide abstraction from the management, architecting, and scaling requirements of core infrastructure. In the following section, you will learn about the different cloud-computing models.

The cloud-computing evolution

Cloud providers offer their services according to four main models: IaaS, PaaS, CaaS, and FaaS. All the aforementioned models are just thousands of servers, disks, routers, and cables under the hood. They just add layers of abstraction on top to make management easier and increase the development velocity.

Infrastructure as a Service

Infrastructure as a Service (IaaS), sometimes abbreviated to IaaS, is the basic cloud-consumption model. It exposes an API built on top of a virtualized platform to access compute, storage, and network resources. It allows customers to scale out their application infinitely (no capacity planning).

In this model, the cloud provider abstracts the hardware and physical servers, and the cloud user is responsible for managing and maintaining the guest operating systems and applications on top of it.

AWS is the leader according to Gartner's Infrastructure as a Service Magic Quadrant. Irrespective of whether you're looking for content delivery, compute power, storage, or other service functionality, AWS is the most advantageous of the various available options when it comes to the IaaS cloud-computing model. It dominates the public cloud market, while Microsoft Azure is gradually catching up with to Amazon, followed by Google Cloud Platform and IBM Cloud.

Platform as a Service

Platform as a Service (PaaS) provides developers with a framework in which they can develop applications. It simplifies, speeds up, and lowers the costs associated with the process of developing, testing, and deploying applications while hiding all implementation details, such as server management, load balancers, and database configurations.

PaaS is built on top of IaaS and thus hides the underlying infrastructure and operating systems, to allow developers to focus on delivering business values and reduce operational overhead.

Among the first to launch PaaS was Heroku, in 2007; later, Google App Engine and AWS Elastic Beanstalk joined the fray.

Container as a Service

Container as a Service (CaaS) became popular with the release of Docker in 2013. It made it easy to build and deploy containerized applications on on-premise data centers or over the cloud.

Containers changed the unit of scale for DevOps and site reliability engineers. Instead of one dedicated VM per application, multiple containers can run on a single virtual machine, which allows better server utilization and reduces costs. Also, it brings developer and operation teams closer together by eliminating the "worked on my machine" joke. This transition to containers has allowed multiple companies to modernize their legacy applications and move them to cloud.

To achieve fault-tolerance, high-availability, and scalability, an orchestrations tool, such as Docker Swarm, Kubernetes, or Apache Mesos, was needed to manage containers in a cluster of nodes. As a result, CaaS was introduced to build, ship, and run containers quickly and efficiently. It also handles heavy tasks, such as cluster management, scaling, blue/green deployment, canary updates, and rollbacks.

The most popular CaaS platform in the market today is AWS as 57% of the Kubernetes workload is running on Amazon **Elastic Container Service (ECS)**, **Elastic Kubernetes Service (EKS)**, and AWS Fargate, followed by Docker Cloud, CloudFoundry, and Google Container Engine.

This model, CaaS, enables you to split your virtual machines further to achieve higher utilization and orchestrate containers across a cluster of machines, but the cloud user still needs to manage the life cycle of containers; as a solution to this, **Function as a Service (FaaS)** was introduced.

Function as a Service

The FaaS model allows developers to run code (called functions) without provisioning or maintaining a complex infrastructure. Cloud Providers deploy customer code to fully-managed, ephemeral, time-boxed containers that are live only during the invocation of the functions. Therefore, business can grow without customers having to worry about scaling or maintaining a complex infrastructure; this is called going serverless.

Amazon kicked off the serverless revolution with AWS Lambda in 2014, followed by Microsoft Azure Functions and Google Cloud Functions.

Serverless architecture

Serverless computing, or FaaS, is the fourth way to consume cloud computing. In this model, the responsibility for provisioning, maintaining, and patching servers is shifted from the customer to cloud providers. Developers can now focus on building new features and innovating, and pay only for the compute time that they consume.

Benefits of going serverless

There are a number of reasons why going serverless makes sense:

- **NoOps**: The server infrastructure is managed by the cloud provider, and this reduces the overhead and increases developer velocity. OS updates are taken care of and patching is done by the FaaS provider. This results in decreased time to market and faster software releases, and eliminates the need for a system administrator.
- **Autoscaling and high-availability**: Function as a unit of scale leads to small, loosely-coupled, and stateless components that, in the long run, lead to scalable applications. It is up to the service provider to decide how to use its infrastructure effectively to serve requests from the customers and horizontally scale functions-based on the load.
- **Cost-optimization**: You pay only for the compute time and resources (RAM, CPU, network, or invocation time) that you consume. You don't pay for idle resources. No work indicates no cost. If the billing period on a Lambda function, for example, is 100 milliseconds, then it could significantly reduce costs.
- **Polygot**: One benefit that the serverless approach brings to the table is that, as a programmer, you can choose between different language runtimes depending on your use case. One part of the application can be written in Java, another in Go, another in Python; it doesn't really matter as long as it gets the job done.

Drawbacks of going serverless

On the other hand, serverless computing is still in its infancy; hence, it is not suitable for all use cases and it does have its limitations:

- **Transparency**: The infrastructure is managed by the FaaS provider. This is in exchange for flexibility; you don't have full control of your application, you cannot access the underlying infrastructure, and you cannot switch between platform providers (vendor lock-in). In future, we expect increasing work toward the unification of FaaS; this will help avoid vendor lock-in and allow us to run serverless applications on different cloud providers or even on-premise.
- **Debugging**: Monitoring and debugging tools were built without serverless architecture in mind. Therefore, serverless functions are hard to debug and monitor. In addition, it's difficult to set up a local environment to test your functions before deployment (pre-integration testing). The good news is that tools will eventually arrive to improve observability in serverless environments, as serverless popularity is rising and multiple open source projects and frameworks have been created by the community and cloud providers (AWS X-Ray, Datadog, Dashbird, and Komiser).
- **Cold starts**: It takes some time to handle a first request by your function as the cloud provider needs to allocate proper resources (AWS Lambda needs to start a container) for your tasks. To avoid this situation, your function must remain in an active state.
- **Stateless**: Functions need to be stateless to provide the provisioning that enables serverless applications to be transparently scalable. Therefore, to persist data or manage sessions, you need to use an external database, such as DynamoDB or RDS, or an in-memory cache engine, such as Redis or Memcached.

Having stated all these limitations, these aspects will change in the future with an increasing number of vendors coming up with upgraded versions of their platforms.

Serverless cloud providers

There are multiple FaaS providers out there, but to keep it simple we'll compare only the biggest three:

- AWS Lambda
- Google Cloud Functions
- Microsoft Azure Functions

The following is a pictorial comparison:

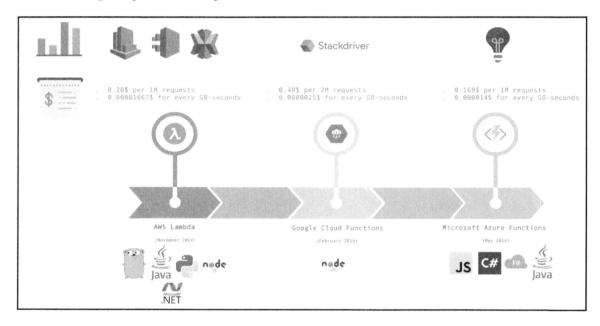

As shown in the preceding diagram, AWS Lambda is the most used, best-known, and the most mature solution in the serverless space today, and that's why upcoming chapters will be fully dedicated to AWS Lambda.

AWS Lambda

AWS Lambda is the center of the AWS serverless platform:

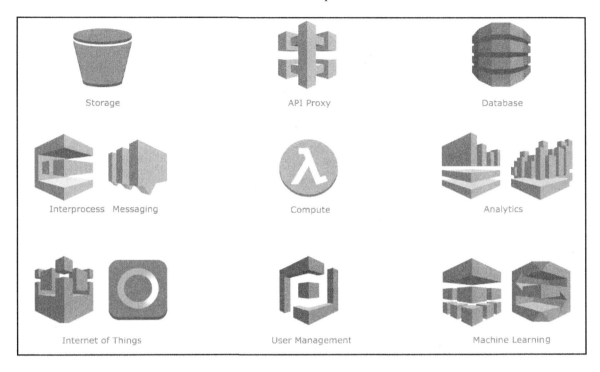

AWS Lambda was launched at re:Invent 2014. It was the first implementation of serverless computing where users could upload their code to Lambda. It performs operational and administrative activities on their behalf, including provisioning capacity, monitoring fleet health, applying security patches, deploying their code, and publishing realtime logs and metrics to Amazon CloudWatch.

Lambda follows the event-driven architecture. Your code is triggered in response to events and runs in parallel. Every trigger is processed individually. Moreover, you are charged only per execution, while with EC2 you are billed by the hour. Therefore, you benefit from autoscaling and fault-tolerance for your application with low cost and zero upfront infrastructure investment.

Source events

AWS Lambda runs your code in response to events. Your function will be invoked when these event sources detect events:

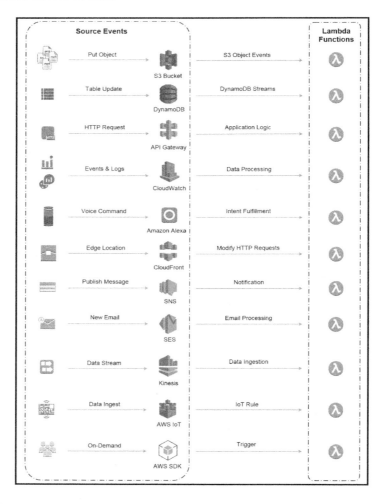

 Amazon is now supporting SQS as a source event for Lambda

Use cases

AWS Lambda can be used for endless application scenarios:

- **Web applications**: Instead of a maintaining a dedicated instance with a web server to host your static website, you can combine S3 and Lambda to benefit from scalability at a cheaper cost. An example of a serverless website is described in the following diagram:

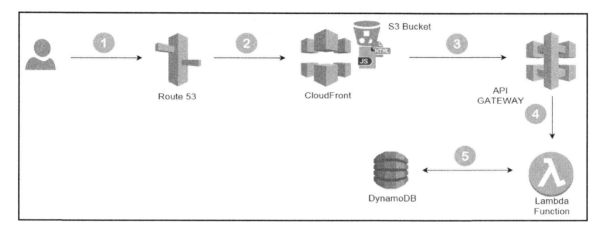

An alias record in **Route 53** points to a **CloudFront** distribution. The **CloudFront** distribution is built on top of an **S3 Bucket** where a static website is hosted. **CloudFront** reduces the response time to static assets (JavaScripts, CSS, fonts, and images), improves webpage load times, and mitigates distributed denial of service (DDoS) attacks. HTTP requests coming from the website then go through **API Gateway** HTTP endpoints that trigger the right **Lambda Function** to handle the application logic and persist data to a fully managed database service, such as **DynamoDB**.

- **Mobile and IoT**: A schematic for building a sensor application, which measures the temperature from a realtime sensor-connected device and sends an SMS alert if the temperature is out of range, can be given as follows:

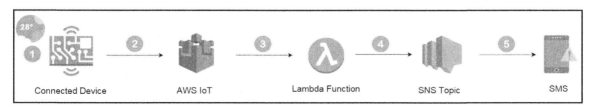

The **Connected Device** will ingest data to **AWS IoT**. **AWS IoT** rules will invoke a **Lambda Function** in order to analyze the data and publish a message to an **SNS Topic** in case of emergency. Once the message is published, Amazon SNS will attempt to deliver that message to every endpoint that is subscribed to the topic. In this case it will be an **SMS**.

- **Data ingestion:** Monitoring your logs and keeping an audit trail is mandatory, and you should be aware of any security breaches in your cloud infrastructure. The following diagram illustrates a realtime log-processing pipeline with Lambda:

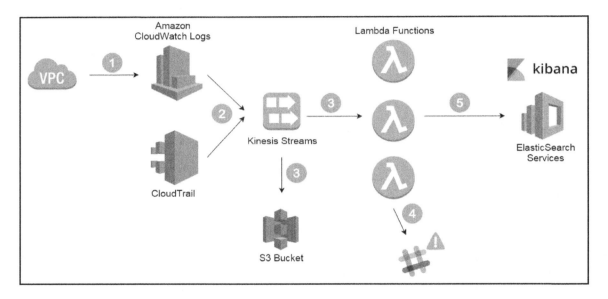

The VPC Flow Logs feature captures information about the IP traffic going to and from network interfaces in your VPC and ships the logs to Amazon CloudWatch Logs. AWS CloudTrail maintains records of all AWS API calls on your account. All logs are aggregated and streamed to AWS Kinesis Data Streams.

Kinesis triggers Lambda Functions, which analyze logs for events or patterns and send a notification to Slack or PagerDuty in the event of abnormal activity. Finally, Lambda posts the dataset to Amazon Elasticsearch with a pre-installed Kibana to visualize and analyze network traffic and logs with dynamic and interactive dashboards. This is done for long-term retention and to archive the logs, especially for organizations with compliance programs. Kinesis will store logs in S3 bucket for backup. The bucket can be configured with a life cycle policy to archive unused logs to Glacier.

- **Scheduling tasks**: Scheduled tasks and events are a perfect fit for Lambda. Instead of keeping an instance up and running 24/7, you can use Lambda to create backups, generate reports, and execute cron-jobs. The following schematic diagram describes how to use AWS Lambda to perform a post-processing job:

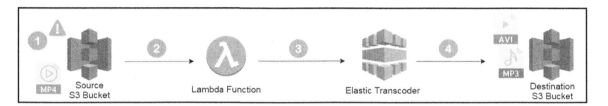

When a video arrives at an S3 bucket, an event will trigger a Lambda Function, which will pass the video filename and path to an Elastic Transcoder pipeline to perform video transcoding, generate multiple video formats (`.avi`, `.h264`, `.webm`, `.mp3`, and so on), and store the results in an S3 bucket.

- **Chatbots and voice assistants:** You can use a **Natural Language Understanding (NLU)** or **Automatic Speech Recognition (ASR)** service, such as Amazon Lex, to build application bots that can trigger Lambda Functions for intent fulfillment in response to voice commands or text. The following diagram describes a use case for building a personal assistant with Lambda:

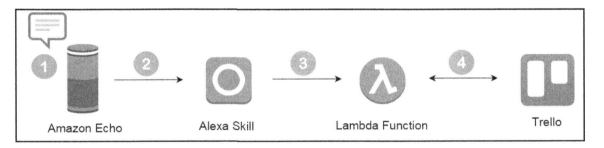

A user can ask **Amazon Echo** about its to-do list. Echo will intercept the user's voice command and pass it to a custom **Alexa Skill**, which will carry out speech recognition and transform the user's voice commands into intents, which will trigger a **Lambda Function** that in turn will query **Trello** API to fetch a list of tasks for today.

Due to Lambda's limitation in terms of memory, CPU, and timeout execution, it's not suited for long-running workflows and other massive workloads.

Go serverless

AWS announced its support for Go as the language for AWS Lambda in January 2018. There were already some open source frameworks and libraries with which to shim Go applications that used Node.js (Apex serverless Framework), but now Go is officially supported and added to list of programming languages that you can use to write your Lambda Functions:

- Go
- Node.js
- Java
- Python
- .NET

But which language should we use to write efficient Lambda Functions? One of the reasons to go serverless is being a polygot. Regardless of the language you choose, there is a common pattern to writing code for a Lambda Function. Meanwhile, you need to pay extra attention to performance and cold starts. That's where Go comes into play. The following diagram highlights the main advantages of using Go for serverless applications in AWS Lambda:

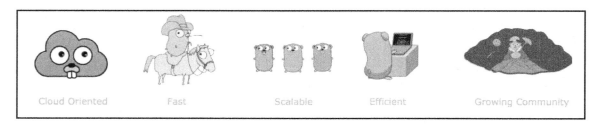

- **Cloud-oriented**: It was designed by Google primarily for the cloud with scalability in mind, and to reduce the amount of build time. Go is a solid language for distributed systems and infrastructure tools. Docker, Kubernetes, Terraform, etcd, Prometheus, and many orchestration, provisioning, and monitoring tools are built using Go.
- **Fast**: Go complies into a single binary. Therefore, you provide a precompiled Go binary to AWS Lambda. AWS does not compile the Go source files for you and this has certain consequences, such as Fast cold-boot time. Lambda doesn't need to set up a runtime environment; Java, on the other hand, requires spinning up a JVM instance to make your function hot. Go has a clean syntax and clear language specifications. This delivers an easy language for developers to learn and shows good results quickly while producing maintainable code.
- **Scalable**: Go has built-in concurrency with goroutines instead of threads. They consume almost 2 Kb memory from the heap and work faster than threads; hence, you can spin up millions of goroutine at any time. For software development, there is no need for a framework; the Golang community has built many tools that are natively supported by Go's language core:
    - Go's error-handling is elegant.
    - Lightweight framework for unit testing.
    - Solid standard library—HTTP protocol support out of the box.
    - Common data type and structure supported—maps, array, structs, and so on.
- **Efficient**: It involves efficient execution and compilation. Go is a compiled language; it compiles into a single binary. It uses static linking to combine all dependencies and modules into one single binary file. Also, its faster compilation speed allows for rapid feedback. Speedy development saves time and money; thus, this is certainly the most significant advantage for someone with a tight budget. Moreover, it provides efficient memory utilization with garbage collector.

- **Growing community**: The following screenshot shows the rising popularity and usage (as observed in the StackOverflow Survey 2017) for the most loved, dreaded, and wanted programming languages:

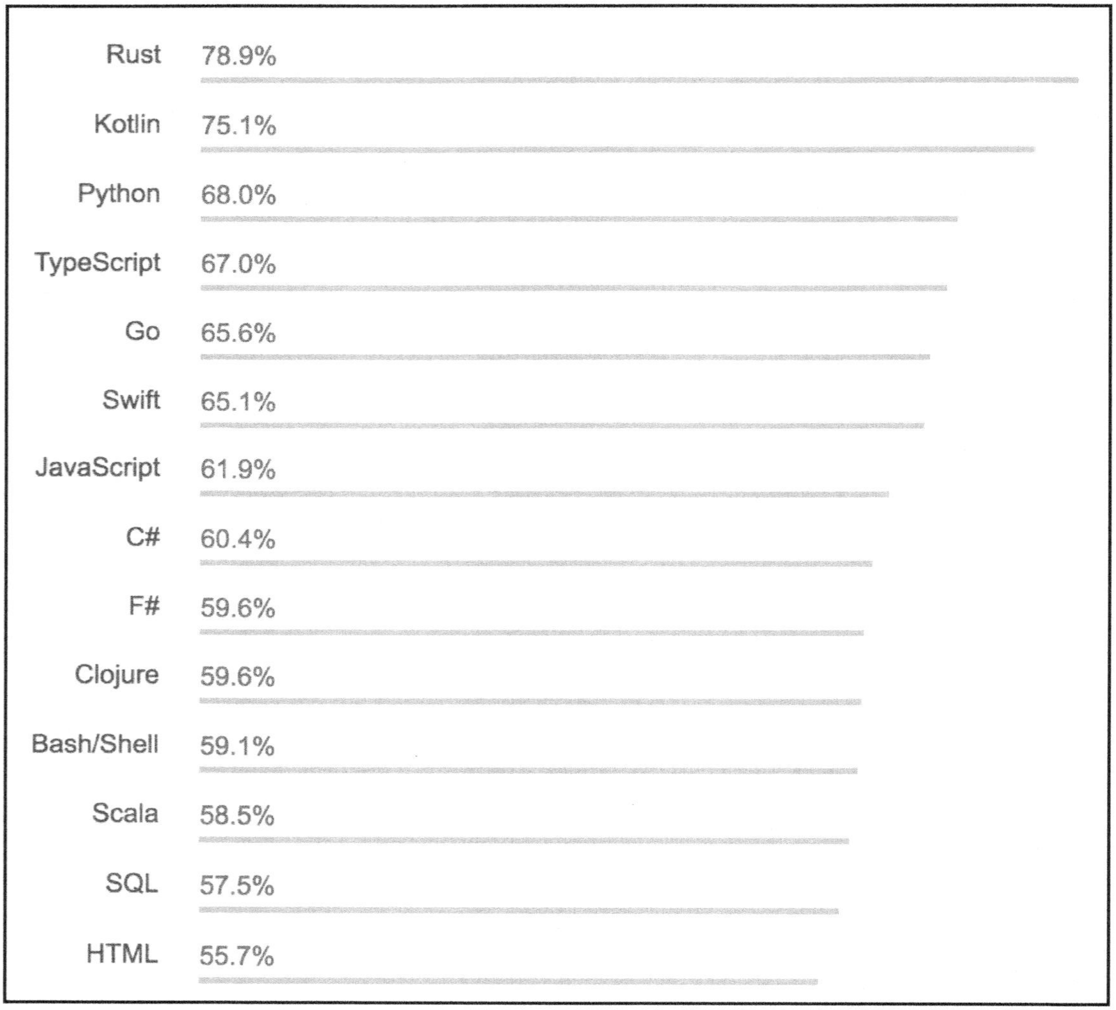

Language	Percentage
Rust	78.9%
Kotlin	75.1%
Python	68.0%
TypeScript	67.0%
Go	65.6%
Swift	65.1%
JavaScript	61.9%
C#	60.4%
F#	59.6%
Clojure	59.6%
Bash/Shell	59.1%
Scala	58.5%
SQL	57.5%
HTML	55.7%

In addition, Go is backed by Google and has a large, growing ecosystem and numerous contributors to the language on GitHub, and great IDE support (IntelliJ, VSCode, Atom, GoGland) and debugging.

Summary

AWS Lambda is the first successful implementation of serverless computing or FaaS. It gives users freedom from managing servers, increases development velocity, decreases system complexity, and enables small business to go big with zero upfront infrastructure investment.

Go support for AWS Lambda provides significant cost-saving and performance benefits for those running their business on Lambda. So If you are looking for a modern, fast, safe, and easy language, Go is the one for you.

In the next chapter, you will get started with AWS Lambda Console and set up your Golang development environment.

Questions

1. What are the advantages of using the serverless approach?
2. What makes Lambda a time-saving approach?
3. How does serverless architecture enable microservices?
4. What is the maximum time limit for an AWS Lambda function
5. Which of the following are supported event-sources for AWS Lambda?
    - Amazon Kinesis Data Streams
    - Amazon RDS
    - AWS CodeCommit
    - AWS CloudFormation
6. Explain what a goroutine is in Go. How can you stop goroutines?
7. What's Lambda@Edge in AWS?
8. What's the difference between Function as a Service and Platform as a Service?
9. What's an AWS Lambda cold start?
10. Can AWS Lambda functions be stateless or stateful?

Getting Started with AWS Lambda

2

This chapter supplies guidelines for setting up an AWS environment alongside Go runtime and development environments. You'll be introduced to the powerful AWS CLI, which will make deploying serverless applications more efficient and increase your productivity immensely.

In addition, you will be given a set of tips and recommendations on how to choose your Go **Integrated Development Environment (IDE)**.

Technical requirements

Before proceeding with the installation and configuration of the AWS and Go environments, it is recommended that you follow along with this chapter with on a laptop (Windows, Linux, or macOS X) with Python 2 version 2.6.5+ or Python 3 version 3.3+ preinstalled and an AWS account set up so you can easily execute the given commands. The code bundle for this chapter is hosted on GitHub at `https://github.com/PacktPublishing/Hands-On-serverless-Applications-with-Go`.

Setting up the AWS environment

This section will walk you through how to install and configure the AWS command line. The CLI is a solid and mandatory tool and it will be covered in upcoming chapters; it will save us substantial time by automating the deployment and configuration of Lambda functions and other AWS services.

The AWS command line

The AWS CLI is a powerful tool for managing your AWS services and resources from a terminal session. It was built on top of the AWS API, and hence everything that can be done through the AWS Management Console can be done with the CLI; this makes it a handy tool that can be used to automate and control your AWS infrastructure through scripts. Later chapters will provide information on the use of the CLI to manage Lambda functions and create other AWS services around Lambda.

Let's go through the installation process for the AWS CLI; you can find information on its configuration and testing in the *AWS Management Console* section.

Installing the AWS CLI

To get started, open a new terminal session and then use the `pip` Python package manager to install the latest stable release of `awscli`:

```
pip install awscli
```

If you have the CLI installed, it's recommended you upgrade to the latest version for security purposes:

```
pip install --upgrade awscli
```

 Windows users can also use MSI Installer (https://s3.amazonaws.com/aws-cli/AWSCLI64.msi or https://s3.amazonaws.com/aws-cli/AWSCLI32.msi), which doesn't require Python to be installed.

Once installed, you need to add the AWS binary path to the PATH environment variable as follows:

- For Windows, press the Windows key and type **Environment Variables**. In the **Environment Variables** window, highlight the PATH variable in the **System variables** section. Edit it and add a path by placing a semicolon right after the last path, enter the complete path to the folder where the CLI binary is installed.
- For Linux, Mac, or any Unix system, open your shell's profile script (`.bash_profile`, `.profile`, or `.bash_login`) and add the following line to the end of the file:

```
export PATH=~/.local/bin:$PATH
```

Finally, load the profile into your current session:

```
source ~/.bash_profile
```

Verify that the CLI is correctly installed by opening a new terminal session and typing the following command:

```
aws --version
```

You should be able to see the AWS CLI version; in my case, 1.14.60 is installed:

```
[serverless:~ mlabouardy$ aws --version
aws-cli/1.14.60 Python/3.6.5 Darwin/17.3.0 botocore/1.9.13
serverless:~ mlabouardy$
```

Let's test it out and list Lambda functions in the Frankfurt region as an example:

```
aws lambda list-functions --region eu-central-1
```

The previous command will display the following output:

```
serverless:~ mlabouardy$ aws lambda list-functions --region eu-central-1
Unable to locate credentials. You can configure credentials by running "aws configure".
serverless:~ mlabouardy$
```

When using the CLI, you'll generally need your AWS credentials to authenticate with AWS services. There are multiple ways to configure AWS credentials:

- **Environment Credentials**: The AWS_ACCESS_KEY_ID and AWS_SECRET_KEY variables.

- **The Shared Credentials file**: The ~/.aws/credentials file.

- **IAM Roles**: If you're using the CLI in an EC2 instance, these remove the need to manage credential files in production.

In the next section, I will show you how to create a new user for CLI with the **AWS Identity and Access Management (IAM)** service.

AWS Management Console

IAM is a service that allows you to manage users, groups, and their level of access to AWS services.

It's strongly recommended that you do not use the AWS root account for any task except billing tasks, as it has the ultimate authority to create and delete IAM users, change billing, close the account, and perform all other actions on your AWS account. Hence, we will create a new IAM user and grant it the permissions it needs to access the right AWS resources following the *Principle of least privilege*. In this case, the user will have full access to AWS Lambda services:

1. Sign into AWS Management Console (`https://console.aws.amazon.com/console/home`) using your AWS email address and password.
2. Open the **IAM** console from the **Security, Identity & Compliance** section:

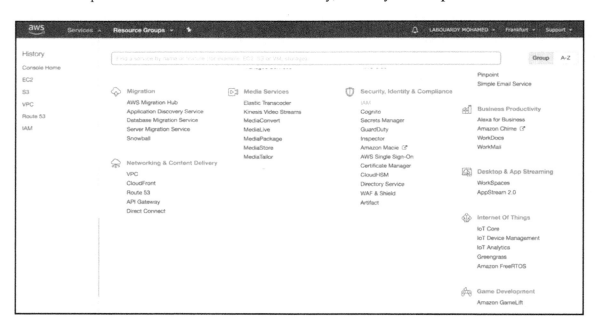

3. From the navigation pane, choose **Users** and click on the **Add user** button, then set a name for the user and select **Programmatic access** (also select **AWS Management Console** access if you want the same user to have access to the console):

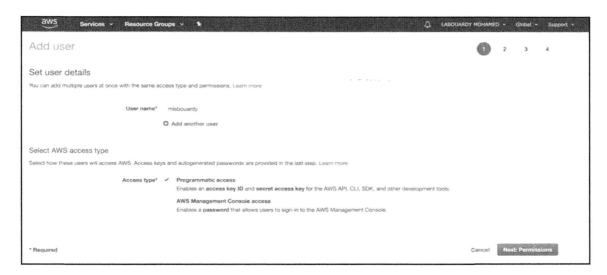

4. In the **Set permissions** section, assign the **AWSLambdaFullAccess** policy to the user:

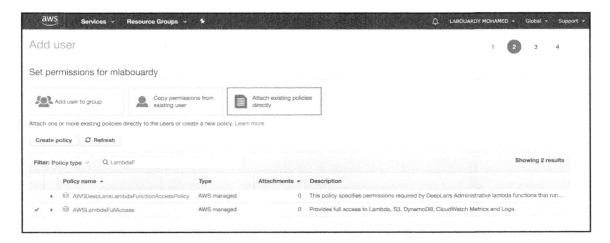

5. On the final page, you should see the user's AWS credentials:

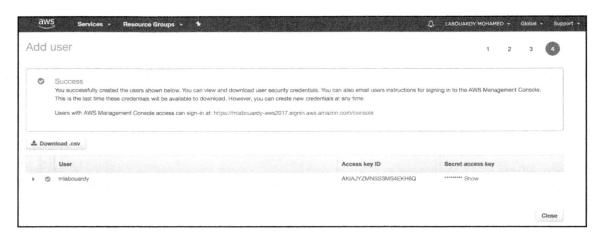

Make sure you save the access keys in a safe location as you won't be able to see them again:

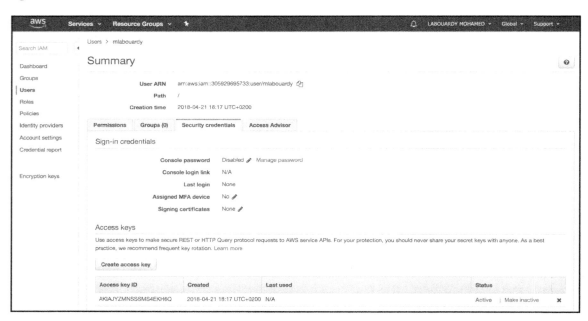

Configuration

Our IAM user has been created. Let's provide the access key and secret key along with a default region. This can be done using the `aws configure` command:

```
serverless:~ mlabouardy$ aws configure
AWS Access Key ID [None]: AKIAJYZMNSSSMS4EKH6Q
AWS Secret Access Key [None]: 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
Default region name [eu-central-1]:
Default output format [None]:
serverless:~ mlabouardy$
```

The CLI will store credentials specified in the preceding command in a local file under `~/.aws/credentials` (or in `%UserProfile%\.aws/credentials` on Windows) with the following content:

```
[default]
aws_access_key_id = AKIAJYZMNSSSMS4EKH6Q
aws_secret_access_key = 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
region=eu-central-1
```

Testing

That should be it; try out the following command and, if you have any Lambda functions, you should be able to see them listed:

```
serverless:~ mlabouardy$ aws lambda list-functions
{
    "Functions": [
        {
            "FunctionName": "Random",
            "FunctionArn": "arn:aws:lambda:eu-central-1:305929695733:function:Random",
            "Runtime": "nodejs6.10",
            "Role": "arn:aws:iam::305929695733:role/service-role/lambda-role-execute",
            "Handler": "index.getRandomNumber",
            "CodeSize": 281,
            "Description": "",
            "Timeout": 3,
            "MemorySize": 128,
            "LastModified": "2017-10-19T15:43:32.517+0000",
            "CodeSha256": "XxXme/lvk5GcoHIDnja0kFHLTK5SLqKJWez9xREujnQ=",
            "Version": "$LATEST",
            "VpcConfig": {
                "SubnetIds": [],
                "SecurityGroupIds": [],
                "VpcId": ""
            },
            "TracingConfig": {
                "Mode": "PassThrough"
            },
            "RevisionId": "687ba47f-d8b7-47f9-8825-268ad53b7637"
        }
    ]
}
serverless:~ mlabouardy$
```

The default output is JSON. You can change the output format for commands by adding the --output option (supported values: *json, table, text*). The following are the results shown in a table format:

```
[serverless:~ mlabouardy$ aws lambda list-functions --output table
-------------------------------------------------------------------------------
|                                ListFunctions                                |
+-----------------------------------------------------------------------------+
||                               Functions                                   ||
|+---------------+-----------------------------------------------------------+|
||  CodeSha256   | XxXme/1vk5GcoHIDnja0kFHLTK5SLqKJWez9xREujnQ=              ||
||  CodeSize     | 281                                                       ||
||  Description  |                                                           ||
||  FunctionArn  | arn:aws:lambda:eu-central-1:305929695733:function:Random  ||
||  FunctionName | Random                                                    ||
||  Handler      | index.getRandomNumber                                     ||
||  LastModified | 2017-10-19T15:43:32.517+0000                              ||
||  MemorySize   | 128                                                       ||
||  RevisionId   | 687ba47f-d8b7-47f9-8825-268ad53b7637                      ||
||  Role         | arn:aws:iam::305929695733:role/service-role/lambda-role-execute ||
||  Runtime      | nodejs6.10                                                ||
||  Timeout      | 3                                                         ||
||  Version      | $LATEST                                                   ||
|+---------------+-----------------------------------------------------------+|
|||                            TracingConfig                                |||
||+---------------------------------+---------------------------------------+||
|||  Mode                           | PassThrough                           |||
||+---------------------------------+---------------------------------------+||
|||                              VpcConfig                                   |||
||+------------------------------------------+------------------------------+||
|||  VpcId                                    |                              |||
||+------------------------------------------+------------------------------+||
serverless:~ mlabouardy$ @
```

Moreover, you can use the --query option to extract the output elements from this JSON document. For example, to output the function name attribute, the following command can be used:

```
aws lambda list-functions --query Functions[].FunctionName
```

The output should be similar to the following:

```
[serverless:~ mlabouardy$ aws lambda list-functions --query Functions[].FunctionName
[
    "Random"
]
serverless:~ mlabouardy$
```

A tool such as `jq` can be used to manipulate JSON. It enables us to filter, map, count, and perform other advanced JSON processes against the JSON returned by the CLI:

```
aws lambda list-functions | jq '.Functions[].FunctionName'
```

The Console will display the following output:

```
[serverless:~ mlabouardy$ aws lambda list-functions | jq '.Functions[].FunctionName'
"Random"
serverless:~ mlabouardy$
```

Setting up the Go environment

This section will walk you through how to download and install Go on multiple platforms, how to build a simple Hello World application, and how to use an IDE to speed up your Go development. Along the way, you will become familiar with the Go commands that you will need to write Lambda functions in Go.

The runtime environment

Download the appropriate package for your operating system and architecture from the Go download page (https://golang.org/dl/):

- **For macOS X:** Download the `goVersion.darwin.amd64.pkg` file and follow the installation prompt. You may need to restart any open Terminal sessions for the change to take effect.
- **For Windows**: Download the MSI installer and follow the wizard. The installer will set up environment variables for you.
- **For Linux**: Open a new terminal session and type the following commands (at the time of writing, the current version is 1.10):

  ```
  curl
  https://golang.org/doc/install?download=go1.10.1.linux-amd64.tar.gz
  -O /tmp/go1.10.tar.gz
  tar -C /usr/local -xzf /tmp/go1.10.tar.gz
  ```

The previous commands will download the latest Go package using `curl`. Then, it will use `tar` to unpack the package. Next, add the `/usr/local/go/bin` to the `PATH` environment variable by adding the following line to your shell's profile script:

```
export PATH=$PATH:/usr/local/go/bin
```

If you install Go in a custom directory, rather than /usr/local, you must set the GOROOT environment variable to point to the directory in which it was installed:

```
export GOROOT=PATH/go
export PATH=$PATH:$GOROOT/bin
```

Then you have to reload the user profile to apply the changes:

```
$ source ~/.bash_profile
```

Now that Go is properly installed and the paths are set for your machine, let's test it out. Create a workspace on which we will build our serverless applications throughout the book:

```
mkdir -p $HOME/go/src
```

The Go source code lives in a workspace; by default, it should be $HOME/go. If you'd like to use a different directory, you will need to set the GOPATH environment variable.

To validate that the Go workspace is configured correctly, you can run the go env command:

```
[serverless:~ mlabouardy$ go env
GOARCH="amd64"
GOBIN=""
GOCACHE="/Users/mlabouardy/Library/Caches/go-build"
GOEXE=""
GOHOSTARCH="amd64"
GOHOSTOS="darwin"
GOOS="darwin"
GOPATH="/Users/mlabouardy/go"
GORACE=""
GOROOT="/usr/local/go"
GOTMPDIR=""
GOTOOLDIR="/usr/local/go/pkg/tool/darwin_amd64"
GCCGO="gccgo"
CC="clang"
CXX="clang++"
CGO_ENABLED="1"
CGO_CFLAGS="-g -O2"
CGO_CPPFLAGS=""
CGO_CXXFLAGS="-g -O2"
CGO_FFLAGS="-g -O2"
CGO_LDFLAGS="-g -O2"
PKG_CONFIG="pkg-config"
GOGCCFLAGS="-fPIC -m64 -pthread -fno-caret-diagnostics -Qunused-arguments -fmessage-length=0 -fdebug-prefix-ma
p=/var/folders/z0/yhy5td5s1mz3_kh8n8361rl00000gn/T/go-build445470133=/tmp/go-build -gno-record-gcc-switches -f
no-common"
serverless:~ mlabouardy$ 
```

If the `GOPATH` variable is set, you're ready to go. Within the workspace, create a `main.go` file using `vim` with the following content:

```
package main
import "fmt"

func main(){
    fmt.Println("Welcome to 'Hands-On serverless Applications with Go'")
}
```

Compile the file with the following command:

```
go run main.go
```

The file will show `Welcome to 'Hands-On serverless Applications with Go'` if it runs successfully; this shows that Go is compiling files correctly.

Go is a compiled language, and hence you can generate a single binary for your application using the following command:

```
go build -o app main.go
```

If you want to build an executable for a specific OS and architecture, you can override the `GOOS` and `GOARCH` parameters:

```
GOOS=linux GOARCH=amd64 go build -o app main.go
```

Editing Go using the vim text editor is not optimal; therefore, in the next section, I will show you how to use VSCode as a Go editor to enhance your development productivity/experience.

The development environment

Having an IDE can increase your development velocity and save a lot of time, which could be spent debugging and searching for the correct syntax. Plus, you can navigate and search your Lambda function code with ease.

But which one should we use? There are many solutions out there; these solutions can be divided into three main categories:

- **IDEs**: GoLand, Eclipse, Komodo
- **Editors**: Atom, VSCode, Sublime Text
- **Cloud-based IDEs**: Cloud9, Codeanywhere, CodeEnvy

The Go ecosystem provides a variety of editors and IDEs; ensure you play around with them to find the one that suits you best.

I opted to go with Visual Studio Code (VS Code) as it meets all my criteria:

- Open Source
- Supports multiple languages
- Plugin-driven tool
- Great community and support

VSCode has strong support for Go development, including syntax-highlighting out of the box, built-in GIT integration, integration of all Go tools, and the Delve Debugger.

In addition to the native support of Go, the open source community has built some useful and powerful plugins that you can install from VSCode Marketplace:

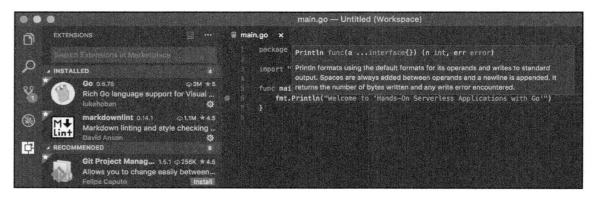

VSCode is also cross-platform, and hence you can use it with Mac, Linux, or Windows. With Visual Studio Code, you can extend functionalities with the array of available plugins that come with so many powerful and robust additions, such as the following:

- **Autocompletion**: As you type in a Go file, you can see IntelliSense providing you with suggested completions:

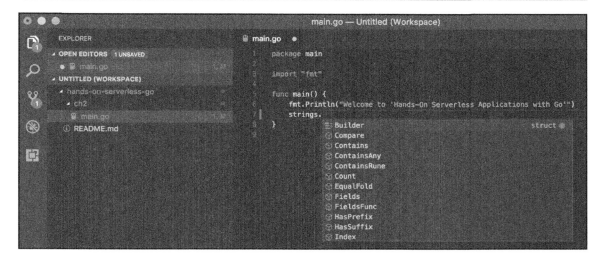

- **Signature help**: Hovering on any variable, function, or struct will give you information on that item, such as documentation, signature, expected input, and output parameters. For example, the following screenshot shows the information on `Println`, which was acquired from hovering on the `main.go` file:

- **Code formatting:** It automatically formats your Go source code on save, using the **gofmt** tool so your code becomes easier to write, read, and maintain.
- **Integrated debugger:** You can set breakpoints and conditional breakpoints, and view the stack trace and local and global variables in each frame.

- **Auto-import Go packages**: It automatically imports required Go packages on save.
- **Test runner**: It lets you run, stop, and restart unit tests as well as integration tests.

I'm looking forward to the stable release of GoLand by JetBrains: it looks like a very promising Go IDE and I'm excited to see where it goes.

And that's all it takes! You're ready to start building and deploying serverless applications in Go.

Summary

In this chapter, we learned how to install, configure, and use the AWS CLI. This tool will be very helpful when it comes to managing AWS services and automating the deployment of Lambda functions. Then, we covered how to create a user and generate AWS credentials from IAM with the least amount of privilege necessary. That way, if your access keys end up in the wrong hands, there is a limited capability to do harm. Also, we learned how to set up the Go environment, with a step-by-step installation of Go for multiple platforms (Windows, macOS X, and Linux) and compiled our first Hello World application in Go. Along the way, we covered the most important commands in Go, which will help you follow later chapters with ease.

In the next chapter, we will finally get our hands dirty and write our first Lambda function in Go.

Questions

1. Which format is not supported by the AWS CLI?
   - JSON
   - Table
   - XML
   - Text

2. Is it recommended to use the AWS root account for everyday interaction with AWS? If yes, why?
3. What environment variables do you need to set to use the AWS CLI?
4. How do you use the AWS CLI with named profiles?
5. Explain the GOPATH environment variable.
6. Which command-line command compiles a program in Go?
   - `go build`
   - `go run`
   - `go fmt`
   - `go doc`

7. What's the Go workspace?

3
Developing a Serverless Function with Lambda

In this chapter, we will finally learn how to write our very first Go-based Lambda function from scratch, followed by how to configure, deploy, and test a Lambda function manually from the AWS Lambda Console. Along the way, you will be given a set of tips on how to grant access to your function so that it can interact with other AWS services in a secure way.

We will be covering the following topics:

- Writing a Lambda function in Go
- Execution role
- Deployment package
- Event testing

Technical requirements

In order to follow along with this chapter, you will need to set up and configure your Go and AWS development environment as described in the previous chapter. Familiarity with Go is preferred but not required. The code bundle for this chapter is hosted on GitHub at https://github.com/PacktPublishing/Hands-On-Serverless-Applications-with-Go.

Writing a Lambda function in Go

Follow the steps in this section to create your first Lambda function in Go from scratch:

1. To write a Lambda function, we need to install some dependencies. Hence, open a new terminal session, and install the Go Lambda package using the following command:

```
go get github.com/aws/aws-lambda-go/lambda
```

2. Next, open your favorite Go IDE or editor; in my case, I will work with VS Code. Create a new project directory in your **GOPATH** and then paste the following content into a `main.go` file:

```
package main

import "github.com/aws/aws-lambda-go/lambda"

func handler() (string, error){
  return "Welcome to Serverless world", nil
}

func main() {
  lambda.Start(handler)
}
```

The previous code uses the `lambda.Start()` method to register an entry-point handler that contains the code that will be executed when a Lambda function is invoked. Each language supported by Lambda has its own requirements for how a function handler can be defined. For Golang, the handler signature must meet the following criteria:

- It must be a function
- It can have between 0 and 2 arguments
- It must return an error

3. Next, sign in to the AWS Management Console (`https://console.aws.amazon.com/console/home`) and choose **Lambda** from the **Compute** section:

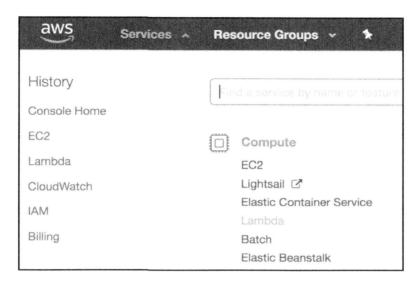

4. In the AWS Lambda Console, click on the **Create function** button and follow the wizard to create your first Lambda function:

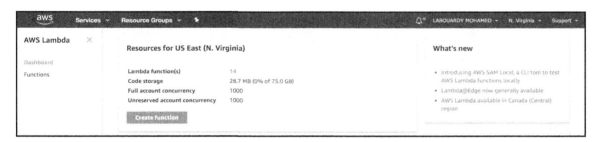

5. Select the **Author from Scratch** option, give your function a name, and then choose **Go 1.x** as the **Runtime** environment from the list of supported languages:

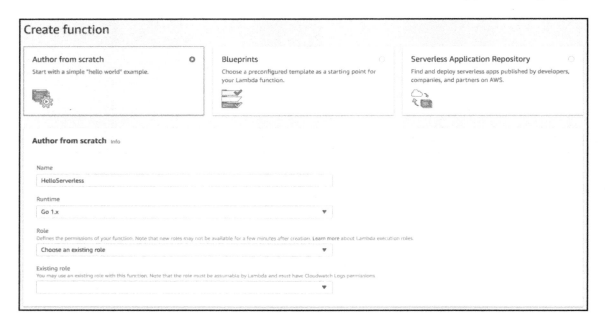

You must assign an IAM role (called an execution role) to your Lambda function. The IAM policies attached to that role define what AWS services your function code is authorized to interact with.

Execution role

1. Now that we have learned how to write our first Go Lambda function, let's create a new IAM role from Identity and Access Management (https://console.aws.amazon.com/iam/home) to grant the function access to AWS CloudWatch Logs:

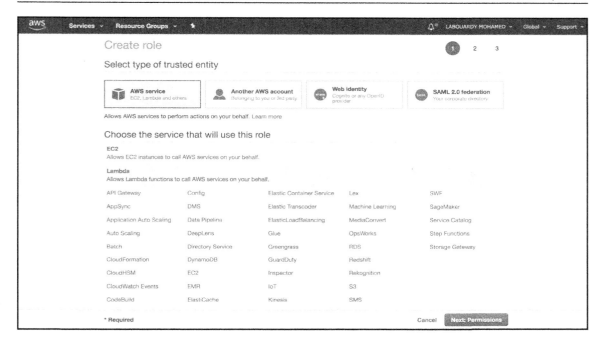

2. In the permissions page, you can either choose an existing AWS managed policy called **CloudWatchFullAccess** or (as shown in Step 3) create a least-privilege IAM role (the second option is recommended by AWS; a chapter dedicated to this will discuss security best practices for Lambda functions in depth):

3. Go ahead and click on the **Create policy** button, and create a policy by selecting the appropriate service (CloudWatch) from the visual editor:

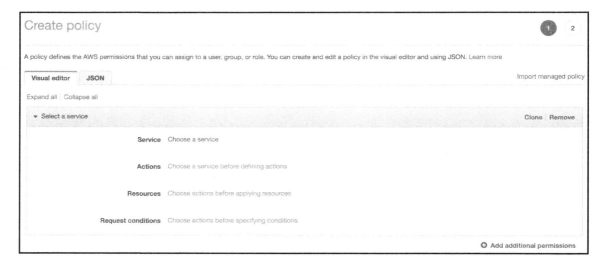

4. For readers familiar with the JSON format, a JSON policy document can be used instead in the **JSON** tab. The document must have one statement that grants permissions to create log groups and log streams, and to upload log events to AWS CloudWatch:

```
{
  "Version": "2012-10-17",
  "Statement": [
      {
        "Sid": "VisualEditor0",
        "Effect": "Allow",
        "Action": [
            "logs:CreateLogStream",
            "logs:CreateLogGroup",
            "logs:PutLogEvents"
        ],
        "Resource": "*"
      }
  ]
}
```

5. On the **Review policy** page, type a **Name** and a **Description** for the policy:

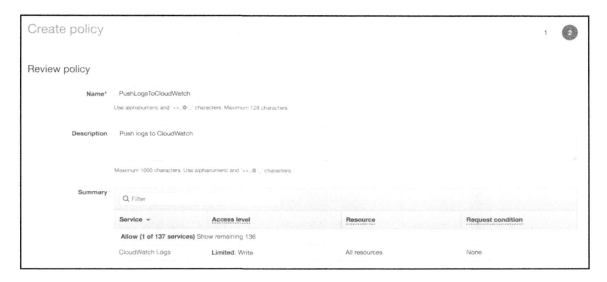

6. Go back to the **Create role** page and click on **Refresh**; you should see the policy that we created previously:

7. On the **Review** page, type a name for the role and choose **Create role**:

8. Now that our role is defined, head back to the Lambda form creation and select the IAM role (you might need to refresh the page for the changes to take effect) from the **Existing role** drop-down list. Then, click the **Create function** button:

Optionally, you can deploy a Lambda function using the AWS CLI. A more comprehensive discussion of this and its step-by-step process is reserved for Chapter 6, *Deploying Your Serverless Application*.

The Lambda console will display a success message in green, indicating that your function has been successfully created:

After we write, package, and create the Lambda function, we have various configuration options to set that define how the code should be executed within Lambda. As shown in the preceding screenshot, you can trigger the Lambda function by different AWS services (called triggers).

Leave the rest of the advanced settings unchanged (VPC, resource usage, versions, aliases, and concurrency) as they will be discussed in-depth in further chapters.

Because Go is a recently added language, the developers behind it haven't added the capability for an inline editor yet, so you must provide an executable binary in a ZIP file format or reference an S3 bucket and object key where you have uploaded the package:

Deployment package

In this section, we will see how to build a deployment package for the function and how to deploy it to the AWS Lambda console.

Uploading a ZIP file

As mentioned in Chapter 1, *Go Serverless*, Go is a compiled language. Therefore, you must generate an executable binary using the following Shell script:

```bash
#!/bin/bash

echo "Build the binary"
GOOS=linux GOARCH=amd64 go build -o main main.go

echo "Create a ZIP file"
zip deployment.zip main

echo "Cleaning up"
rm main
```

The Lambda runtime environment is based on an **Amazon Linux AMI**; therefore, the handler should be compiled for Linux (note the use of the GOOS flag).

For Windows users, it's recommended you to use the `build-lambda-zip` tool to create a working ZIP file for Lambda.

Execute the Shell script as follows:

```
[serverless:ch3 mlabouardy$ chmod +x build.sh
[serverless:ch3 mlabouardy$ ./build.sh
 Build the binary
 Create a zip file
   adding: main (deflated 65%)
 Cleaning up
[serverless:ch3 mlabouardy$ ls
 build.sh          deployment.zip   main.go          policy.json
 serverless:ch3 mlabouardy$
```

Now our ZIP file has been generated; you can now go back to the Lambda console and upload the ZIP file, making sure to update the **Handler** to **main** and save the results:

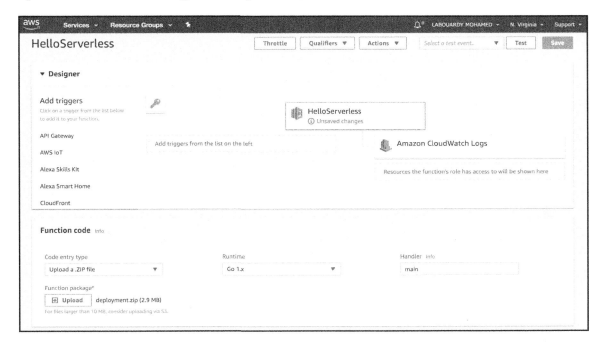

The **Handler** configuration property must match the name of the executable file. If you build (`go build -o NAME`) the binary with a different name, you must update the **Handler** property accordingly.

Uploading from Amazon S3

Another way to upload the deployment package to Lambda is by using an AWS S3 bucket to store the ZIP file. Under **Storage**, choose **S3** to open the Amazon S3 console:

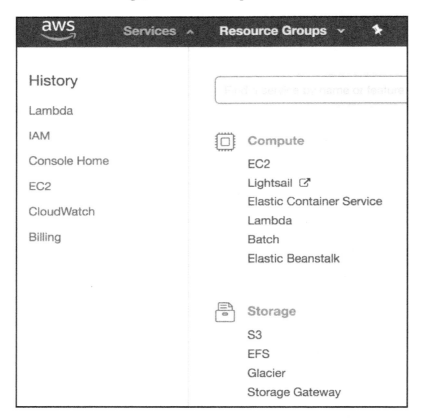

Before you can upload the ZIP to Amazon S3, you must create a new bucket in the same AWS region where you created the Lambda function, as described in the following screenshot:

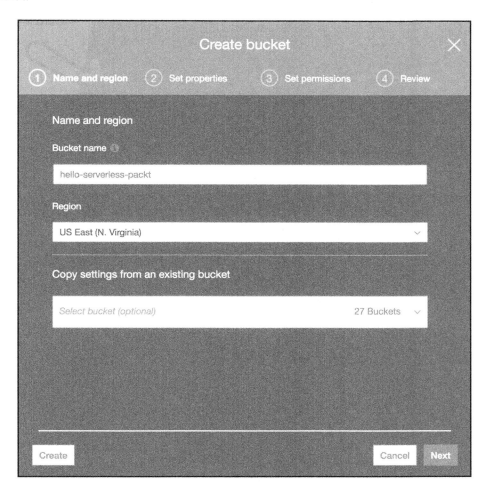

 S3 buckets have a global namespace. Hence, it must be globally unique across all existing bucket names in Amazon S3.

Now that you've created a bucket, drag and drop the ZIP file that you generated in the previous section into the destination bucket or use the **Upload** button:

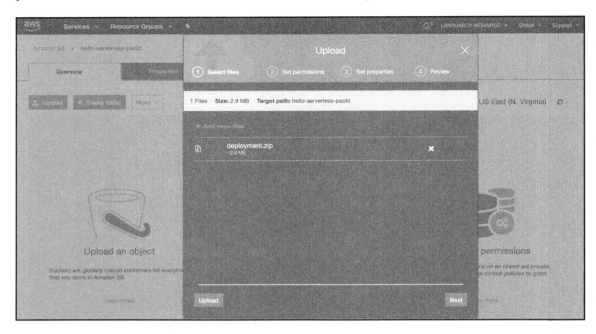

AWS CLI might be used to upload a deployment package to the S3 bucket as follows:

```
aws s3 cp deployment.zip s3://hello-serverless-packt
```

 Ensure that the `s3:PutObject` permission is granted to the IAM user to be able to upload an object using the AWS command line.

Once uploaded, select the ZIP file and copy the **Link** value to the clipboard:

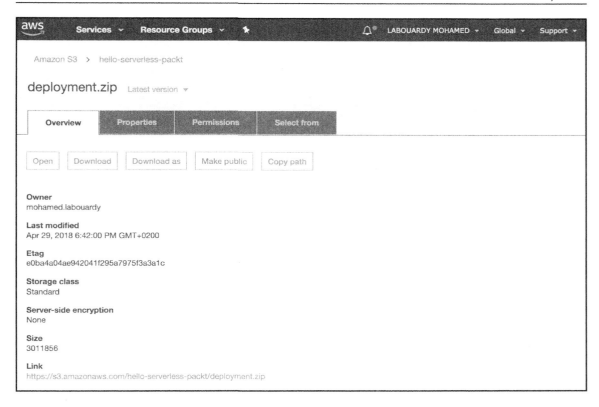

Go back to the Lambda Dashboard and select **Upload a file from Amazon S3** from the **Code entry type** drop-down list, then paste the path in the deployment package in S3:

Once saved, you're ready to test the Lambda function in the AWS Lambda Console.

Event testing

The following procedure will demonstrate how to invoke the Lambda function from the Console:

1. Now that the function has been deployed, let's invoke it manually using the sample event data by clicking on the **Test** button in the top right of the console.
2. Selecting **Configure test event** opens a new window that has a drop-down. The items in the drop-down are sample JSON event templates which are mocks for source events or triggers (recall Chapter 1, *Go Serverless*) that can be consumed by the Lambda in order to test its functionality:

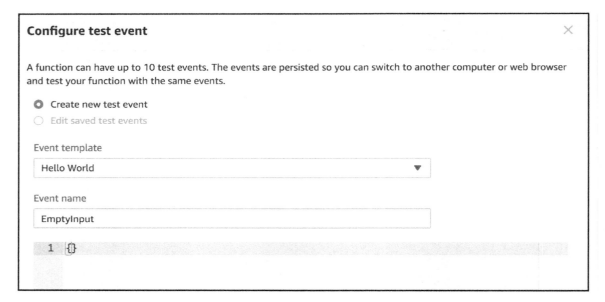

3. Retain the default **Hello World** option. Type an event name and provide an empty JSON object:

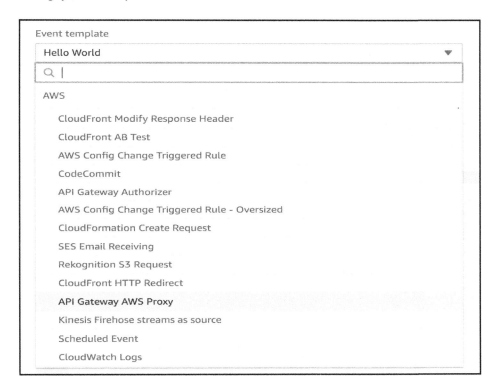

4. Choose **Create**. After it's been saved, you should see **EmptyInput** in the **Test** list:

5. Click on the **Test** button again. AWS Lambda will execute your function and display the following output:

In addition to the results returned by the function, we will be able to see **Welcome to Serverless world**, which is a global overview about the resource use and execution duration of the Lambda function, plus the logs written to CloudWatch by the Lambda function.

 Advanced monitoring with CloudWatch metrics and logging with CloudWatch logs and CloudTrail will be discussed in `Chapter 11`, *Monitoring and Troubleshooting*.

Congratulations! You have just set up and deployed your first Lambda function. The real power of Lambda comes in when you use triggers or source events with your Lambda function so that it executes based on events that happen. We will take a look at that in the next chapter.

Summary

In this chapter, we learned how to a write a Lambda function in Go from scratch. Then, we covered how to create an execution role for Lambda to generate event logs to AWS CloudWatch. We further learned how to test and invoke this function manually from the AWS Lambda Console.

In the next chapter, I will walk you through how to use triggers to invoke Lambda functions automatically and how to build an unified RESTful API on top using the AWS API Gateway to execute Lambda functions in response to HTTP requests.

Questions

1. What's the command-line command to create an IAM role for an AWS Lambda function?
2. What's the command-line command to create a new S3 bucket in the Virginia region (*us-east-1*) and upload a Lambda deployment package to it?
3. What are the Lambda package size limits?
   - 10 MB
   - 50 MB
   - 250 MB
4. AWS Lambda Console supports editing Go source code.
   - True
   - False
5. What's the underlying AWS Lambda execution environment?
   - Amazon Linux Image
   - Microsoft Windows Server
6. How are events represented in AWS Lambda?

4
Setting up API Endpoints with API Gateway

In the previous chapter, we learned how to build our first Lambda function with Go. We also learned how to invoke it manually from the console. To leverage the power of Lambda, in this chapter, we are going to learn how to trigger this Lambda function in response to incoming HTTP requests (event-driven architecture) using the AWS API Gateway service. At the end of this chapter, you will be familiar with API Gateway advanced topics such as resources, deployment stages, debugging, and much more.

We will be covering the following topics:

- Getting started with API Gateway
- Building a RESTful API

Technical requirements

This chapter is a follow-up of the previous one, and hence it's recommended to read the previous chapter first to follow this part with ease. In addition, basic knowledge of RESTful API design and practices is needed. The code bundle for this chapter is hosted on GitHub at `https://github.com/PacktPublishing/Hands-On-Serverless-Applications-with-Go`.

Getting started with API Gateway

API Gateway is an AWS serverless API proxy service that allows you to create a single and unified entry point for all of your Lambda functions. It proxies and routes the incoming HTTP requests to the appropriate Lambda function (mapping). From a server-side perspective, it's a facade or a wrapper that sits on top of Lambda functions. However, from a client's perspective, it's just a single monolithic application.

In addition to providing a single interface to the clients, and its scalability, API Gateway provides powerful features such as the following:

- **Caching**: You can cache endpoint responses, hence reducing the number of requests made to the Lambda functions (cost optimization) and enhancing the response time.
- **CORS configuration**: By default, the browsers deny access to resources from a different domain. This policy can be overridden by enabling **Cross Origin Resource Sharing** (**CORS**) in the API Gateway.

> CORS will be discussed in-depth in Chapter 9, *Building a Frontend with S3*, with a practical example.

- **Deployment stages/life cycle**: You can manage and maintain multiple API versions and environments (Sandbox, QA, staging, and production).
- **Monitoring**: Troubleshooting and debugging incoming requests and outgoing responses is simple and is done by enabling CloudWatch integration with API Gateway. It will push a stream of log events to AWS CloudWatch Logs and you can expose a set of metrics to CloudWatch, including:
    - Client-side errors, including 4XX and 5XX status codes
    - Total number of API requests in a given period
    - Endpoint response time (latency)
- **Visual editing**: You can describe your API resources and methods directly from the console without any coding or RESTful API knowledge.
- **Documentation**: You can generate API documentation for each version of your API with the ability to export/import and publish the documentation to a Swagger specification.
- **Security and authentication**: You can secure your RESTful API endpoints with IAM roles and policies. API Gateway can also act as a firewall against DDoS attacks and SQL/scripts injection. Moreover, rate limiting or throttling can be enforced at this level.

That's enough theory. In the next section, we will go through how to set up API Gateway to trigger our Lambda function each time an HTTP request is received.

> In addition to its support for AWS Lambda, API Gateway can be used to invoke other AWS Services (EC2, S3, Kinesis, CloudFront, and so on) or external HTTP endpoints in response to HTTP requests.

Setting up an API endpoint

The following section describes how to trigger a Lambda function using API Gateway:

1. To set up an API endpoint, sign in into the **AWS Management Console** (`https://console.aws.amazon.com/console/home`), navigate to the AWS Lambda Console, and select the Lambda function **HelloServerless** that we built in the previous chapter:

2. Search for **API Gateway** from the list of triggers available and click on it:

The list of available triggers may change depending on which AWS region you're using because AWS Lambda-supported source events are not available in all AWS regions.

3. At the bottom of the page, a **Configure triggers** section will be displayed, as shown in the following screenshot:

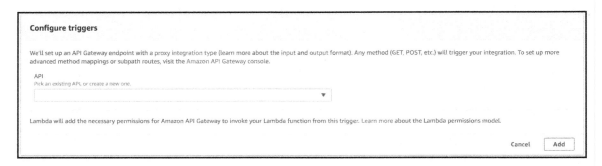

4. Create a new API, give it a name, set the deployment stage as `staging`, and make the API **open** to the public:

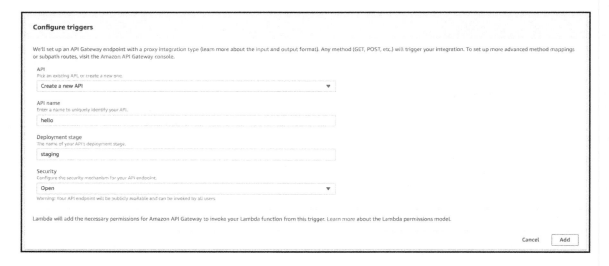

The form will have to be filled in with the following parameters:

- **API name**: A unique identifier of the API.
- **Deployment stage**: The API stage environment, which helps separate and maintain different API environments (dev, staging, production, and so on) and versions/releases (major, minor, beta, and so on). Plus, it's very handy if a Continuous Integration/Continuous Deployment pipeline is implemented.
- **Security**: It defines if the API endpoint will be public or private:
    - **Open**: Publicly accessible and can be invoked by everyone
    - **AWS IAM**: Will be invoked by users with granted IAM permissions
    - **Open with Access Key**: Requires an AWS access key to be invoked

5. Once the API is defined, the following section will be displayed:

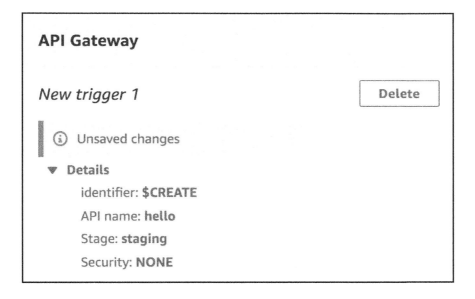

6. Click on the **Save** button at the top of the page to create the API Gateway trigger. Once saved, the API Gateway Invoke URL will be generated with the following format: `https://API_ID.execute-api.AWS_REGION.amazonaws.com/DEPLOYMENT_ STAGE/FUNCTION_NAME`, as shown in the following screenshot:

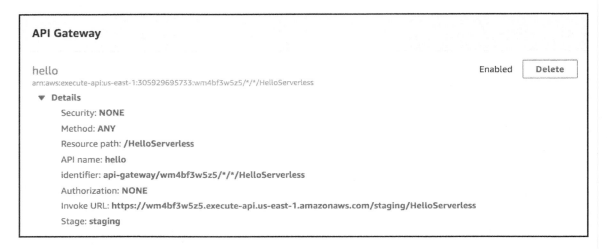

7. Open your favorite browser with the API **Invoke URL**; you should see a message like the one shown in the following screenshot:

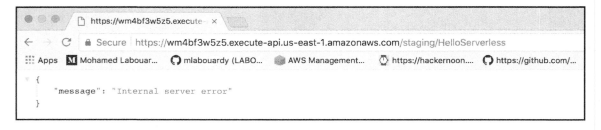

8. The **Internal server error message** means that something went wrong on Lambda's side. To help us troubleshoot and debug the issue, we will enable the logging feature in the API Gateway.

Debugging and troubleshooting

In order to troubleshoot the API Gateway server error, we need to enable logs as follows:

1. First, we need to grant the **API Gateway** access to **CloudWatch** in order to be able to push **API Gateway** log events to **CloudWatch Logs**. Therefore, we need to create a new IAM role from identity and access management.

 Some parts have been skipped to avoid me repeating myself. If you need a step by step procedure, make sure that you've followed on from the previous chapter.

The following screenshot will give you a glimpse of how to create a IAM role:

Choose the service that will use this role

EC2
Allows EC2 instances to call AWS services on your behalf.

Lambda
Allows Lambda functions to call AWS services on your behalf.

API Gateway	Config	Elastic Container Service	Lex	SWF
AppSync	DMS	Elastic Transcoder	Machine Learning	SageMaker
Application Auto Scaling	Data Pipeline	ElasticLoadBalancing	MediaConvert	Service Catalog
Auto Scaling	DeepLens	Glue	OpsWorks	Step Functions
Batch	Directory Service	Greengrass	RDS	Storage Gateway
CloudFormation	DynamoDB	GuardDuty	Redshift	
CloudHSM	EC2	Inspector	Rekognition	
CloudWatch Events	EMR	IoT	S3	
CodeBuild	ElastiCache	Kinesis	SMS	
CodeDeploy	Elastic Beanstalk	Lambda	SNS	

Select your use case

API Gateway
Allows API Gateway to push logs to CloudWatch Logs.

* Required   Cancel   **Next: Permissions**

---

2. Select **API Gateway** from the list of AWS services, then, on the permissions page, you can do either of the following:
   - Select an existing policy called **AmazonAPIGatewayPushToCloudWatchLogs**, as shown in the following screenshot:

   - Create a new Policy document with the following JSON:

```
{
  "Version": "2012-10-17",
  "Statement": [
  {
  "Effect": "Allow",
      "Action": [
          "logs:CreateLogGroup",
          "logs:CreateLogStream",
          "logs:DescribeLogGroups",
          "logs:DescribeLogStreams",
          "logs:PutLogEvents",
          "logs:GetLogEvents",
          "logs:FilterLogEvents"
      ],
      "Resource": "*"
  }
  ]
}
```

3. Next, assign a name to the role and copy the **Role ARN (Amazon Resource Name)** to the clipboard:

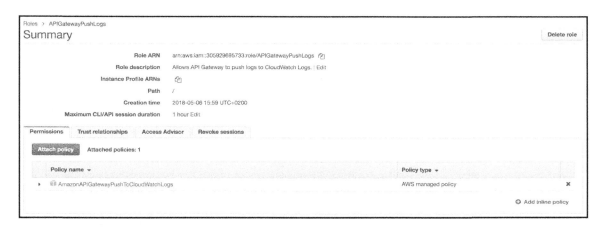

4. Then, select **API Gateway** from the **Networking & Content Delivery** section. Click on **Settings** and paste the **IAM role ARN** that we created earlier:

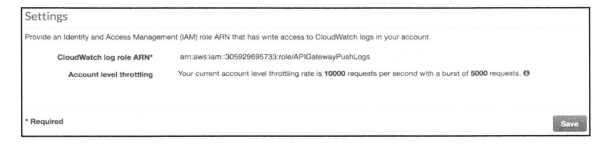

5. Save it and select the API created by the Lambda function. Click on **Stages** in the navigation pane:

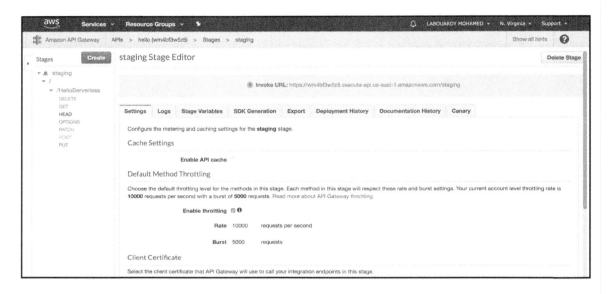

6. Then, click the **Logs** tab and under **CloudWatch Settings**, click on **Enable CloudWatch Logs** and select the **Log level** you want to catch. In this case, we are interested in error logs:

7. Try to invoke the Lambda again with the API URL and jump to the **AWS CloudWatch Logs** Console; you will see that a new **Log Group** has been created with the format **API-Gateway-Execution-Logs_AP_ID/DEPLOYMENT_STAGE**:

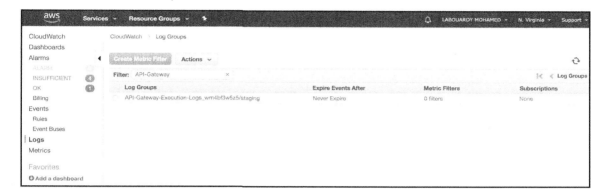

8. Click on the log group and you will see log streams generated by the **API Gateway**:

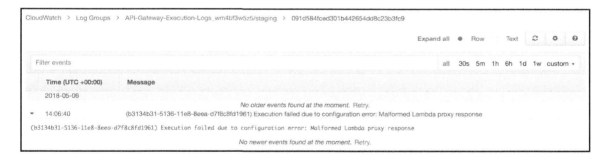

9. The preceding log states that the response returned from the Lambda function is not in the correct format. The correct format of response should contain the following attributes:

- **Body**: It is a required attribute that contains the function's actual output.
- **Status Code**: This is the function response status code, as described in the HTTP/1.1 standard (`https://tools.ietf.org/html/rfc7231#section-6`). It's mandatory, otherwise the API Gateway will display a 5XX error, as seen in the previous section.
- **Optional parameters**: It include things like `Headers` and `IsBase64Encoded`.

In the upcoming section, we will fix this incorrect response by formatting the response returned by the Lambda function to meet the format expected by the API Gateway.

Invoking the function with an HTTP request

As seen in the previous section, we need to fix the response returned by the Lambda function. Instead of returning a simple string variable, we will return a `struct` variable with a `Body` attribute which will contain the actual string value, and a `StatusCode` with `200` value to tell API Gateway that the request was successful. To do so, update the `main.go` file to match the following signature:

```go
package main

import "github.com/aws/aws-lambda-go/lambda"

type Response struct {
  StatusCode int `json:"statusCode"`
  Body string `json:"body"`
}

func handler() (Response, error) {
  return Response{
    StatusCode: 200,
    Body: "Welcome to Serverless world",
  }
, nil
}

func main() {
  lambda.Start(handler)
}
```

Once updated, build the deployment package with the Shell script provided in the previous chapter and upload the package to Lambda using the AWS Lambda Console or use the following AWS CLI command:

```
aws lambda update-function-code --function-name HelloServerless \
    --zip-file fileb://./deployment.zip \
    --region us-east-1
```

Ensure that you grant `lambda:CreateFunction` and `lambda:UpdateFunctionCode` permissions to the IAM user to be able to use the AWS command line throughout this chapter.

Head back to your web browser and invoke the API Gateway URL again:

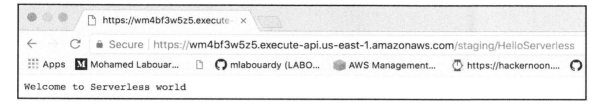

Congratulations! You have just built your first event-driven function with Lambda and API Gateway.

For quick reference, the Lambda Go package offers an easier way to integrate Lambda with the API Gateway by using the APIGatewayProxyResponse structure as follows:

```go
package main

import (
  "github.com/aws/aws-lambda-go/events"
  "github.com/aws/aws-lambda-go/lambda"
)

func handler() (events.APIGatewayProxyResponse, error) {
  return events.APIGatewayProxyResponse{
    StatusCode: 200,
    Body: "Welcome to Serverless world",
  }, nil
}

func main() {
  lambda.Start(handler)
}
```

Now that we know how to invoke our Lambda function in response to HTTP requests, let's go further and build a RESTful API with API Gateway.

Building a RESTful API

In this section, we will design, build, and deploy a RESTful API from scratch to explore some advanced topics involving Lambda and API Gateway.

API architecture

Before going into further detail about the architecture, we will look at an AIP that will help a local movie rental shop in managing their available movies. The following diagram shows how the API Gateway and Lambda fit into the API architecture:

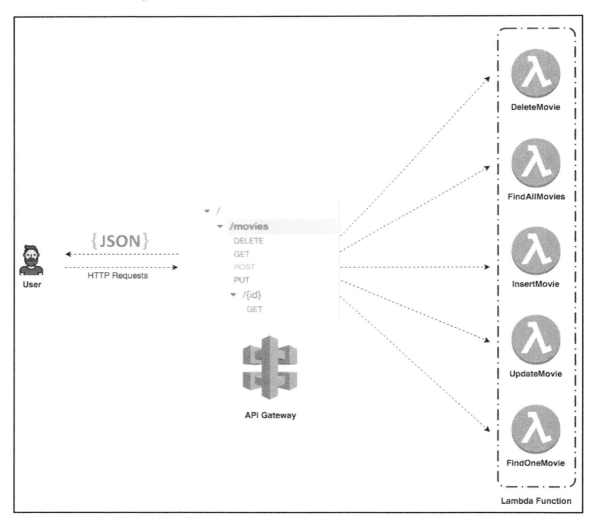

AWS Lambda empowers microservice development. That being said, each endpoint triggers a different Lambda function. These functions are independent of one another and can be written in different languages. Hence, this leads to scaling at function level, easier unit testing, and loose coupling.

All requests from clients first go through the API Gateway. It then routes the incoming request to the right Lambda function accordingly.

 Note that a single Lambda function can `Handle` multiple HTTP methods (`GET`, `POST`, `PUT`, `DELETE`, and so on). In order to leverage the power of microservices, we will create multiple Lambda functions for each functionality. However, building a single Lambda function to handle multiple endpoints could be a good exercise.

Endpoints design

Now that the architecture has been defined, we will go through the implementation of the functionalities described in the previous diagram.

The GET method

The first feature to implement is listing movies. That's where the `GET` method comes into play. The following steps are to be referred to in order to do this:

1. Create a Lambda function that registers a `findAll` handler. This handler transforms a list of `movies` structure to a `string`, and then returns this string wrapped by the `APIGatewayProxyResponse` variable along with a 200 HTTP status code. It also handles errors in case of conversion failure. The handler implementation is as follows:

```go
package main

import (
  "encoding/json"

  "github.com/aws/aws-lambda-go/events"
  "github.com/aws/aws-lambda-go/lambda"
)

var movies = []struct {
  ID int `json:"id"`
  Name string `json:"name"`
```

```
}{
    {
      ID: 1,
      Name: "Avengers",
    },
    {
      ID: 2,
      Name: "Ant-Man",
    },
    {
      ID: 3,
      Name: "Thor",
    },
    {
      ID: 4,
      Name: "Hulk",
    }, {
      ID: 5,
      Name: "Doctor Strange",
    },
}

func findAll() (events.APIGatewayProxyResponse, error) {
  response, err := json.Marshal(movies)
  if err != nil {
    return events.APIGatewayProxyResponse{}, err
  }

  return events.APIGatewayProxyResponse{
    StatusCode: 200,
    Headers: map[string]string{
      "Content-Type": "application/json",
    },
    Body: string(response),
  }, nil
}

func main() {
  lambda.Start(findAll)
}
```

Instead of hardcoding the HTTP status code, you can use the
net/http Go package and use a built-in status code variables such as
http.StatusOK, http.StatusCreated, http.StatusBadRequest,
http.StatusInternalServerError, and so on.

2. Next, create a new Lambda function using the AWS CLI after building the ZIP file:

```
aws lambda create-function --function-name FindAllMovies \
    --zip-file fileb://./deployment.zip \
    --runtime go1.x --handler main \
    --role arn:aws:iam::ACCOUNT_ID:role/FindAllMoviesRole \
    --region us-east-1
```

 `FindAllMoviesRole` should be created in advance, as described in the previous chapter, with permissions to allow streaming Lambda logs to AWS CloudWatch.

3. Heading back to the AWS Lambda Console; you should see that the function has been created successfully:

4. Create a sample event with an empty JSON, as the function doesn't expect any argument, and click on the **Test** button:

You will notice in the previous screenshot that the function returns the expected output in a JSON format.

5. Now that the function has been defined, we need to create a new API Gateway in order to trigger it:

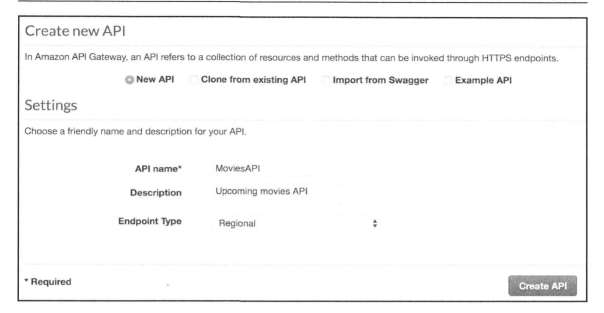

6. Next, from the **Actions** drop-down list, select **Create resource** and name it **movies**:

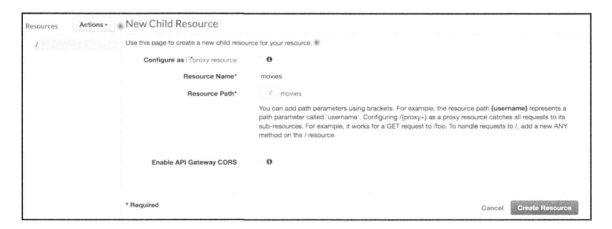

7. Expose a GET method on this `/movies` resource by clicking on **Create Method**. Choose **Lambda Function** under the **Integration type** section and select the **FindAllMovies** function:

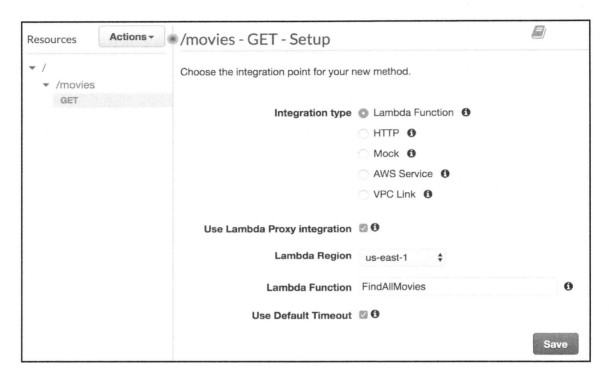

8. To deploy the API, select **Deploy API** from the **Actions** drop-down list. You will be prompted to create a new deployment stage:

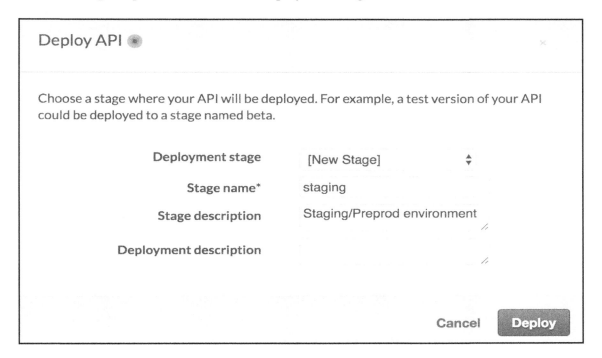

9. Once the deployment stage is created, an invocation URL will be displayed:

10. Point your browser to the URL given or use a modern REST client like Postman or Insomnia. I opted to go with the cURL tool as it is installed by default on almost all operating systems:

```
curl -sX GET
https://51cxzthvma.execute-api.us-east-1.amazonaws.com/staging/movi
es | jq '.'
```

The preceding command will return a list of movies in a JSON format:

```json
[
    {
      "id": 1,
      "name": "Avengers"
    },
    {
      "id": 2,
      "name": "Ant-Man"
    },
    {
      "id": 3,
      "name": "Thor"
    },
    {
      "id": 4,
      "name": "Hulk"
    },
    {
      "id": 5,
      "name": "Doctor Strange"
    }
]
```

When calling the GET endpoint, the request will go through the API Gateway, which will trigger the findAll handler. This returns a response which is proxied by the API Gateway to the client in a JSON format.

Now that the findAll function has been deployed, we can implement a findOne function to search for a movie by its ID.

The GET method with parameters

The findOne handler expects the APIGatewayProxyRequest argument that contains the event input. Then, it uses the PathParameters method to get the movie ID and validate it. If the ID provided is not a valid number, the Atoi method will return an error and a 500 error code will be returned to the client. Otherwise, a movie will be fetched based on the index and returned to the client with a 200 OK status wrapped in APIGatewayProxyResponse:

```go
func findOne(req events.APIGatewayProxyRequest)
(events.APIGatewayProxyResponse, error) {
  id, err := strconv.Atoi(req.PathParameters["id"])
  if err != nil {
    return events.APIGatewayProxyResponse{
      StatusCode: 500,
      Body:       "ID must be a number",
    }, nil
  }

  response, err := json.Marshal(movies[id-1])
  if err != nil {
    return events.APIGatewayProxyResponse{
      StatusCode: 500,
      Body:       err.Error(),
    }, nil
  }

  return events.APIGatewayProxyResponse{
    StatusCode: 200,
    Headers: map[string]string{
      "Content-Type": "application/json",
    },
    Body: string(response),
  }, nil
}

func main() {
  lambda.Start(findOne)
}
```

 Note that in the preceding code, we have used both methods of handling errors. The first is the `err.Error()` method, which returns a built-in Go error message that's raised when the encoding fails. The second one is a user-defined error, which is error-specific and easy to understand and debug from the client's perspective.

Similarly to the `FindAllMovies` function, create a new Lambda function for searching for a movie:

```
aws lambda create-function --function-name FindOneMovie \
    --zip-file fileb://./deployment.zip \
    --runtime go1.x --handler main \
    --role arn:aws:iam::ACCOUNT_ID:role/FindOneMovieRole \
    --region us-east-1
```

Go back to API Gateway console, create a new resource, and expose the GET method, and then link the resource to the FindOneMovie function. Note the use of the {id} placeholder in the path. The value of id will be made available via the APIGatewayProxyResponse object. The following screenshot depicts this:

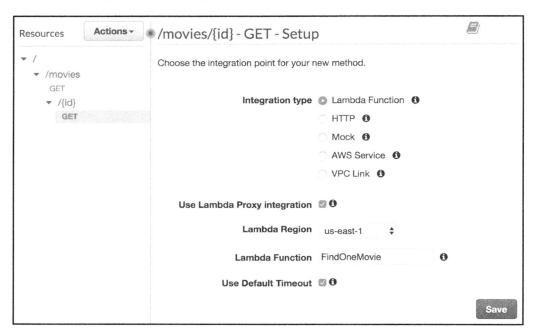

Redeploy the API and use the following cURL command to test the endpoint:

```
curl -sX
https://51cxzthvma.execute-api.us-east-1.amazonaws.com/staging/movies/1 |
jq '.'
```

The following JSON will be returned:

```
{
    "id": 1,
    "name": "Avengers"
}
```

When the API URL is invoked with an ID, the movie corresponding to the ID is returned if it exists.

The POST method

Now we know how the GET method works with and without path parameters. The next step will be to pass a JSON payload to a Lambda function through the API Gateway. The code is self-explanatory. It converts the request input to a movie structure, adds it to the list of movies, and returns the new list of movies in a JSON format:

```go
package main

import (
  "encoding/json"

  "github.com/aws/aws-lambda-go/events"
  "github.com/aws/aws-lambda-go/lambda"
)

type Movie struct {
  ID int `json:"id"`
  Name string `json:"name"`
}

var movies = []Movie{
  Movie{
    ID: 1,
    Name: "Avengers",
  },
  ...
}

func insert(req events.APIGatewayProxyRequest)
(events.APIGatewayProxyResponse, error) {
  var movie Movie
  err := json.Unmarshal([]byte(req.Body), &movie)
  if err != nil {
    return events.APIGatewayProxyResponse{
      StatusCode: 400,
      Body: "Invalid payload",
    }, nil
  }

  movies = append(movies, movie)

  response, err := json.Marshal(movies)
  if err != nil {
    return events.APIGatewayProxyResponse{
      StatusCode: 500,
      Body: err.Error(),
```

```
    }, nil
  }

  return events.APIGatewayProxyResponse{
    StatusCode: 200,
    Headers: map[string]string{
      "Content-Type": "application/json",
    },
    Body: string(response),
  }, nil
}

func main() {
  lambda.Start(insert)
}
```

Next, create a new Lambda function for `InsertMovie` with the following command:

```
aws lambda create-function --function-name InsertMovie \
    --zip-file fileb://./deployment.zip \
    --runtime go1.x --handler main \
    --role arn:aws:iam::ACCOUNT_ID:role/InsertMovieRole \
    --region us-east-1
```

Next, create a `POST` method on the `/movies` resource and link it to the `InsertMovie` function:

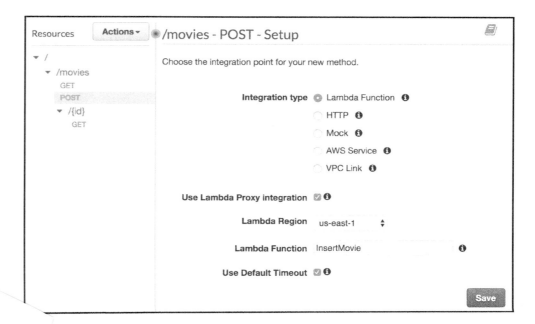

To test it out, use the following cURL command with the POST verb and the -d flag, followed by a JSON string (with the id and name attributes):

```
curl -sX POST -d '{"id":6, "name": "Spiderman:Homecoming"}'
https://51cxzthvma.execute-api.us-east-1.amazonaws.com/staging/movies | jq
'.'
```

The preceding command will return the following JSON response:

```
[
  {
    "id": 1,
    "name": "Avengers"
  },
  {
    "id": 2,
    "name": "Ant-Man"
  },
  {
    "id": 3,
    "name": "Thor"
  },
  {
    "id": 4,
    "name": "Hulk"
  },
  {
    "id": 5,
    "name": "Doctor Strange"
  },
  {
    "id": 6,
    "name": "Spiderman:Homecoming"
  }
]
```

As you can see, the new movie has been inserted successfully. If you test it again, it should work as expected:

```
curl -sX POST -d '{"id":7, "name": "Iron man"}'
https://51cxzthvma.execute-api.us-east-1.amazonaws.com/staging/movies | jq
'.'
```

The preceding command will return the following JSON response:

```json
[
  {
    "id": 1,
    "name": "Avengers"
  },
  {
    "id": 2,
    "name": "Ant-Man"
  },
  {
    "id": 3,
    "name": "Thor"
  },
  {
    "id": 4,
    "name": "Hulk"
  },
  {
    "id": 5,
    "name": "Doctor Strange"
  },
  {
    "id": 6,
    "name": "Spiderman:Homecoming"
  },
  {
    "id": 7,
    "name": "Iron man"
  }
]
```

As you can see, it was successful and the movie was again inserted as expected, but what if we wait few minutes and try to insert a third movie? The following command will be used to execute it again:

```
curl -sX POST -d '{"id":8, "name": "Captain America"}'
https://51cxzthvma.execute-api.us-east-1.amazonaws.com/staging/movies | jq
'.'
```

Once again, a new JSON response will be returned:

```
[
  {
    "id": 1,
    "name": "Avengers"
  },
  {
    "id": 2,
    "name": "Ant-Man"
  },
  {
    "id": 3,
    "name": "Thor"
  },
  {
    "id": 4,
    "name": "Hulk"
  },
  {
    "id": 5,
    "name": "Doctor Strange"
  },
  {
    "id": 8,
    "name": "Captain America"
  }
]
```

You will find that the movies with IDs 6 and 7 have been removed; why did this happen? It's simple. If you remember from `Chapter 1`, *Go Serverless*, the Lambda functions are stateless. When the `InsertMovie` function is invoked for the first time (first insert), AWS Lambda creates a container and deploys the function payload to the container. Then, it remains active for a few minutes before it is terminated (**warm start**), which explains why the second insert passed. In the third insert, the container is already terminated, and hence Lambda creates a new container (**cold start**) to handle the insert.

Therefore, the previous state is lost. The following diagram illustrates the cold/warm start issue:

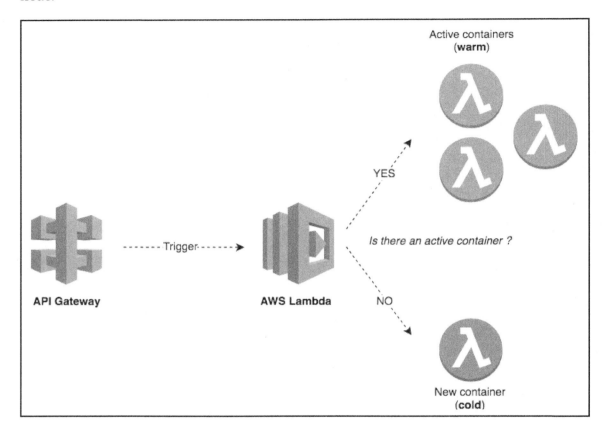

This explains why Lambda functions should be stateless and why we should not make any assumptions that the state will be preserved from one invocation to the next. So, how can we manage data persistency when working with serverless applications? The answer is by using an external database like DynamoDB, which will be the subject of the upcoming chapter.

Summary

In this chapter, you learned how to build a RESTful API from scratch with Lambda and API Gateway. We also covered how to debug and troubleshoot incoming API Gateway requests by enabling the CloudWatch logs feature, plus how to create an API deployment stage and how to create multiple endpoints with different HTTP methods. Finally, we learned about the cold/warm container issue and why Lambda functions should be stateless.

In the upcoming chapter, we will use DynamoDB as a database to manage data persistency for our API.

5
Managing Data Persistence with DynamoDB

In the previous chapter, we learned how to build a RESTful API with Lambda and API Gateway, and we discovered why Lambda functions should be stateless. In this chapter, we will resolve the stateless issue by using AWS DynamoDB for data storage. Moreover, we will also see how to integrate it with the Lambda functions.

We will be covering the following topics:

- Setting up DynamoDB
- Working with DynamoDB

Technical requirements

This chapter is a follow-up of the previous one as it will use the same source code. Hence, some snippets won't be explained to avoid repetition. Also, basic knowledge of NoSQL concepts is preferred so that you can follow this chapter with ease. The code bundle for this chapter is hosted on GitHub at `https://github.com/PacktPublishing/Hands-On-Serverless-Applications-with-Go`.

Setting up DynamoDB

DynamoDB is an AWS NoSQL database. It's a managed AWS service that allows you to store and retrieve data at scale without managing or maintaining a database server.

You need to understand a few key concepts about DynamoDB before digging into its integration with AWS Lambda:

- **Structure and Design**:
    - **Table**: This is a set of items (rows) where each item is a set of attributes (columns) and values.
    - **Partition key**: This is also called a hash key. It's a unique ID used by DynamoDB to determine the partition (physical location) in which the item can be found (read operation) or will be stored (write operation). A sort key might be used to order/sort items in the same partition.
    - **Index**: Similar to relational databases, indexes are used to speed up queries. In DynamoDB, two types of indexes can be created:
        - **Global Secondary Index (GSI)**
        - **Local Secondary Index (LSI)**
- **Operations**:
    - **Scan**: As the name implies, this operation scans the entire table before returning the requested items.
    - **Query**: This operation finds items based on primary key values.
    - **PutItem**: This creates a new item or replaces an old item with a new one.
    - **GetItem**: This finds an item by its primary key.
    - **DeleteItem**: This deletes a single item in a table by its primary key.

 In terms of performance, scan operations are less efficient and more expensive (they consume more throughput) as the operation has to iterate through each item in the table to get the requested items. Therefore, it's always recommended to use query over scan operations.

Now that you're familiar with DynamoDB terminology, we can start by creating our first DynamoDB table to store the API items.

Creating a table

To begin creating a table, sign in to the AWS Management Console (`https://console.aws.amazon.com/console/home`) and select **DynamoDB** from the **Database** section. Click on the **Create table** button to create a new DynamoDB table, as shown in the following screenshot:

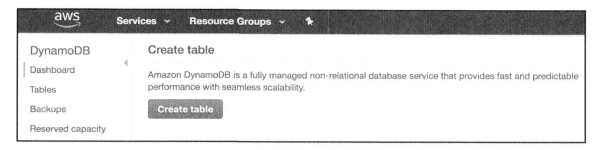

Next, give the table a name such as `movies` in the next example.. Since each movie will be identified by a unique ID, it will be the partition key for the table. Leave all of the other settings as their default states and hit **Create**, shown as follows:

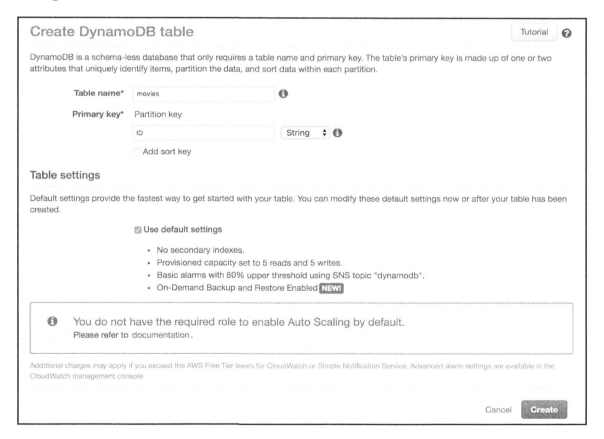

Wait a few seconds while the table is created, shown as follows:

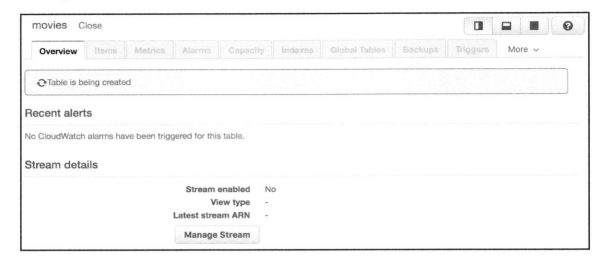

Once the `movies` table is created, a success message will prompt you to confirm its creation. Now, we need to load sample data into the table.

Loading sample data

To populate items in the `movies` table, click on the **Items** tab:

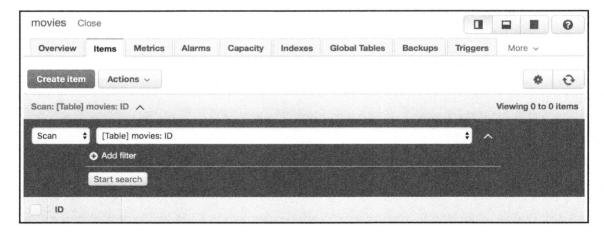

Then, click on **Create item** and insert a new movie, as shown in the following screenshot (you need to use the plus (**+**) button to append an extra column to store the movie name):

Click on **Save**. The table should look something like this:

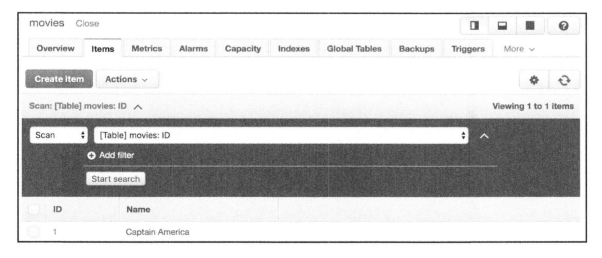

For a real-world application, we won't use the console to populate millions of items. To save time, we will use the AWS SDK to write a small application in Go to load items to the table.

Create a new project in your Go workspace and copy the following content into the `init-db.go` file:

```go
func main() {
  cfg, err := external.LoadDefaultAWSConfig()
  if err != nil {
    log.Fatal(err)
  }

  movies, err := readMovies("movies.json")
  if err != nil {
    log.Fatal(err)
  }

  for _, movie := range movies {
    fmt.Println("Inserting:", movie.Name)
    err = insertMovie(cfg, movie)
    if err != nil {
      log.Fatal(err)
    }
  }

}
```

The preceding code reads a JSON file (https://github.com/PacktPublishing/Hands-On-Serverless-Applications-with-Go/blob/master/ch5/movies.json), which contains a list of movies; encode it into an array of the `Movie` struct as follows:

```go
func readMovies(fileName string) ([]Movie, error) {
  movies := make([]Movie, 0)

  data, err := ioutil.ReadFile(fileName)
  if err != nil {
    return movies, err
  }

  err = json.Unmarshal(data, &movies)
  if err != nil {
    return movies, err
  }

  return movies, nil
```

```
}
```

Then, it iterates through every movie within the movies array. Then, use the `PutItem` method to insert it into a DynamoDB table as follows:

```go
func insertMovie(cfg aws.Config, movie Movie) error {
  item, err := dynamodbattribute.MarshalMap(movie)
  if err != nil {
    return err
  }

  svc := dynamodb.New(cfg)
  req := svc.PutItemRequest(&dynamodb.PutItemInput{
    TableName: aws.String("movies"),
    Item: item,
  })
  _, err = req.Send()
  if err != nil {
    return err
  }
  return nil
}
```

 Be sure to install the AWS Go SDK with the `go get github.com/aws/aws-sdk-go-v2/aws` command from your terminal session.

To load the `movies` table with data, enter the following command:

AWS_REGION=us-east-1 go run init-db.go

You can use the DynamoDB Console to verify the data that you loaded into the `movies` table, as shown in the following screenshot:

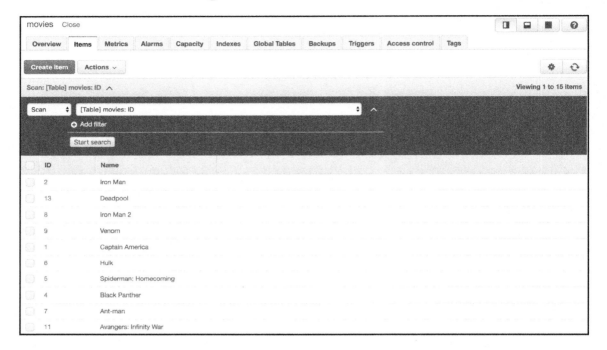

Now that the DynamoDB table is prepared, we need to update each API endpoint function's code to use the table instead of the hardcoded movies list.

Working with DynamoDB

In this section, we will update the existing functions to read and write from/to the DynamoDB table. The following diagram describes the target architecture:

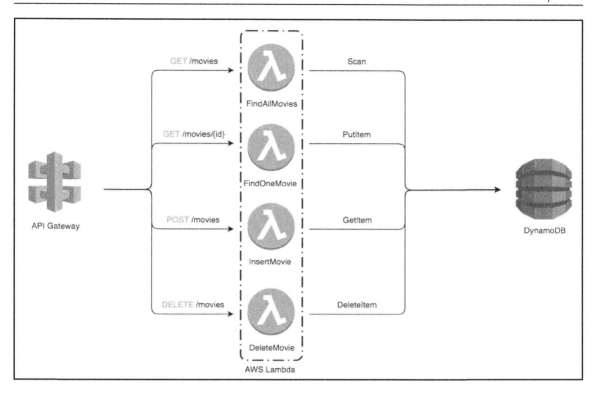

API Gateway will forward incoming requests to the target Lambda function, which will call the corresponding DynamoDB operation on the `movies` table.

Scan request

To get started, we need to implement the function responsible for returning a list of movies; the following steps describe how to achieve that:

1. Update the `findAll` handler endpoint to use the `Scan` method to fetch all items from the table:

```
func findAll() (events.APIGatewayProxyResponse, error) {
  cfg, err := external.LoadDefaultAWSConfig()
  if err != nil {
    return events.APIGatewayProxyResponse{
      StatusCode: http.StatusInternalServerError,
      Body: "Error while retrieving AWS credentials",
    }, nil
```

```
  }

  svc := dynamodb.New(cfg)
  req := svc.ScanRequest(&dynamodb.ScanInput{
    TableName: aws.String(os.Getenv("TABLE_NAME")),
  })
  res, err := req.Send()
  if err != nil {
    return events.APIGatewayProxyResponse{
      StatusCode: http.StatusInternalServerError,
      Body: "Error while scanning DynamoDB",
    }, nil
  }

  response, err := json.Marshal(res.Items)
  if err != nil {
    return events.APIGatewayProxyResponse{
      StatusCode: http.StatusInternalServerError,
      Body: "Error while decoding to string value",
    }, nil
  }

  return events.APIGatewayProxyResponse{
    StatusCode: 200,
    Headers: map[string]string{
      "Content-Type": "application/json",
    },
    Body: string(response),
  }, nil
}
```

 Full implementation of this function can be found in the GitHub repository (https://github.com/PacktPublishing/Hands-On-Serverless-Applications-with-Go/blob/master/ch5/findAll/main.go).

2. Build the deployment package and update the `FindAllMovies` Lambda function code with the following AWS CLI command:

```
aws lambda update-function-code --function-name FindAllMovies \
    --zip-file fileb://./deployment.zip \
    --region us-east-1
```

3. Be sure to update the **FindAllMoviesRole** in order to grant that Lambda function permissions to call the `Scan` operation on the DynamoDB table by adding the following IAM policy:

```
{
  "Version": "2012-10-17",
  "Statement": [
    {
      "Sid": "1",
      "Effect": "Allow",
      "Action": "dynamodb:Scan",
      "Resource": [
        "arn:aws:dynamodb:us-
east-1:ACCOUNT_ID:table/movies/index/ID",
        "arn:aws:dynamodb:us-east-1:ACCOUNT_ID:table/movies"
      ]
    }
  ]
}
```

Once the policy is assigned to the IAM role, it should be part of the attached policies, as shown in the next screenshot:

4. Finally, with the Lambda console or using the AWS CLI, add a new environment variable to point to the DynamoDB table name that we created earlier:

```
aws lambda update-function-configuration --function-name
FindAllMovies \
    --environment Variables={TABLE_NAME=movies} \
    --region us-east-1
```

The following screenshot shows a properly configured **FindAllMovies** function with IAM access to DynamoDB and CloudWatch with a defined TABLE_NAME environment variable:

Properly configured FindAllMovies function

5. Save it and invoke the API Gateway URL with the cURL command as follows:

```
curl -sX GET
https://51cxzthvma.execute-api.us-east-1.amazonaws.com/staging/movi
es | jq '.'
```

6. An array will be returned in a JSON format as follows:

```
[
  {
    "ID": {
      "B": null,
      "BOOL": null,
      "BS": null,
      "L": null,
      "M": null,
      "N": null,
      "NS": null,
      "NULL": null,
      "S": "2",
      "SS": null
    },
    "Name": {
      "B": null,
      "BOOL": null,
      "BS": null,
      "L": null,
      "M": null,
      "N": null,
      "NS": null,
      "NULL": null,
      "S": "Iron Man",
      "SS": null
    }
  },
  {
    "ID": {
      "B": null,
      "BOOL": null,
      "BS": null,
      "L": null,
      "M": null,
      "N": null,
      "NS": null,
      "NULL": null,
      "S": "13",
      "SS": null
    },
    "Name": {
      "B": null,
      "BOOL": null,
      "BS": null,
      "L": null,
      "M": null,
      "N": null,
      "NS": null,
      "NULL": null,
      "S": "Deadpool",
      "SS": null
    }
  },
  {
```

7. The endpoint is working and fetching the movie's items from the table, but the JSON returned is a raw DynamoDB response. We will fix that by returning only the `ID` and `Name` properties as follows:

```
movies := make([]Movie, 0)
for _, item := range res.Items {
  movies = append(movies, Movie{
    ID: *item["ID"].S,
    Name: *item["Name"].S,
  })
}

response, err := json.Marshal(movies)
```

8. Further to this, generate the ZIP file and update the Lambda function code, and then invoke the API Gateway URL with the cURL command given earlier, shown as follows:

```
[
  {
    "id": "2",
    "name": "Iron Man"
  },
  {
    "id": "13",
    "name": "Deadpool"
  },
  {
    "id": "8",
    "name": "Iron Man 2"
  },
  {
    "id": "9",
    "name": "Venom"
  },
  {
    "id": "1",
    "name": "Captain America"
  },
  {
    "id": "6",
    "name": "Hulk"
  },
  {
    "id": "5",
    "name": "Spiderman: Homecoming"
  },
  {
    "id": "4",
    "name": "Black Panther"
  },
  {
    "id": "7",
    "name": "Ant-man"
  },
  {
    "id": "11",
    "name": "Avangers: Infinity War"
  },
  {
    "id": "3",
    "name": "Thor"
  },
  {
    "id": "12",
    "name": "Doctor Strange"
  },
  {
    "id": "10",
    "name": "Guardians of the Galaxy"
  },
  {
    "id": "15",
    "name": "X-Men"
  },
  {
    "id": "14",
    "name": "Captain Marvel"
  }
]
```

Much better, right?

GetItem request

The second function to be implemented will be responsible for returning a single item from DynamoDB, the following steps illustrate how it should be built:

1. Update the `findOne` handler to call the `GetItem` method in DynamoDB. This should return a single item with the identifier passed into the API endpoint parameter:

```
func findOne(request events.APIGatewayProxyRequest)
(events.APIGatewayProxyResponse, error) {
  id := request.PathParameters["id"]

  cfg, err := external.LoadDefaultAWSConfig()
  if err != nil {
    return events.APIGatewayProxyResponse{
      StatusCode: http.StatusInternalServerError,
      Body: "Error while retrieving AWS credentials",
    }, nil
  }

  svc := dynamodb.New(cfg)
  req := svc.GetItemRequest(&dynamodb.GetItemInput{
    TableName: aws.String(os.Getenv("TABLE_NAME")),
    Key: map[string]dynamodb.AttributeValue{
      "ID": dynamodb.AttributeValue{
        S: aws.String(id),
      },
    },
  })
  res, err := req.Send()
  if err != nil {
    return events.APIGatewayProxyResponse{
      StatusCode: http.StatusInternalServerError,
      Body: "Error while fetching movie from DynamoDB",
    }, nil
  }
  ...
}
```

Full implementation of this function can be found in the GitHub repository (https://github.com/PacktPublishing/Hands-On-Serverless-Applications-with-Go/blob/master/ch5/findOne/main.go).

2. Similar to the `FindAllMovies` function, create a ZIP file and update the existing Lambda function code with the following AWS CLI command:

```
aws lambda update-function-code --function-name FindOneMovie \
    --zip-file fileb://./deployment.zip \
    --region us-east-1
```

3. Grant `GetItem` permission on the `movies` table to the `FindOneMovie` Lambda function with the following IAM policy:

```
{
  "Version": "2012-10-17",
  "Statement": [
    {
      "Sid": "1",
      "Effect": "Allow",
      "Action": "dynamodb:GetItem",
      "Resource": "arn:aws:dynamodb:us-
east-1:ACCOUNT_ID:table/movies"
    }
  ]
}
```

4. The IAM role should be configured as shown in the following screenshot:

5. Define a new environment variable with the DynamoDB table name as a value:

```
aws lambda update-function-configuration --function-name
FindOneMovie \
 --environment Variables={TABLE_NAME=movies} \
 --region us-east-1
```

6. Head back to the `FindOneMovie` dashboard and verify that all of the settings have been configured, as shown in the following screenshot:

7. Invoke the API Gateway by issuing the following cURL command:

```
curl -sX GET
https://51cxzthvma.execute-api.us-east-1.amazonaws.com/staging/movi
es/3 | jq '.'
```

8. As expected, the response is a single movie item, with an ID of 3, as requested in the cURL command:

```
{
  "id": "3",
  "name": "Thor"
}
```

PutItem request

So far, we have learned how to list all items and return a single item from DynamoDB. The following section describes how we can implement a Lambda function to add a new item to a database:

1. Update the insert handler to call the PutItem method to insert a new movie into the table:

```go
func insert(request events.APIGatewayProxyRequest)
(events.APIGatewayProxyResponse, error) {
  ...
  cfg, err := external.LoadDefaultAWSConfig()
  if err != nil {
    return events.APIGatewayProxyResponse{
      StatusCode: http.StatusInternalServerError,
      Body: "Error while retrieving AWS credentials",
    }, nil
  }

  svc := dynamodb.New(cfg)
  req := svc.PutItemRequest(&dynamodb.PutItemInput{
    TableName: aws.String(os.Getenv("TABLE_NAME")),
    Item: map[string]dynamodb.AttributeValue{
      "ID": dynamodb.AttributeValue{
        S: aws.String(movie.ID),
      },
      "Name": dynamodb.AttributeValue{
        S: aws.String(movie.Name),
      },
```

```
      },
  })
  _, err = req.Send()
  if err != nil {
    return events.APIGatewayProxyResponse{
      StatusCode: http.StatusInternalServerError,
      Body: "Error while inserting movie to DynamoDB",
    }, nil
  }
  ...
}
```

Full implementation of this function can be found in the GitHub repository (https://github.com/PacktPublishing/Hands-On-Serverless-Applications-with-Go/blob/master/ch5/insert/main.go).

2. Create a deployment package and update the `InsertMovie` Lambda function code with the following command:

```
aws lambda update-function-code --function-name InsertMovie \
    --zip-file fileb://./deployment.zip \
    --region us-east-1
```

3. Allow the function to call the `PutItem` operation on the **movies** table with the IAM policy as follows:

```
{
  "Version": "2012-10-17",
  "Statement": [
    {
      "Sid": "1",
      "Effect": "Allow",
      "Action": "dynamodb:PutItem",
      "Resource": "arn:aws:dynamodb:us-
east-1:ACCOUNT_ID:table/movies"
    }
  ]
}
```

The following screenshot shows that the IAM role is updated to handle the `PutItem` operation's permissions:

4. Create a new environment variable with the DynamoDB table name as follows:

```
aws lambda update-function-configuration --function-name
InsertMovie \
    --environment Variables={TABLE_NAME=movies} \
    --region us-east-1
```

5. Make sure that the Lambda function is configured as follows:

Properly configured InsertMovie function

6. Insert a new movie by calling the following cURL command on the API Gateway URL:

```
curl -sX POST -d '{"id":"17", "name":"The Punisher"}'
https://51cxzthvma.execute-api.us-east-1.amazonaws.com/staging/movi
es | jq '.'
```

7. Verify that the movie is inserted in the DynamoDB Console, as shown in the next screenshot:

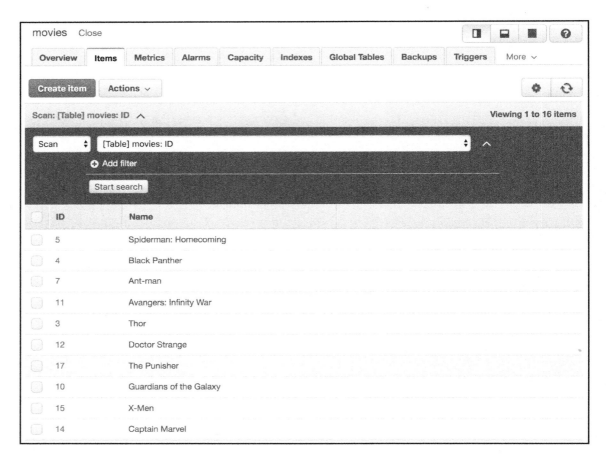

Another way to verify that the insert was well-executed is to use the `findAll` endpoint with a cURL command:

```
curl -sX GET
https://51cxzthvma.execute-api.us-east-1.amazonaws.com/staging/movi
es | jq '.'
```

8. The movie which has an ID of `17` has been created. If the table contained a movie item with the same ID, it would have been replaced instead. The following is the output:

```json
[
  {
    "id": "2",
    "name": "Iron Man"
  },
  {
    "id": "13",
    "name": "Deadpool"
  },
  {
    "id": "8",
    "name": "Iron Man 2"
  },
  {
    "id": "9",
    "name": "Venom"
  },
  {
    "id": "1",
    "name": "Captain America"
  },
  {
    "id": "6",
    "name": "Hulk"
  },
  {
    "id": "5",
    "name": "Spiderman: Homecoming"
  },
  {
    "id": "4",
    "name": "Black Panther"
  },
  {
    "id": "7",
    "name": "Ant-man"
  },
  {
    "id": "11",
    "name": "Avangers: Infinity War"
  },
  {
    "id": "3",
    "name": "Thor"
  },
  {
    "id": "12",
    "name": "Doctor Strange"
  },
  {
    "id": "17",
    "name": "The Punisher"
  },
  {
    "id": "10",
    "name": "Guardians of the Galaxy"
  },
  {
    "id": "15",
    "name": "X-Men"
  },
  {
    "id": "14",
    "name": "Captain Marvel"
  }
]
```

DeleteItem request

Finally, in order to delete an item from DynamoDB, the following Lambda function should be implemented:

1. Register a new handler to delete a movie. The handler will encode the payload in the request body to a `Movie` struct:

```
var movie Movie
err := json.Unmarshal([]byte(request.Body), &movie)
if err != nil {
   return events.APIGatewayProxyResponse{
      StatusCode: 400,
      Body: "Invalid payload",
   }, nil
}
```

2. Then, call the `DeleteItem` method with the movie ID as a parameter to remove it from the table:

```
cfg, err := external.LoadDefaultAWSConfig()
if err != nil {
   return events.APIGatewayProxyResponse{
      StatusCode: http.StatusInternalServerError,
      Body: "Error while retrieving AWS credentials",
   }, nil
}

svc := dynamodb.New(cfg)
req := svc.DeleteItemRequest(&dynamodb.DeleteItemInput{
   TableName: aws.String(os.Getenv("TABLE_NAME")),
   Key: map[string]dynamodb.AttributeValue{
      "ID": dynamodb.AttributeValue{
         S: aws.String(movie.ID),
      },
   },
})
_, err = req.Send()
if err != nil {
   return events.APIGatewayProxyResponse{
      StatusCode: http.StatusInternalServerError,
      Body: "Error while deleting movie from DynamoDB",
   }, nil
}
```

Full implementation of this function can be found in the GitHub repository (`https://github.com/PacktPublishing/Hands-On-Serverless-Applications-with-Go/blob/master/ch5/delete/main.go`).

3. Similar to what we did with the other functions, create a new IAM role called `DeleteMovieRole` with permissions to push logs to CloudWatch and to call the `DeleteItem` operation on the **movies** table, as shown in the next screenshot:

4. Next, create a new Lambda function after building a deployment package:

```
aws lambda create-function --function-name DeleteMovie \
    --zip-file fileb://./deployment.zip \
    --runtime go1.x --handler main \
    --role arn:aws:iam::ACCOUNT_ID:role/DeleteMovieRole \
    --environment Variables={TABLE_NAME=movies} \
    --region us-east-1
```

5. Head back to the Lambda Console. A `DeleteMovie` function should have been created, as shown in the next screenshot:

6. Finally, we need to expose a `DELETE` method on the `/movies` endpoint in the API Gateway. To do so, we won't use the API Gateway console, but we will use the AWS CLI so that you can get familiar with it.

7. To create a `DELETE` method on `movies` resources, we will use the following command:

```
aws apigateway put-method --rest-api-id API_ID \
    --resource-id RESOURCE_ID \
    --http-method DELETE \
    --authorization-type "NONE" \
    --region us-east-1
```

8. However, we need to supply the API ID as well as the resource ID. Those IDs can be found easily in the API Gateway Console, shown as follows:

For CLI enthusiasts like myself, you can also get this information by running the following commands:

- REST API ID:

```
aws apigateway get-rest-apis --query
"items[?name==\`MoviesAPI\`].id" --output text
```

- Resource ID:

```
aws apigateway get-resources --rest-api-id API_ID --query
"items[?path==\`/movies\`].id" --output text
```

9. Now that the IDs have been defined, update the `aws apigateway put-method` command with your IDs and execute the command.

10. Next, set the `DeleteMovie` function as the target for the `DELETE` method:

```
aws apigateway put-integration \
  --rest-api-id API_ID \
  --resource-id RESOURCE_ID \
  --http-method DELETE \
  --type AWS_PROXY \
  --integration-http-method DELETE \
  --uri arn:aws:apigateway:us-
east-1:lambda:path/2015-03-31/functions/arn:aws:lambda:us-
east-1:ACCOUNT_ID:function:DeleteMovie/invocations \
  --region us-east-1
```

11. Finally, tell the API Gateway to skip any translation and to pass it without any modification the response returned by the Lambda function:

```
aws apigateway put-method-response \
    --rest-api-id API_ID \
    --resource-id RESOURCE_ID \
    --http-method DELETE \
    --status-code 200 \
    --response-models '{"application/json": "Empty"}' \
    --region us-east-1
```

12. In the **Resources** panel, a `DELETE` method should be defined as follows:

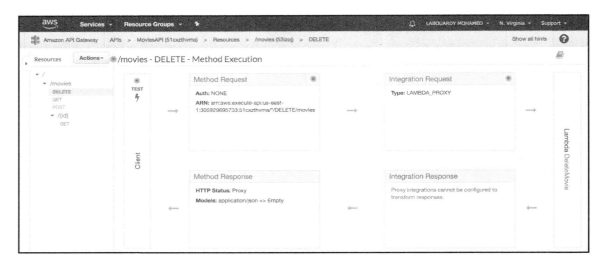

13. Redeploy the API with the following AWS CLI command:

```
aws apigateway create-deployment \
    --rest-api-id API_ID \
    --stage-name staging \
    --region us-east-1
```

14. Use the following cURL command to delete a movie:

```
curl -sX DELETE -d '{"id":"1", "name":"Captain America"}'
https://51cxzthvma.execute-api.us-east-1.amazonaws.com/staging/movi
es | jq '.'
```

15. Verify that the movie had been deleted by calling the `findAll` endpoint with the following cURL command:

```
curl -sX GET
https://51cxzthvma.execute-api.us-east-1.amazonaws.com/staging/movi
es | jq '.'
```

16. The movie with ID as 1 won't be part of the list that's being returned. You can verify in the DynamoDB Console that the movie has been successfully deleted, shown as follows:

```
[
    {
        "id": "2",
        "name": "Iron Man"
    },
    {
        "id": "13",
        "name": "Deadpool"
    },
    {
        "id": "8",
        "name": "Iron Man 2"
    },
    {
        "id": "9",
        "name": "Venom"
    },
    {
        "id": "6",
        "name": "Hulk"
    },
    {
        "id": "5",
        "name": "Spiderman: Homecoming"
    },
    {
        "id": "4",
        "name": "Black Panther"
    },
    {
        "id": "7",
        "name": "Ant-man"
    },
    {
        "id": "11",
        "name": "Avangers: Infinity War"
    },
    {
        "id": "3",
        "name": "Thor"
    },
    {
        "id": "12",
        "name": "Doctor Strange"
    },
    {
        "id": "17",
        "name": "The Punisher"
    },
    {
        "id": "10",
        "name": "Guardians of the Galaxy"
    },
    {
        "id": "15",
        "name": "X-Men"
    },
    {
        "id": "14",
        "name": "Captain Marvel"
    }
]
```

Indeed, the movie having ID as 1, no longer exists in the `movies` table.

At this point, we have created a serverless RESTful API with AWS Lambda, API Gateway, and DynamoDB.

Summary

In this chapter, you learned how to build an event-driven API with Lambda and API Gateway, and how to store data in DynamoDB. In later chapters, we will go further and add a security layer on top of the API Gateway, build a CI/CD pipeline to automate the deployment, and much more.

In the next chapter, we will go through some advanced AWS CLI commands and options that you can use while building serverless functions in AWS Lambda to save time. We will also see how to create and maintain multiple versions and releases of Lambda functions.

Questions

1. Implement an `update` handler to update an existing movie item.
2. Create a new PUT method in API Gateway to trigger the `update` Lambda function.
3. Implement a single Lambda function to handle all type of events (GET, POST, DELETE, PUT).
4. Update the `findOne` handler to return a proper response code for a valid request but an empty data (for example, no movie for the ID requested).
5. Implement a pagination system on the `findAll` endpoint using a `Range` header and using a `Query` string.

6
Deploying Your Serverless Application

In previous chapters, we learned how to build a serverless API from scratch. In this chapter, we will try to accomplish the following:

- Build, deploy, and manage our Lambda functions going through some advanced AWS CLI commands
- Publish multiple versions of the API
- Learn how to separate multiple deployment environments (sandbox, staging, and production) with aliases
- Cover the usage of the API Gateway stage variables to change the method endpoint's behavior.

Lambda CLI commands

In this section, we will go through the various AWS Lambda commands that you might use while building your Lambda functions. We will also learn how you use them to automate your deployment process.

The list-functions command

If you recall, this command was introduced in `Chapter 2`, *Getting Started with AWS Lambda*. As its name implies, it lists all Lambda functions in the AWS region you provided. The following command will return all Lambda functions in the North Virginia region:

```
aws lambda list-functions --region us-east-1
```

For each function, the response includes the function's configuration information (`FunctionName`, **Resources** usage, `Environment` variables, IAM Role, `Runtime` environment, and so on), as shown in the following screenshot:

```
{
    "FunctionName": "FindAllMovies",
    "FunctionArn": "arn:aws:lambda:us-east-1:305929695733:function:FindAllMovies",
    "Runtime": "go1.x",
    "Role": "arn:aws:iam::305929695733:role/FindAllMoviesRole",
    "Handler": "main",
    "CodeSize": 4033405,
    "Description": "",
    "Timeout": 3,
    "MemorySize": 128,
    "LastModified": "2018-05-19T12:36:42.983+0000",
    "CodeSha256": "1Ct1BXdozq77l3WZlzIhrY6KnDSooENyl5SDpPl7glk=",
    "Version": "$LATEST",
    "Environment": {
        "Variables": {
            "TABLE_NAME": "movies"
        }
    },
    "TracingConfig": {
        "Mode": "PassThrough"
    },
    "RevisionId": "097648db-5238-40b0-805b-117ceac4acfb"
},
```

To list only some attributes, such as the function name, you can use the `query` filter option, as follows:

```
aws lambda list-functions --query Functions[].FunctionName[]
```

The create-function command

If you've read through the preceding chapters, you should be familiar with this command as it has been used multiple times to create a new Lambda function from scratch.

In addition to the function's configuration, you can use the command to provide the deployment package (ZIP) in two ways:

- **ZIP file**: It provides the path to the ZIP file of the code you are uploading with the `--zip-file` option:

```
aws lambda create-function --function-name UpdateMovie \
    --description "Update an existing movie" \
    --runtime go1.x \
    --role arn:aws:iam::ACCOUNT_ID:role/UpdateMovieRole \
```

```
--handler main \
--environment Variables={TABLE_NAME=movies} \
--zip-file fileb://./deployment.zip \
--region us-east-1a
```

- **S3 Bucket object**: It provides the S3 bucket and object name with the `--code` option:

```
aws lambda create-function --function-name UpdateMovie \
--description "Update an existing movie" \
--runtime go1.x \
--role arn:aws:iam::ACCOUNT_ID:role/UpdateMovieRole \
--handler main \
--environment Variables={TABLE_NAME=movies} \
--code S3Bucket=movies-api-deployment-
package,S3Key=deployment.zip \
--region us-east-1
```

The as-mentioned commands will return a summary of the function's settings in a JSON format, as follows:

```
{
    "FunctionName": "UpdateMovie",
    "FunctionArn": "arn:aws:lambda:us-east-1:305929695733:function:UpdateMovie",
    "Runtime": "go1.x",
    "Role": "arn:aws:iam::305929695733:role/UpdateMovieRole",
    "Handler": "main",
    "CodeSize": 4038140,
    "Description": "Update an existing movie",
    "Timeout": 3,
    "MemorySize": 128,
    "LastModified": "2018-05-28T20:31:34.064+0000",
    "CodeSha256": "6+F7yAbM5nhWgnR5PtKUdQSBEHYnCqJH/xtaT/WHgAw=",
    "Version": "$LATEST",
    "Environment": {
        "Variables": {
            "TABLE_NAME": "movies"
        }
    },
    "TracingConfig": {
        "Mode": "PassThrough"
    },
    "RevisionId": "7ca628ca-0b65-4af7-ab22-eb34df3ebfff"
}
```

It's worth mentioning that while creating your Lambda function, you might override the compute usage and network settings based on your function's behavior with the following options:

- `--timeout`: The default execution timeout is three seconds. When the three seconds are reached, AWS Lambda terminates your function. The maximum timeout you can set is five minutes.
- `--memory-size`: The amount of memory given to your function when executed. The default value is 128 MB and the maximum is 3,008 MB (increments of 64 MB).
- `--vpc-config`: This deploys the Lambda function in a private VPC. While it might be useful if the function requires communication with internal resources, it should ideally be avoided as it impacts the Lambda performance and scaling (this will be discussed in upcoming chapters).

 AWS doesn't allow you to set the CPU usage of your function as it's calculated automatically based on the memory allocated for your function. CPU usage is proportional to the memory.

The update-function-code command

In addition to AWS Management Console, you can update your Lambda function's code with AWS CLI. The command requires the target Lambda function name and the new deployment package. Similarly to the previous command, you can provide the package as follows:

- The path to the new `.zip` file:

```
aws lambda update-function-code --function-name UpdateMovie \
    --zip-file fileb://./deployment-1.0.0.zip \
    --region us-east-1
```

- The S3 bucket where the `.zip` file is stored:

```
aws lambda update-function-code --function-name UpdateMovie \
    --s3-bucket movies-api-deployment-packages \
    --s3-key deployment-1.0.0.zip \
    --region us-east-1
```

This operation prints a new unique ID (called `RevisionId`) for each change in the Lambda function's code:

```
{
    "FunctionName": "UpdateMovie",
    "FunctionArn": "arn:aws:lambda:us-east-1:305929695733:function:UpdateMovie",
    "Runtime": "go1.x",
    "Role": "arn:aws:iam::305929695733:role/UpdateMovieRole",
    "Handler": "main",
    "CodeSize": 4038140,
    "Description": "Update an existing movie",
    "Timeout": 3,
    "MemorySize": 128,
    "LastModified": "2018-05-28T20:37:20.253+0000",
    "CodeSha256": "6+F7yAbM5nhWgnR5PtKUdQSBEHYnCqJH/xtaT/WHgAw=",
    "Version": "$LATEST",
    "Environment": {
        "Variables": {
            "TABLE_NAME": "movies"
        }
    },
    "TracingConfig": {
        "Mode": "PassThrough"
    },
    "RevisionId": "885bd218-a7b9-435a-bd21-d9d759bf288c"
}
```

The get-function-configuration command

In order to retrieve the configuration information of a Lambda function, issue the following command:

```
aws lambda get-function-configuration --function-name UpdateMovie --region
us-east-1
```

The preceding command will provide the same information in the output that was displayed when the `create-function` command was used.

 To retrieve configuration information for a specific Lambda version or alias (following section), you can use the `--qualifier` option.

The invoke command

So far, we invoked our Lambda functions directly from AWS Lambda Console and through HTTP events with API Gateway. In addition to that, Lambda can be invoked from the AWS CLI with the `invoke` command:

```
aws lambda invoke --function-name UpdateMovie result.json
```

The preceding command will invoke the `UpdateMovie` function and save the function's output in `result.json` file:

```
{
  "statusCode": 400,
  "headers": null,
  "body": "Invalid payload"
}
```

The status code is 400, which is normal, as `UpdateFunction` is expecting a JSON input. Let's see how to provide a JSON to our function with the `invoke` command.

Head back to the DynamoDB `movies` table, and pick up a movie that you want to update. In this example, we will update the movie with the **ID** as **13**, shown as follows:

Create a JSON file with a `body` attribute that contains the new movie item attribute, as the Lambda function is expecting the input to be in the API Gateway Proxy request format:

```
{
    "body": "{\"id\":\"13\", \"name\":\"Deadpool 2\"}"
}
```

Finally, run the `invoke` function command again with the JSON file as the input parameter:

```
aws lambda invoke --function UpdateMovie --payload file://input.json
result.json
```

If you print the `result.json` content, the updated movie should be returned, shown as follows:

```
{
    "statusCode": 200,
    "headers": {
        "Content-Type": "application/json"
    },
    "body": "{\"id\":\"13\",\"name\":\"Deadpool 2\"}"
}
```

You can verify that the movie's name is updated in the DynamoDB table by invoking the `FindAllMovies` function:

```
aws lambda invoke --function-name FindAllMovies result.json
```

The `body` attribute should contain the new updated movie, shown as follows:

```
{
  "statusCode": 200,
  "headers": {
    "Content-Type": "application/json"
  },
  "body": "[{\"id\":\"2\",\"name\":\"Iron Man\"},{\"id\":\"13\",\"name\":\"Deadpool 2\"},{\"id\":\"8\",\"name\":\"Iron Man 2\"},{\"id\":\"9\",\"name\":\"Venom\"},{\"id\":\"6\",\"name\":\"Hulk\"},{\"id\":\"5\",\"name\":\"Spiderman: Homecoming\"},{\"id\":\"4\",\"name\":\"Black Panther\"},{\"id\":\"7\",\"name\":\"Ant-man\"},{\"id\":\"11\",\"name\":\"Avengers: Infinity War\"},{\"id\":\"3\",\"name\":\"Thor\"},{\"id\":\"12\",\"name\":\"Doctor Strange\"},{\"id\":\"17\",\"name\":\"The Punisher\"},{\"id\":\"10\",\"name\":\"Guardians of the Galaxy\"},{\"id\":\"15\",\"name\":\"X-Men\"},{\"id\":\"14\",\"name\":\"Captain Marvel\"}]"
}
```

Head back to DynamoDB Console; the movie with the **ID** of **13** should have a new name, as shown in the following screenshot:

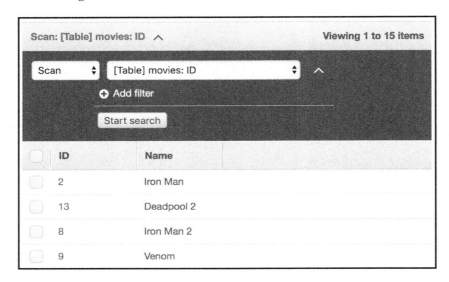

The delete-function command

To delete a Lambda function, you can use the following command:

```
aws lambda delete-function --function-name UpdateMovie
```

By default, the command will delete all function versions and aliases. To delete a specific version or alias, you might want to use the --qualifier option.

By now, you should be familiar with all the AWS CLI commands you might use and need while building your serverless applications in AWS Lambda. In the upcoming section, we will see how to create different versions of your Lambda functions and maintain multiple environments with aliases.

Versions and aliases

When you're building your serverless application, you must separate your deployment environments to test new changes without impacting your production. Therefore, having multiple versions of your Lambda functions makes sense.

Versioning

A version represents a state of your function's code and configuration in time. By default, each Lambda function has the $LATEST version pointing to the latest changes of your function, as shown in the following screenshot:

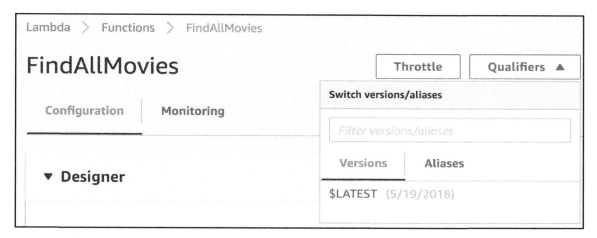

In order to create a new version from the $LATEST version, click on **Actions** and **Publish new version**. Let's call it 1.0.0, as shown in the next screenshot:

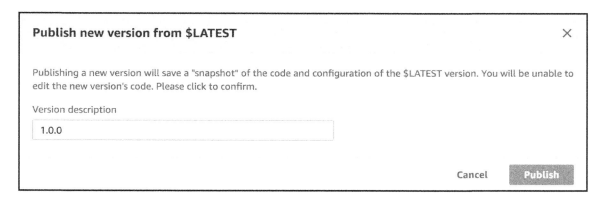

The new version will be created with an ID=1 (incremental). Note the ARN Lambda function at the top of the window in the following screenshot; it has the version ID:

Once the version is created, you cannot update the function code, shown as follows:

Moreover, advanced settings, such as IAM roles, network configuration, and compute usage, cannot be changed, shown as follows:

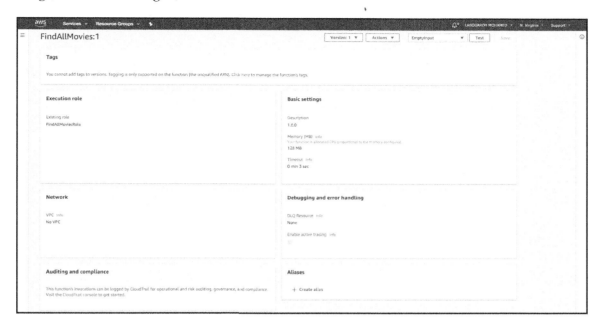

Versions are called **immutable**, which means they cannot be changed once they're published; only the $LATEST version is editable.

Now, we know how to publish a new version from the console. Let's publish a new version with the AWS CLI. But first, we need to update the FindAllMovies function as we cannot publish a new version if no changes were made to $LATEST since publishing version 1.0.0.

The new version will have a pagination system. The function will return only the number of items requested by the user. The following code will read the Count header parameter, convert it to a number, and use the Scan operation with the Limit parameter to fetch the movies from DynamoDB:

```
func findAll(request events.APIGatewayProxyRequest)
(events.APIGatewayProxyResponse, error) {
  size, err := strconv.Atoi(request.Headers["Count"])
  if err != nil {
    return events.APIGatewayProxyResponse{
      StatusCode: http.StatusBadRequest,
      Body: "Count Header should be a number",
```

```
    }, nil
}

...

svc := dynamodb.New(cfg)
req := svc.ScanRequest(&dynamodb.ScanInput{
  TableName: aws.String(os.Getenv("TABLE_NAME")),
  Limit: aws.Int64(int64(size)),
})
...
}
```

Next, we update the `FindAllMovies` Lambda function's code with the `update-function-code` command:

```
aws lambda update-function-code --function-name FindAllMovies \
    --zip-file fileb://./deployment.zip
```

Then, publish a new version, `1.1.0`, based on the current configuration and code with the following command:

```
aws lambda publish-version --function-name FindAllMovies --description
1.1.0
```

Go back to AWS Lambda Console and navigate to your `FindAllMovies`; a new version should be created with a new ID=2, as shown in the following screenshot:

Now that our versions are created, let's test them out by using the AWS CLI `invoke` command.

FindAllMovies v1.0.0

Invoke the `FindAllMovies` v1.0.0 version with its ID in the qualifier parameter with the following command:

```
aws lambda invoke --function-name FindAllMovies --qualifier 1 result.json
```

`result.json` should have all the movies in the DynamoDB `movies` table, shown as follows:

The output showing all the movies in the DynamoDB movies table

FindAllMovies v1.1.0

Create a new file called `input.json`, and paste in the following content. This function's version expects a Header parameter, called `Count`, with a number of movies to return:

```
{
  "headers": {
    "Count": "4"
  }
}
```

Execute the function, but this time, use the `--payload` parameter with the path location to the `input.json` file:

```
aws lambda invoke --function-name FindAllMovies --payload file://input.json
    --qualifier 2 result.json
```

`result.json` should contain only four movies, as expected, shown as follows:

That's how to create multiple versions of your Lambda function. But, what are the best practices for Lambda function versioning?

Semantic Versioning

When you publish a new version of your Lambda function, you should give it a significant and meaningful version name that allows you to track different changes made to your function through its development cycle.

When you're building a public serverless API that will be used by millions of customers, the way you name your different API versions is critical as it allows your customers to know whether the new release introduces breaking changes. It also lets them choose the right time to upgrade to the newest version without taking much risk of breaking up their pipeline.

That's where Semantic Versioning (`https://semver.org`) comes into play, it's a version scheme that uses a sequence of three digits:

Each digit is incremented based on the following rules:

- **Major**: Increment if the Lambda function is not backward-compatible with previous releases.
- **Minor**: Increment if the new functionality or features have been added to the function and it's still backward-compatible.
- **Patch**: Increment if bugs and issues have been fixed and the function is still backward-compatible.

For example, the `FindAllMovies` function's version `1.1.0` is the first major release, with one minor version bringing a new feature (Pagination system).

Aliases

The alias is a pointer to a specific version, it allows you to promote a function from one environment to another (such as staging to production). Aliases are mutable, unlike versions, which are immutable.

To illustrate the concept of aliases, we will create two aliases, as illustrated in the following diagram: a `Production` alias pointing to `FindAllMovies` Lambda function `1.0.0` version, and a `Staging` alias that points to function `1.1.0` version. Then, we will configure API Gateway to use these aliases instead of the `$LATEST` version:

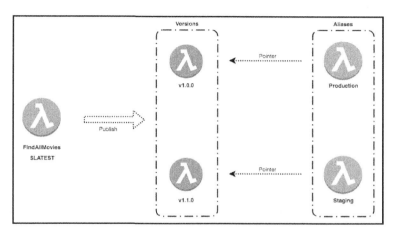

Head back to the `FindAllMovies` configuration page. If you click on the **Qualifiers** drop-down list, you should see a default alias called `Unqualified` pointing to your `$LATEST` version, as shown in the following screenshot:

To create a new alias, click on **Actions** and then **Create a new alias** called `Staging`. Select the 5 version as the target, shown as follows:

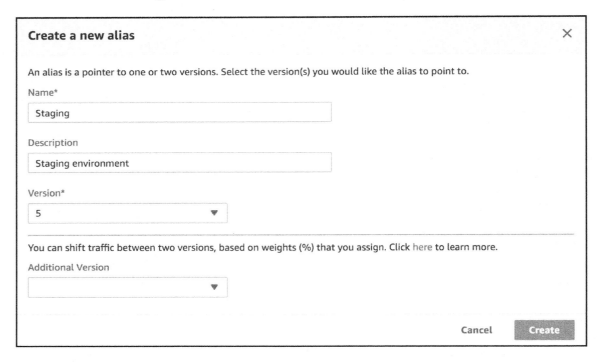

Once created, the new version should be added to the list of **Aliases**, shown as follows:

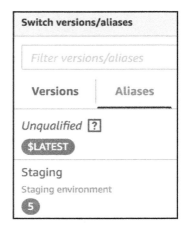

Next, create a new alias for the `Production` environment that points to version `1.0.0` using the AWS command line:

```
aws lambda create-alias --function-name FindAllMovies \
    --name Production --description "Production environment" \
    --function-version 1
```

Similarly, the new alias should be successfully created:

Now that our aliases have been created, let's configure the API Gateway to use those aliases with **Stage variables**.

Stage variables

Stage variables are environment variables that can be used to change the behavior at runtime of the API Gateway methods for each deployment stage. The following section will illustrate how to use stage variables with API Gateway.

On the API Gateway Console, navigate to the `Movies` API, click on the `GET` method, and
update the target **Lambda Function** to use a stage variable instead of a hardcoded Lambda
function name, as shown in the following screenshot:

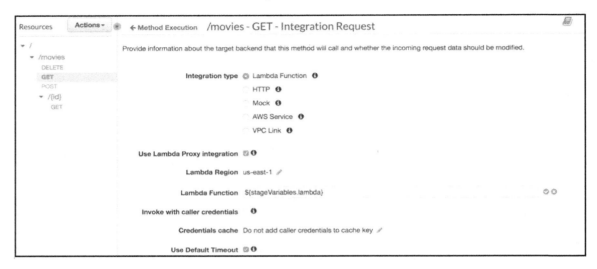

When you save it, a new prompt will ask you to grant the permissions to API Gateway to
call your Lambda function aliases, as shown in the following screenshot:

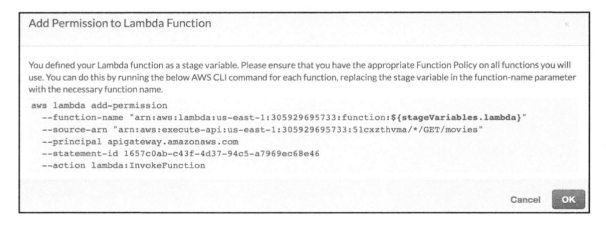

Execute the following commands to allow API Gateway to invoke the `Production` and `Staging` aliases:

- **Production alias**:

```
aws lambda add-permission --function-name "arn:aws:lambda:us-
east-1:ACCOUNT_ID:function:FindAllMovies:Production" \
    --source-arn "arn:aws:execute-api:us-
east-1:ACCOUNT_ID:API_ID/*/GET/movies" \
    --principal apigateway.amazonaws.com \
    --statement-id STATEMENT_ID \
    --action lambda:InvokeFunction
```

- **Staging alias:**

```
aws lambda add-permission --function-name "arn:aws:lambda:us-
east-1:ACCOUNT_ID:function:FindAllMovies:Staging" \
    --source-arn "arn:aws:execute-api:us-
east-1:ACCOUNT_ID:API_ID/*/GET/movies" \
    --principal apigateway.amazonaws.com \
    --statement-id STATEMENT_ID \
    --action lambda:InvokeFunction
```

Then, create a new stage called `production`, as shown in next screenshot:

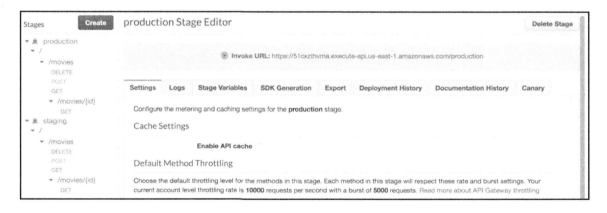

Next, click on the **Stages Variables** tab, and create a new stage variable called `lambda` and set `FindAllMovies:Production` as a value, shown as follows:

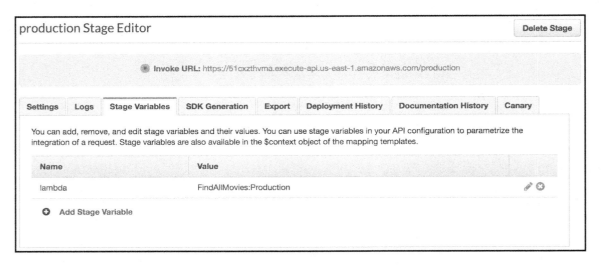

Do the same for the `staging` environment with the `lambda` variable pointing to the Lambda function's `Staging` alias, shown as follows:

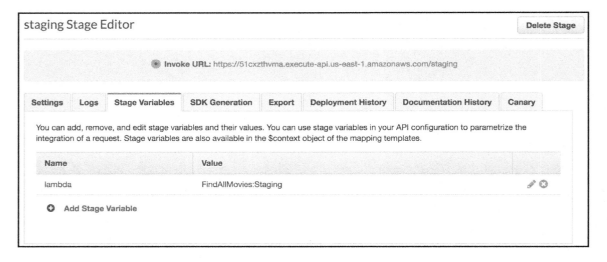

To test the endpoint, use the cURL command or any REST client you're familiar with. I opt for Postman. A GET method on the API Gateway's production stage invoked URL should return all the movies in the database, shown as follows:

Do the same for the staging environment, with a new `Header` key called `Count=4`; you should have only four movies items in return, shown as follows:

That's how you can maintain multiple environments of your Lambda functions. You can now easily promote the `1.1.0` version into production by changing the `Production` pointer to point to `1.1.0` instead of `1.0.0`, and roll back in case of failure to the previous working version without changing the API Gateway settings.

Summary

AWS CLI can be very useful for creating automation scripts to manage AWS Lambda functions.

Versions are immutable and cannot be changed once they're published. On the other hand, aliases are dynamic and their binding can be changed at any time to implement code-promotion or rollback. Adopting Semantic Versioning for the Lambda function's versions can make tracking changes easier.

In the next chapter, we will learn how to set up a CI/CD pipeline from scratch to automate the process of deploying Lambda functions to production. We will also cover how aliases and versions can be used in the Continuous Integration workflow.

Implementing a CI/CD Pipeline

7

This chapter will discuss advanced concepts, such as:

- How to set up a highly resilient and fault-tolerant CI/CD pipeline to automate the deployment of your serverless application
- The importance of having a centralized code repository for your Lambda functions
- How to automatically deploy your code changes to production.

Technical requirements

Before starting this chapter, make sure that you create and upload the source code of the functions built in previous chapters to a centralized GitHub repository. In addition, previous experience with CI/CD concepts is highly recommended. The code bundle for this chapter is hosted on GitHub at `https://github.com/PacktPublishing/Hands-On-Serverless-Applications-with-Go`.

Continuous Integration and deployment workflow

Continuous Integration, continuous deployment, and continuous delivery are an excellent way to accelerate the time-to-market of your software and drive innovation from feedback while ensuring you're building high-quality products through each iteration. But what do these practices mean? And how can they be applied when you're building serverless applications in AWS Lambda?

Continuous Integration

Continuous Integration (CI) is the process of having a centralized code repository and making all the changes and features go through a complex pipeline before integrating them into the central repository. A classic CI pipeline triggers a build whenever a code commit occurs, runs the unit tests and all pre-integration tests, builds the artifact, and pushes the result to an artifacts-management repository.

Continuous Deployment

Continuous Deployment (CD) is an extension of Continuous Integration. Every change that passes all stages of your Continuous Integration pipeline is released automatically to your staging environment.

Continuous Delivery

Continuous Delivery (CD) is similar to CD but requires human intervention or a business decision before deploying the release to production.

Now that the practices are defined, you can use these concepts to leverage the power of automation and build an end-to-end deployment process, as described in the following diagram:

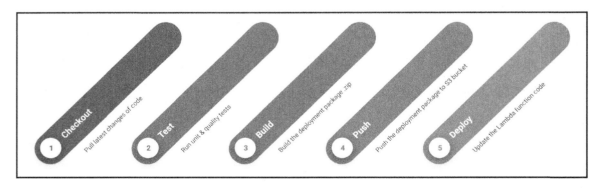

In the upcoming sections, we will go through how to build this pipeline with the most-used CI solutions.

To illustrate the concepts, only the `FindAllMovies` function's code will be used, but the same steps can be applied over the rest of the Lambda functions.

Automating the deployment of Lambda functions

In this section, we will see how to build a pipeline to automate the deployment process of the Lambda functions built in the previous chapter in the following different ways:

- AWS-managed solutions, such as CodePipeline and CodeBuild
- On-premise solutions, such as Jenkins
- SaaS solutions, such as Circle CI

Continuous Deployment with CodePipeline and CodeBuild

AWS CodePipeline is a workflow-management tool that allows you to automate the release and deployment process of your software. The user defines a set of steps that form a CI workflow that can be executed on AWS-managed services, such as CodeBuild and CodeDeploy, or third-party tools, such as Jenkins.

In this example, AWS CodeBuild will be used to test, build, and deploy your Lambda function. Therefore, a build specification file with the name of `buildspec.yml` should be created in the code repository.

`buildspec.yml` defines a set of steps that will be executed on the CI server as follows:

```
version: 0.2
env:
  variables:
    S3_BUCKET: "movies-api-deployment-packages"
    PACKAGE: "github.com/mlabouardy/lambda-codepipeline"

phases:
  install:
    commands:
      - mkdir -p "/go/src/$(dirname ${PACKAGE})"
      - ln -s "${CODEBUILD_SRC_DIR}" "/go/src/${PACKAGE}"
```

```
      - go get -u github.com/golang/lint/golint

  pre_build:
    commands:
      - cd "/go/src/${PACKAGE}"
      - go get -t ./...
      - golint -set_exit_status
      - go vet .
      - go test .

  build:
    commands:
      - GOOS=linux go build -o main
      - zip $CODEBUILD_RESOLVED_SOURCE_VERSION.zip main
      - aws s3 cp $CODEBUILD_RESOLVED_SOURCE_VERSION.zip s3://$S3_BUCKET/

  post_build:
    commands:
      - aws lambda update-function-code --function-name FindAllMovies --s3-
  bucket $S3_BUCKET --s3-key $CODEBUILD_RESOLVED_SOURCE_VERSION.zip
```

The build specification is divided into the following four phases:

- **Install**:
  - Set up Go workspace
  - Install Go linter

- **Pre-build**:
  - Install Go dependencies
  - Check whether our code is well formatted and follows Go best practices and common conventions
  - Run unit tests with the go test command

- **Build**:
  - Build a single binary with the go build command
  - Create a deployment package, .zip, from the generated binary
  - Store the .zip file in the S3 bucket

- **Post-build**:
  - Update the Lambda function's code with the new deployment package

The unit test command will return an empty response as we will write unit tests of our Lambda functions in an upcoming chapter.

Source provider

Now that our workflow is defined, let's create a continuous deployment pipeline. Open the AWS Management Console (`https://console.aws.amazon.com/console/home`), navigate to AWS CodePipeline from the **Developer Tools** section, and create a new pipeline called **MoviesAPI,** as shown in the following screenshot, shown as follows:

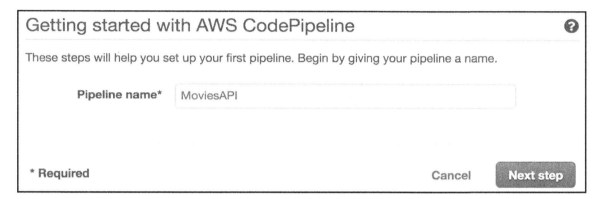

On the **Source location** page, select **GitHub** as the **Source provider**, shown as follows:

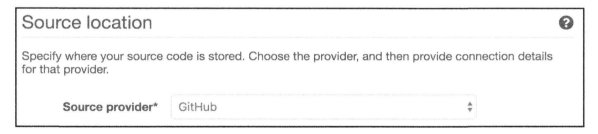

In addition to GitHub, AWS CodePipeline supports Amazon S3 and AWS CodeCommit as code-source providers.

Click on the **Connect to GitHub** button and authorize CodePipeline to access to your GitHub repositories; then, select the Github repository on which your code is stored and the target git branch you want to build, shown as follows:

Connect to GitHub

Choose a repository from the list of repositories, and then select the branch you want to use. You must have, at minimum, read-only access to the repository. Learn more

Repository*	mlabouardy/lambda-codepipeline
Branch*	master

> ℹ **We will use webhooks to detect changes**
> AWS CodePipeline will create a webhook for you. You can opt-out in the options below.

▸ Change detection options

* Required   Cancel   Previous   **Next step**

Build provider

On the **Build** stage, choose **AWS CodeBuild** as the build server. Jenkins and Solano CI are also a supported build providers. Note the following screenshot:

The next step in the creation of the pipeline is to define a new CodeBuild project, shown as follows:

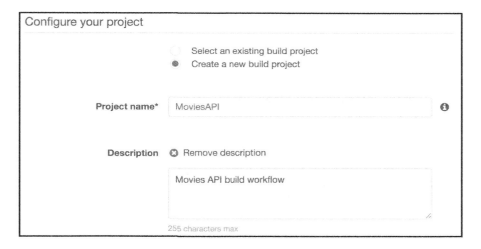

Set the build server to be an **Ubuntu** instance with **Golang** as the **Runtime** environment, as shown in the next screenshot:

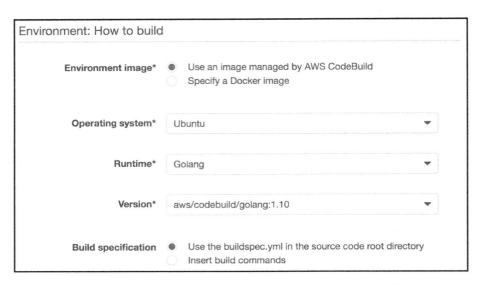

The build environment can also be based on a Docker image publicly available on DockerHub or in a private registry, such as **Elastic Container Registry (ECR)**.

CodeBuild will store the artifacts (the deployment package) in an S3 bucket and update the Lambda function's FindAllMovies code. Hence, an IAM role with the following policy should be attached:

```
{
  "Version": "2012-10-17",
  "Statement": [
    {
      "Sid": "VisualEditor0",
      "Effect": "Allow",
      "Action": [
        "s3:PutObject",
        "s3:GetObject",
        "lambda:UpdateFunctionCode"
      ],
      "Resource": [
        "arn:aws:s3:::movies-api-deployment-packages/*",
        "arn:aws:lambda:us-east-1:305929695733:function:FindAllMovies"
      ]
```

```
      }
   ]
}
```

 In the preceding code block the `arn:aws:lambda:us-east-1` account ID should be replaced with you account ID.

Deploy provider

With our project built, the next step to configure in the pipeline is the deployment to an environment. For this chapter, we will select the **No Deployment** option, and let CodeBuild deploy the new code to Lambda using the AWS CLI, as shown in the next screenshot:

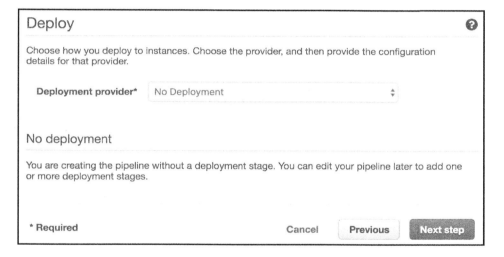

This deployment process requires an explanation of Serverless Application Model and CloudFormation, which will be explained in further chapters in detail.

Review the details; when you're ready, click on **Save**, and a new pipeline should be created as follows:

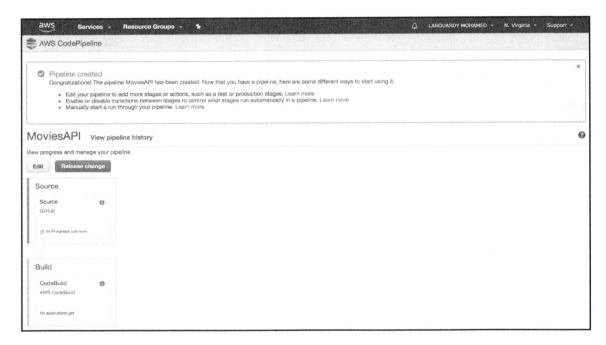

The pipeline will be started, and the Build stage will fail, as shown in the following screenshot:

If we click on the **Details** link, it will bring you to the CodeBuild project page for that particular build. The phases describing the build specification file can be seen here:

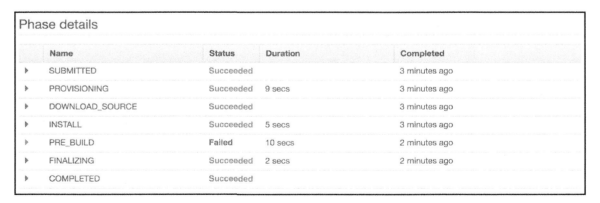

	Name	Status	Duration	Completed
▶	SUBMITTED	Succeeded		3 minutes ago
▶	PROVISIONING	Succeeded	9 secs	3 minutes ago
▶	DOWNLOAD_SOURCE	Succeeded		3 minutes ago
▶	INSTALL	Succeeded	5 secs	3 minutes ago
▶	PRE_BUILD	Failed	10 secs	2 minutes ago
▶	FINALIZING	Succeeded	2 secs	2 minutes ago
▶	COMPLETED	Succeeded		

As shown, the **Pre-build** phase has failed; in the logs section at the bottom, we can see it's due to the `golint` command:

```
Build logs
Showing the last 10000 lines of build log below. View entire log
16   [Container] 2018/06/10 09:34:00 Entering phase INSTALL
17   [Container] 2018/06/10 09:34:00 Running command mkdir -p "/go/src/$(dirname ${PACKAGE})"
18
19   [Container] 2018/06/10 09:34:00 Running command ln -s "${CODEBUILD_SRC_DIR}" "/go/src/${PACKAGE}"
20
21   [Container] 2018/06/10 09:34:00 Running command go get -u github.com/golang/lint/golint
22
23   [Container] 2018/06/10 09:34:06 Phase complete: INSTALL Success: true
24   [Container] 2018/06/10 09:34:06 Phase context status code:  Message:
25   [Container] 2018/06/10 09:34:06 Entering phase PRE_BUILD
26   [Container] 2018/06/10 09:34:06 Running command cd "/go/src/${PACKAGE}"
27
28   [Container] 2018/06/10 09:34:06 Running command go get -t ./...
29
30   [Container] 2018/06/10 09:34:16 Running command golint -set_exit_status
31   main.go:15:6: exported type Movie should have comment or be unexported
32   Found 1 lint suggestions; failing.
33
34   [Container] 2018/06/10 09:34:16 Command did not exit successfully golint -set_exit_status exit status 1
35   [Container] 2018/06/10 09:34:16 Phase complete: PRE_BUILD Success: false
36   [Container] 2018/06/10 09:34:16 Phase context status code: COMMAND_EXECUTION_ERROR Message: Error while executing command:
         golint -set_exit_status. Reason: exit status 1
37
```

In Golang, all top-level, exported names (uppercase) should have doc comments. Hence, a new comment on top of the Movie struct declaration should be added as follows:

```go
// Movie entity
type Movie struct {
  ID string `json:"id"`
  Name string `json:"name"`
}
```

Commit the new changes to GitHub, and a new build will trigger the execution of the pipeline:

You might be wondering how pushing the code change to the code repository triggered a new build. The answer is GitHub webhooks. When you created your CodeBuild project, a new Webhook is created automatically in your GitHub repository. Therefore, all changes to your code repository go through the CI pipeline, as shown in the next screenshot:

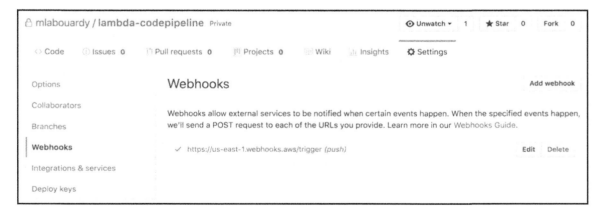

Once the pipeline is completed, all CodeBuild phases should be passed, as shown in the next screenshot:

	Name	Status	Duration	Completed
▶	SUBMITTED	Succeeded		3 minutes ago
▶	PROVISIONING	Succeeded	7 secs	3 minutes ago
▶	DOWNLOAD_SOURCE	Succeeded		3 minutes ago
▶	INSTALL	Succeeded	4 secs	3 minutes ago
▶	PRE_BUILD	Succeeded	10 secs	3 minutes ago
▶	BUILD	Succeeded	2 secs	3 minutes ago
▶	POST_BUILD	Succeeded	1 sec	3 minutes ago
▶	UPLOAD_ARTIFACTS	Succeeded		3 minutes ago
▶	FINALIZING	Succeeded	2 secs	3 minutes ago
▶	COMPLETED	Succeeded		

Open the S3 Console, then click on the **bucket** used by the pipeline; a new deployment package should be stored with a key name identical to the commit ID:

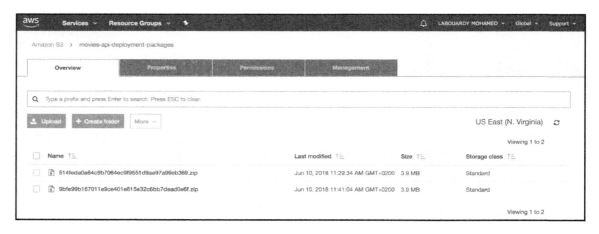

Finally, CodeBuild will update the Lambda function's code with the `update-function-code` command.

Continuous Pipeline with Jenkins

For many years, Jenkins has been the tool of choice. It's an open source continuous-integration server written in Java, built on top of the Hudson project. It's highly extensible due to its plugin-driven architecture and rich ecosystem.

In the upcoming sections, we will write our first *Pipeline as Code* with Jenkins but first we need to set up our Jenkins environment.

Distributed builds

To get started, install Jenkins by following the official instructions from this guide: `https://jenkins.io/doc/book/installing/`. Once Jenkins is up and running, point your browser to `http://instance_ip:8080`. This link will bring up the Jenkins dashboard, as shown in the next screenshot:

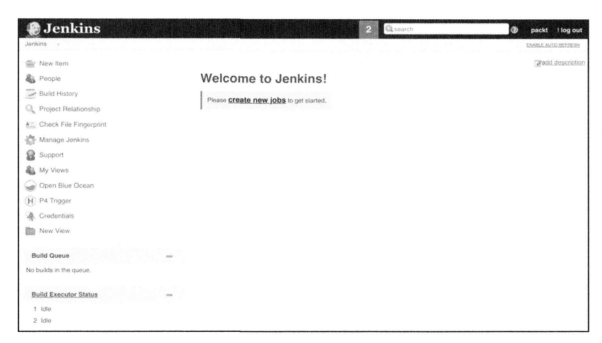

One of the advantages of using Jenkins is its master/slave architecture. It allows you to set up a Jenkins cluster with multiple workers (agents) responsible for building your application. This architecture has many benefits:

- Response time, not a lot of jobs waiting in the queue to be built
- Increased number of concurrent builds
- Supports multiple platforms

The following steps describe the configuration process for bringing up a new worker for use with the Jenkins build server. The worker is an EC2 instance, with `JDK8` and `Golang`, the latest stable version installed (see `Chapter 2`, *Getting Started with AWS Lambda*, for instructions).

Once the worker is running, copy its IP address to the clipboard, head back to the Jenkins master dashboard, click on **Manage Jenkins** and then click on **Manage Nodes**. Click on **New Node**, give the worker a name, and select **Permanent Agent**, as shown in the next screenshot:

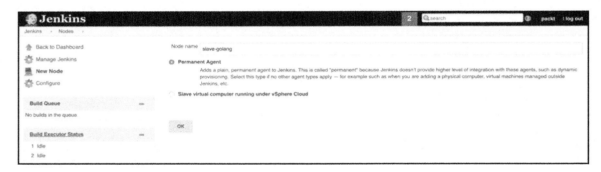

Then, set the node root directory to the Go workspace and paste the IP address of the node and select the SSH key, shown as follows:

If everything is configured correctly, the node will be brought online, shown as follows:

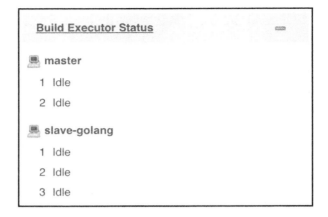

Setting up a Jenkins job

Now that our cluster is deployed, we can write our first Jenkins pipeline. This pipeline is defined in a text file called `Jenkinsfile`. This definition file must be committed to the Lambda function's code repository.

> The `Pipeline` plugin must be installed on Jenkins to use the *Pipeline as Code* feature. This feature offers a number of immediate benefits, such as code review, rollbacks, and versioning.

Consider the following `Jenkinsfile`, which implements a basic five-stage continuous-delivery pipeline for the `FindAllMovies` Lambda function:

```
def bucket = 'movies-api-deployment-packages'

node('slave-golang'){
    stage('Checkout'){
        checkout scm
    }

    stage('Test'){
        sh 'go get -u github.com/golang/lint/golint'
        sh 'go get -t ./...'
        sh 'golint -set_exit_status'
        sh 'go vet .'
        sh 'go test .'
    }
```

```
    stage('Build'){
        sh 'GOOS=linux go build -o main main.go'
        sh "zip ${commitID()}.zip main"
    }

    stage('Push'){
        sh "aws s3 cp ${commitID()}.zip s3://${bucket}"
    }

    stage('Deploy'){
        sh "aws lambda update-function-code --function-name FindAllMovies \
            --s3-bucket ${bucket} \
            --s3-key ${commitID()}.zip \
            --region us-east-1"
    }
}

def commitID() {
    sh 'git rev-parse HEAD > .git/commitID'
    def commitID = readFile('.git/commitID').trim()
    sh 'rm .git/commitID'
    commitID
}
```

The pipeline uses a **domain-specific language** (**DSL**) based on Groovy's syntax and it will be executed on the node we added earlier to the cluster. Each time a change is pushed to the GitHub repository, your changes will go through multiple stages:

- Checking out code-form source control
- Running unit and quality tests
- Building the deployment package and storing this artifact to an S3 bucket
- Updating the `FindAllMovies` function's code

Note the usage of the git commit ID as a name for the deployment package to give a meaningful and significant name for each release and be able to roll back to a specific commit if things go wrong.

Now that our pipeline is defined, we need to create a new job on Jenkins by clicking on **New Item**. Then, enter a name for the job and select **Multibranch Pipeline**. Set the GitHub repository on which your Lambda function's code is stored and the path to the `Jenkinsfile` as follows:

 Prior to the build, an IAM instance role with write access to S3 and the update operation to Lambda must be configured on the Jenkins workers.

Once saved, the pipeline will be executed on the master branch and the job should go to green, as shown:

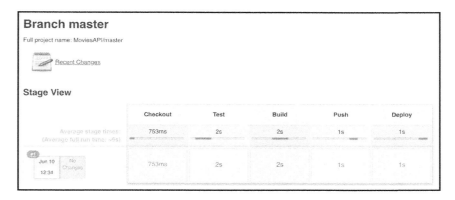

Once the pipeline is completed, you can click on each stage to see execution logs. In the following example, we can see the logs of the `Deploy` stage:

Git Hooks

Finally, to make Jenkins trigger the build when you push to the code repository, click on **Settings** from your GitHub repository, then on **Integrations & Services** search for **Jenkins (GitHub plugin)**, and fill it in with a URL similar to the following:

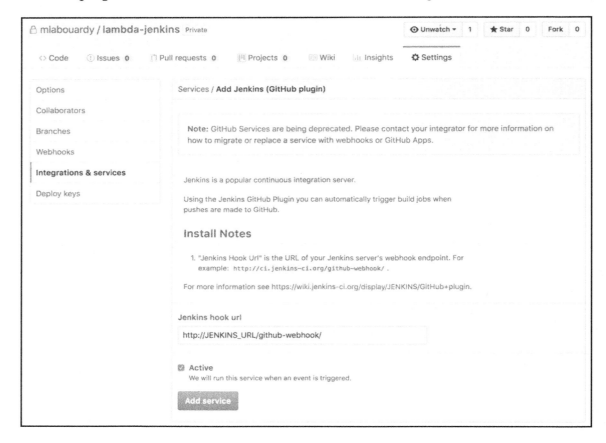

Now, any time you push code to your GitHub repository, the full Jenkins pipeline will be triggered, shown as follows:

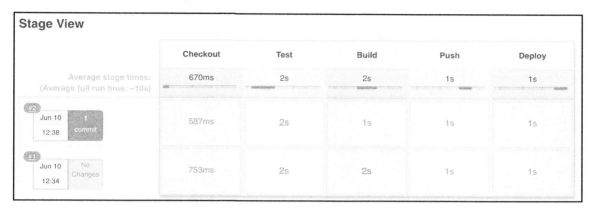

 Another way to make Jenkins create a build if it detects changes is by polling the target git repository periodically (cron job). This solution is a bit inefficient, but might be useful if your Jenkins instance is in a private network.

Continuous Integration with Circle CI

CircleCI is a "CI/CD as a Service". It's a platform that integrates very well with GitHub- and BitBuckets-based projects and has built-in support for Golang applications.

In the following section, we will see how to use CircleCI to automate the deployment process of our Lambda functions.

Identity and access management

Sign into Circle CI (`https://circleci.com/vcs-authorize/`) with your GitHub account. Then, select the repository on which your Lambda function's code is stored, then click on the **Set Up project** button so Circle CI can infer settings automatically, as shown in the following screenshot:

Similar to Jenkins and CodeBuild, CircleCI will need access to a few AWS services. Therefore, an IAM user is needed. Head back to AWS Management Console, and create a new IAM user called **circleci**. Generate the AWS credentials, click on **Settings** from the CircleCI project, and then paste the AWS access and secret keys, as shown in the following screenshot:

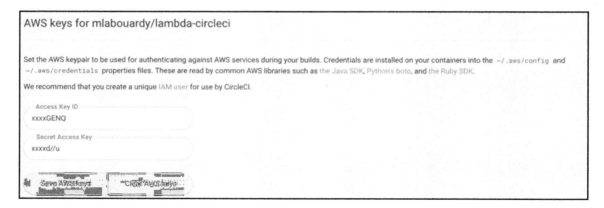

Be sure to attach IAM policies with permissions to read/write the S3 bucket and Lambda functions to the IAM user.

Configuring the CI Pipeline

Now that our project is set up, we need to define the CI workflow; to do so, we need to create a definition file, called the `config.yml` file, inside the `.circleci` folder with the following content:

```
version: 2
jobs:
  build:
    docker:
      - image: golang:1.8

    working_directory: /go/src/github.com/mlabouardy/lambda-circleci

    environment:
        S3_BUCKET: movies-api-deployment-packages

    steps:
      - checkout

      - run:
         name: Install AWS CLI & Zip
         command: |
          apt-get update
          apt-get install -y zip python-pip python-dev
          pip install awscli

      - run:
          name: Test
          command: |
           go get -u github.com/golang/lint/golint
           go get -t ./...
           golint -set_exit_status
           go vet .
           go test .

      - run:
         name: Build
         command: |
          GOOS=linux go build -o main main.go
          zip $CIRCLE_SHA1.zip main
```

```
    - run:
        name: Push
        command: aws s3 cp $CIRCLE_SHA1.zip s3://$S3_BUCKET

    - run:
        name: Deploy
        command: |
          aws lambda update-function-code --function-name FindAllMovies \
              --s3-bucket $S3_BUCKET \
              --s3-key $CIRCLE_SHA1.zip --region us-east-1
```

The build environment will be a Go official Docker image in DockerHub. From this image, a new container will be created and the commands listed in the *steps* section will be executed as follows:

1. Check out the code from the GitHub repository.
2. Install the AWS CLI and the ZIP command.
3. Execute automated tests.
4. Build a single binary from the source code and zipp up a deployment package. The commit ID corresponding to the build will be used as a name for the zip file (note the usage of the CIRCLE_SHA1 environment variable).
5. Save the artefact in the S3 bucket.
6. Update the Lambda function's code using the AWS CLI.

Once the template is defined and committed to the GitHub repository, a new build will be triggered as follows:

When the pipeline is successfully running, it will look like this:

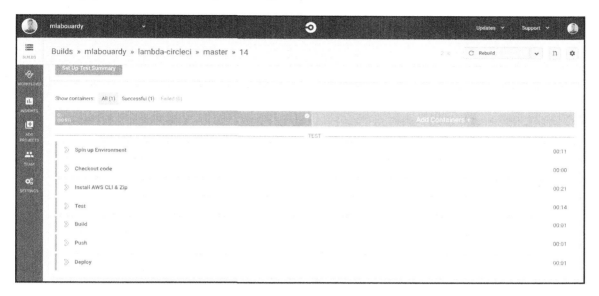

That's pretty much it. This chapter merely scratches the surface of what can be done with the CI/CD pipeline, but should provide enough of a foundation for you to start experimenting and build your end-to-end workflow for your Lambda functions.

Summary

In this chapter, we learned how to set up a CI/CD pipeline from scratch to automate the deployment process of Lambda functions and how this solution can be implemented using different CI tools and services starting with an AWS-managed service to a highly extensible build server.

In the next chapter, we will build an improved version of this pipeline by writing automated unit and integration tests for our serverless API and build a single page app with REST backend backed with serverless functions.

Questions

1. Implement a CI/CD pipeline for other Lambda functions with CodeBuild and CodePipeline.
2. Implement a similar workflow using Jenkins Pipeline.
3. Implement the same pipeline with CircleCI.
4. Add a new stage to the existing pipeline to publish a new version if the current git branch is the master.
5. Configure the pipeline to send a notification on a Slack channel every time a new Lambda function is deployed or updated.

Scaling Up Your Application

8

This chapter is a short break from the previous technical chapters, where we will go in-depth on the following:

- How serverless autoscaling works
- How Lambda can handle traffic demands during peak-service usage with no capacity planning or scheduled scaling
- How AWS Lambda uses concurrency to create multiple executions in parallel to your function's code
- How it can impact your cost and application performance.

Technical requirements

This chapter is a follow-up of the previous chapter as it will use the serverless API built in the previous one; it's recommended to read the previous chapter first before tackling this section.

Load testing and scaling

In this part, we will generate random workloads to see how Lambda acts when incoming requests increase. To achieve that, we will use a load-testing tool, such as **Apache Bench**. In this chapter, I will be using `hey`, which is a Go-based tool, and is very efficient and faster than classic `HTTP` benchmarking tools due to Golang's built-in concurrency. You can download it by installing the following `Go` package from your terminal:

```
go get -u github.com/rakyll/hey
```

Be sure that the $GOPATH variable is set to be able to execute the hey command regardless of your current directory, or you can add the $HOME/go/bin folder to the $PATH variable.

Lambda autoscaling

Now, we are ready to run our first harness or load testing by executing the following command:

```
hey -n 1000 -c 50
https://51cxzthvma.execute-api.us-east-1.amazonaws.com/staging/movies
```

If you prefer apache benchmark, the same command can be used by replacing the **hey** keyword with **ab.**

The command will open 50 connections and send 1,000 requests against the API Gateway endpoint URL for the FindAllMovies function. At the end of the test, **hey** will display information about the total response time and in-depth details about each request, as follows:

```
Summary:
  Total:        7.5889 secs
  Slowest:      2.5742 secs
  Fastest:      0.1340 secs
  Average:      0.3305 secs
  Requests/sec: 131.7718

  Total data:   495000 bytes
  Size/request: 495 bytes

Response time histogram:
  0.134 [1]     |
  0.378 [823]   |••••••••••••••••••••••••••••••••••••••••••••
  0.622 [35]    |••
  0.866 [66]    |•••
  1.110 [41]    |••
  1.354 [27]    |•
  1.598 [2]     |
  1.842 [1]     |
  2.086 [3]     |
  2.330 [0]     |
  2.574 [1]     |

Status code distribution:
  [200] 1000 responses
```

Make sure to replace the invocation URL with your own. Also, please note that some parts of the screenshot have been cropped to focus only on the useful content.

In addition to the total response time, **hey** gives an output of a response-time histogram that shows the first requests taking more time (around 2 seconds) to respond, which can be explained with the **cold start** since Lambda has to download the deployment package and initialize a new container. However, the rest of the requests were fast (less than 800 milliseconds), due to the **warm start** and the usage of existing containers from previous requests.

From the previous benchmark, we can say that Lambda keeps its promise of autoscaling when traffic is raised; while that might be a good thing, it has downsides, which we will see in the next section.

Downstream resources

In our example of the Movies API, a DynamoDB table has been used to resolve the stateless issue. This table requires the user to define the read and write throughput capacity, in advance, to create the necessary underlying infrastructure to handle the defined traffic. While creating the table in Chapter 5, *Managing Data Persistence with DynamoDB*, we used the default throughput, which is five read-capacity units and five write-capacity units. The five read-capacity units work as a charm for APIs that aren't read-heavy. In the previous load test, we created 50 concurrent executions, that is, 50 reads in parallel to the movies table. As a result, the table will be suffering from high read throughput, and the Scan operation will be slower and DynamoDB might start throttling requests.

We can verify this by going to the DynamoDB console and clicking on the **Metrics** tab from the `movies` table, as shown in the following screenshot:

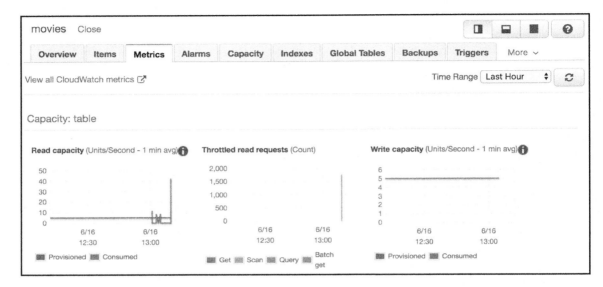

Clearly, the read-capacity graph experienced a high peak, which resulted in throttling read requests, and the table was overwhelmed by all of these incoming requests.

DynamoDB's throttling requests can be fixed by enabling the autoscaling mechanism to increase the provisioned read and write capacity to handle a sudden increase in traffic, or by reusing the query's results stored in the in-memory cache engine (a solution such as AWS ElastiCache with Redis or Memcached engine can be used) to avoid overwhelming the table and cutting several milliseconds off your function's execution time. However, you can't limit and protect your database resource from being overloaded in response to your Lambda function's scaling event.

Private Lambda functions

Another issue of concurrency can arise if your Lambda function is running inside a private VPC, since it will need to attach an **Elastic Network Interface** (**ENI**) to the Lambda container and wait for it to assign itself an IP. AWS Lambda uses the ENI to connect securely to internal resources in the VPC.

In addition to poor performance (attaching ENI takes an average of 4 seconds), a VPC-enabled Lambda function forces you to maintain and configure a NAT instance for internet access and a number of VPC subnets in multiple availability zones capable of supporting the ENI scaling requirements of your function, which might cause the VPC to run out of IP addresses.

To sum up, the Lambda function's autoscaling is a double-edged sword; it doesn't require capacity planning from your side. However, it might result in bad performance and surprising monthly bills. That's where the **concurrent execution** model comes into play.

Concurrent execution

AWS Lambda dynamically scales capacity in response to increased traffic. However, there's a limited number of an executed function's code at any given time. This number is called concurrent execution, and it's defined per AWS region. The default limit of concurrency is 1,000 per AWS region. So, what happens if your function crosses this defined threshold? Read on to find out.

Lambda throttling

Lambda applies throttling (rate limiting) to your function if the concurrent execution count is exceeding the limit. Hence, the remaining incoming requests won't invoke the function.

The invoking client is responsible for retrying the failed requests due to throttling by implementing a back-off strategy based on the HTTP code returned (429 = too many requests). It's worth mentioning that Lambda functions can be configured to store unprocessed events, after a certain number of retries, to a queue called the **dead letter queue**.

Throttling might be useful in some cases, as the concurrent execution capacity is shared across all functions (in our example, the find, update, insert, and delete functions). You may want to ensure that one function doesn't consume all the capacity and avoids starvation of the rest of the Lambda functions. This situation can happen frequently if one of your functions is used more than others. For example, consider the FindAllMovies function. Supposing it's the holiday season, a lot of customers will use your application to see a list of movies available to rent, which might result in several instances of the invocation of the FindAllMovies Lambda function.

Luckily, AWS has added a new feature that lets you reserve and define, in advance, a concurrent execution value per Lambda function. This property allows you to specify a number of reserved concurrency for your function so you are sure that your function always has enough capacity to handle upcoming events or requests. For instance, you could set rate limiting for your functions as follows:

- The `FindAllMovies` function: 500
- The `InsertMovie` function : 100
- The `UpdateMovie` function: 50
- The remaining will be shared among the others

In the upcoming section, we will see how to define a reserved concurrency for `FindAllMovies` and how it can impact the performance of the API.

 You can estimate the concurrent execution count with the following formula: `events/requests per second * function duration.`

Concurrency reservation

Navigate to the AWS Lambda Console (`https://console.aws.amazon.com/lambda/home`) and click on the **FindAllMovies** function. Under the **Concurrency** section, we can see that our function is only limited by the total amount of concurrency available in the account, which is **1000**, shown in the following screenshot:

Concurrency

Unreserved account concurrency **1000**

◉ Use unreserved account concurrency

◯ Reserve concurrency

We will change that by defining 10 in the reserved account's concurrency field. This ensures only 10 parallel executions of the function at any given time. This value will be deducted from the unreserved account's concurrency pool, shown as follows:

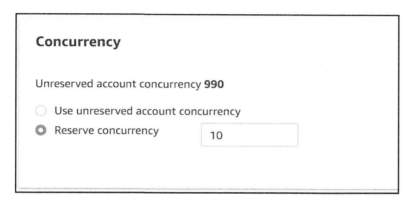

 The maximum reserved concurrency you can set is 900, as AWS Lambda reserves 100 for other functions so they can still process requests and events.

Alternatively, AWS CLI can be used with the put-function-concurrency command to set a concurrency limit:

```
aws lambda put-function-concurrency --function FindAllMovies --reserved-concurrent-executions 10
```

Once again, generate some workloads using the same command given previously:

```
hey -n 1000 -c 50
https://51cxzthvma.execute-api.us-east-1.amazonaws.com/staging/movies
```

This time, the result will be different, as 171 of 1,000 requests fail with the 502 code error, shown as follows:

```
Summary:
  Total:         12.2144 secs
  Slowest:        8.2846 secs
  Fastest:        0.1170 secs
  Average:        0.3482 secs
  Requests/sec:  81.8703

  Total data:    416511 bytes
  Size/request:  416 bytes

Response time histogram:
  0.117 [1]      |
  0.934 [924]    |••••••••••••••••••••••••••••••••••••••••••••
  1.751 [68]     |•••
  2.567 [6]      |
  3.384 [0]      |
  4.201 [0]      |
  5.018 [0]      |
  5.834 [0]      |
  6.651 [0]      |
  7.468 [0]      |
  8.285 [1]      |
Status code distribution:
  [200] 829 responses
  [502] 171 responses
```

Beyond 10 concurrent executions, a throttling is applied and part of the request is refused with the 502 response code.

We can confirm this by heading back to the function console; we should see a warning message similar to that shown in the following screenshot:

If you open the metrics related to the `movies` table and jump to the read-capacity chart, you can see that our read capacity will still be under control and below the defined 5 read-units capacity:

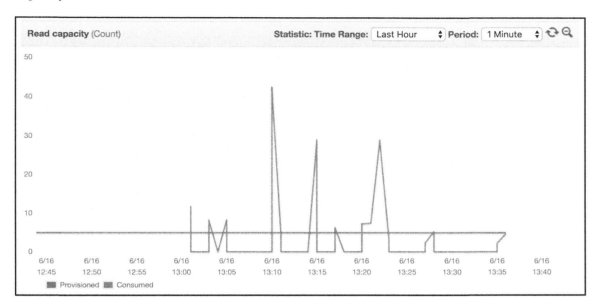

Throttling can be used if you're planning maintenance on a Lambda function and you want to stop its invocation temporarily, this can be done by setting the function concurrency to 0.

Throttle is working as expected and you are now protecting your downstream resources from too much load from your Lambda function.

Summary

In this chapter, we learned that Lambda cannot scale infinitely due the execution limit set per AWS region. This limit can be raised by contacting the AWS support team. We also covered how the concurrency reservation at the function level might help you to protect your downstream resources, match the subnet size if you're using a VPC-enabled Lambda function, and control your costs during the development and testing of your functions.

In the next chapter, we will build a user-friendly UI on top of the serverless API with an S3 static-hosted website feature.

Building the Frontend with S3

9

In this chapter, we will learn the following:

- How to build a static website that consumes API Gateway responses using AWS Simple Storage Service
- How to optimize the access to your website assets such as JavaScript, CSS, images with CloudFront distribution
- How to set up a custom domain name for a serverless application
- How to create an SSL certificate to show your content with HTTPS
- Automating the deployment process of the web application using a CI/CD pipeline.

Technical requirements

Before proceeding with this chapter, you should have a basic understanding of web development and knowledge of how DNS works. The code bundle for this chapter is hosted on GitHub at `https://github.com/PacktPublishing/Hands-On-Serverless-Applications-with-Go`.

Single Page Application

In this section, we will learn how to build a web application that will call the API Gateway invocation URL that we built in previous chapters and list the movies, as follows:

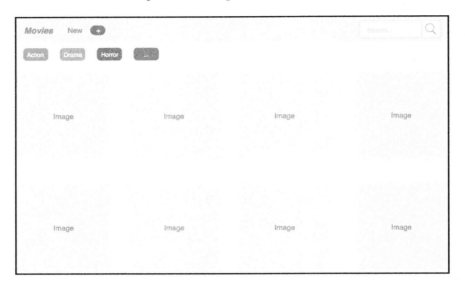

For each movie, we will display its cover image and title. In addition, a user can filter the movies by their categories by clicking on the button to the right of **Horror** . Finally, to add a new movie to the database, a modal will pop up if the user clicks on the **New** button on the navigation bar. The modal will ask the user to fill in the following fields:

Now that the application mock-ups are defined, we will use a JavaScript framework to build the web application quickly. For example, I will be using **Angular 5**, which is currently the latest stable version of Angular.

Developing web applications with Angular

Angular is a fully-integrated framework developed by Google. It allows you to build dynamic web applications without thinking about which libraries to select and how to deal with everyday problems. Keep in mind that the goal is to reach a large audience, Angular was chosen because it's one of the most commonly-used frameworks. However, it's up to you to choose whichever framework you're familiar with, such as React, Vue, or Ember.

In addition to built-in ready-to-use modules, Angular leverages the power of the **Single Page Application (SPA)** architecture. This architecture allows you to navigate between pages without refreshing the browser, hence allowing a better user experience as the application is more fluid and responsive, including better performance (you can preload and cache extra pages).

 Angular comes with its own CLI. You can install it by going to https://cli.angular.io for a step-by-step guide. This book is dedicated to Lambda. Hence, only the basic concepts of Angular are covered in the upcoming sections, to make this chapter easy to understand for those who aren't web developers.

Once the **Angular CLI** is installed, we need to create a new Angular application using the following command:

```
ng new frontend
```

The CLI will generate the basic templates files and install all the required **npm** dependencies to run an Angular 5 application. The file structure looks as follows:

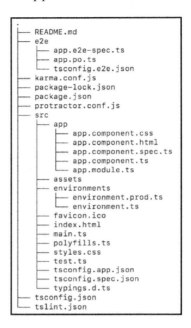

```
.
├── README.md
├── e2e
│   ├── app.e2e-spec.ts
│   ├── app.po.ts
│   └── tsconfig.e2e.json
├── karma.conf.js
├── package-lock.json
├── package.json
├── protractor.conf.js
├── src
│   ├── app
│   │   ├── app.component.css
│   │   ├── app.component.html
│   │   ├── app.component.spec.ts
│   │   ├── app.component.ts
│   │   └── app.module.ts
│   ├── assets
│   ├── environments
│   │   ├── environment.prod.ts
│   │   └── environment.ts
│   ├── favicon.ico
│   ├── index.html
│   ├── main.ts
│   ├── polyfills.ts
│   ├── styles.css
│   ├── test.ts
│   ├── tsconfig.app.json
│   ├── tsconfig.spec.json
│   └── typings.d.ts
├── tsconfig.json
└── tslint.json
```

Next, on the `frontend` directory, start a local web server with this command:

```
ng serve
```

The command will compile all the `TypeScripts` files, build the project, and start a web server on port `4200`:

```
** NG Live Development Server is listening on localhost:4200, open your browser on http://localhost:4200/ **
Date: 2018-06-23T18:05:23.375Z
Hash: 4cfeaf6b7f8f1f176347
Time: 5528ms
chunk {inline} inline.bundle.js (inline) 3.85 kB [entry] [rendered]
chunk {main} main.bundle.js (main) 17.9 kB [initial] [rendered]
chunk {polyfills} polyfills.bundle.js (polyfills) 555 kB [initial] [rendered]
chunk {styles} styles.bundle.js (styles) 41.5 kB [initial] [rendered]
chunk {vendor} vendor.bundle.js (vendor) 7.43 MB [initial] [rendered]
```

Open your browser and navigate to `http://localhost:4200`. This is what you should see in your browser:

Now that our sample app is built and running, let's create our web application. The Angular structure is based on either a components and services architecture (similar to Model-View-Controller).

Generating your first Angular component

For those who haven't had much experience with Angular, a component is basically a Lego brick for the UI. Your web application can be divided into multiple components. Each component has the following files:

- **COMPONENT_NAME.component.ts**: The component-logic definition written in TypeScript
- **COMPONENT_NAME.component.html**: The HTML code of the component
- **COMPONENT_NAME.component.css**: The CSS structure of the component
- **COMPONENT_NAME.component.spec.ts**: The unit test of the component class

In our example, we will need at least three components:

- The Navigation Bar component
- The List of Movies component
- The Movie component

Before we create our first component, let's install **Bootstrap**, which is a frontend web framework developed by Twitter to build attractive user interfaces. It comes with a set of CSS-based design templates for forms, buttons, navigation, and other interface components, as well as optional JavaScript extensions.

Go ahead and install Bootstrap 4 from your terminal:

```
npm install bootstrap@4.0.0-alpha.6
```

Next, import the Bootstrap CSS classes in the `.angular-cli.json` file in order to make the CSS directives available in all components of the application:

```
"styles": [
    "styles.css",
    "../node_modules/bootstrap/dist/css/bootstrap.min.css"
]
```

Now we are ready to create our navigation bar component by issuing the following command:

```
ng generate component components/navbar
```

Override the HTML code generated by default in `navbar.component.html` to use the navigation bar provided by the Bootstrap framework:

```
<nav class="navbar navbar-toggleable-md navbar-light bg-faded">
  <button class="navbar-toggler navbar-toggler-right" type="button" data-
toggle="collapse" data-target="#navbarSupportedContent" aria-
controls="navbarSupportedContent" aria-expanded="false" aria-label="Toggle
navigation">
    <span class="navbar-toggler-icon"></span>
  </button>
  <a class="navbar-brand" href="#">Movies</a>

  <div class="collapse navbar-collapse" id="navbarSupportedContent">
    <ul class="navbar-nav mr-auto">
      <li class="nav-item active">
        <a class="nav-link" href="#">New <span class="sr-
only">(current)</span></a>
      </li>
    </ul>
    <form class="form-inline my-2 my-lg-0">
      <input class="form-control mr-sm-2" type="text" placeholder="Search
...">
      <button class="btn btn-outline-success my-2 my-sm-0" type="submit">GO
!</button>
    </form>
```

```
    </div>
  </nav>
```

Open `navbar.component.ts` and update the selector property to `movies-navbar`. The selector here is nothing but a tag that can be used to reference the component on other components:

```
@Component({
  selector: 'movies-navbar',
  templateUrl: './navbar.component.html',
  styleUrls: ['./navbar.component.css']
})
export class NavbarComponent implements OnInit {
    ...
}
```

The `movies-navbar` selector needs to be added in the `app.component.html` file, as follows:

```
<movies-navbar></movies-navbar>
```

The Angular CLI uses live reload. Hence, every time our code is changed, the CLI will recompile, re-inject if needed, and ask the browser to refresh the page:

When the `movies-navbar` tag is added, everything that is present in the `navbar.component.html` file of the new component will be displayed in the browser.

Similarly, we will create a new component for the movie item:

```
ng generate component components/movie-item
```

We are going to display movies as cards in our interface; replace the `movie-item.component.html` code with the following:

```
<div class="card" style="width: 20rem;">
  <img class="card-img-top" src="http://via.placeholder.com/185x287"
alt="movie title">
  <div class="card-block">
    <h4 class="card-title">Movie</h4>
    <p class="card-text">Some quick description</p>
```

```
        <a href="#" class="btn btn-primary">Rent</a>
    </div>
</div>
```

In the browser, you should see something similar to this:

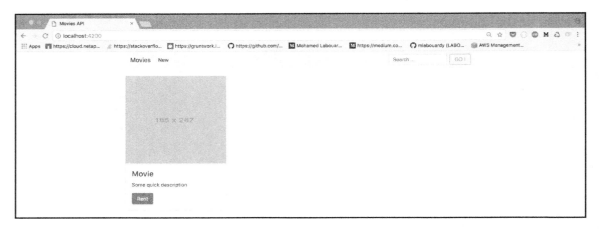

Create another component to display the list of movies:

```
ng generate component components/list-movies
```

This component will use the Angular ngFor directive to iterate over movie in the movies array and print out the movie by calling the movie-item component (this is known as composition):

```
<div class="row">
  <div class="col-sm-3" *ngFor="let movie of movies">
    <movie-item></movie-item>
  </div>
</div>
```

The movies array is declared in list-movies.component.ts and initialized in the class constructor:

```
import { Component, OnInit } from '@angular/core';
import { Movie } from '../../models/movie';

@Component({
  selector: 'list-movies',
  templateUrl: './list-movies.component.html',
  styleUrls: ['./list-movies.component.css']
})
export class ListMoviesComponent implements OnInit {
```

```
  public movies: Movie[];

  constructor() {
    this.movies = [
      new Movie("Avengers", "Some description",
"https://image.tmdb.org/t/p/w370_and_h556_bestv2/cezWGskPY5x7GaglTTRN4Fugfb
8.jpg"),
      new Movie("Thor", "Some description",
"https://image.tmdb.org/t/p/w370_and_h556_bestv2/bIuOWTtyFPjsFDevqvF3QrD1au
n.jpg"),
      new Movie("Spiderman", "Some description"),
    ]
  }
  ...


}
```

The `Movie` class is a simple entity with three fields, namely, `name`, `cover`, and `description`, and getters and setters to access and modify the class attributes:

```
export class Movie {
  private name: string;
  private cover: string;
  private description: string;

  constructor(name: string, description: string, cover?: string){
    this.name = name;
    this.description = description;
    this.cover = cover ? cover : "http://via.placeholder.com/185x287";
  }

  public getName(){
    return this.name;
  }

  public getCover(){
    return this.cover;
  }

  public getDescription(){
    return this.description;
  }

  public setName(name: string){
    this.name = name;
  }

  public setCover(cover: string){
```

```
      this.cover = cover;
  }

  public setDescription(description: string){
    this.description = description;
  }
}
```

If we run the preceding code, we will see three movies displayed in the browser:

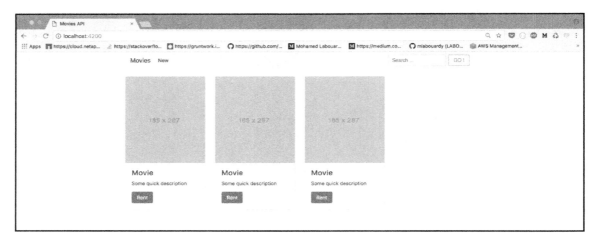

By now, the movie attributes are hardcoded in the HTML page, in order to change that, we need to pass the movie item to the `movie-item` element. Update `movie-item.component.ts` to add a new movie field and use the `Input` annotation to use the Angular input binding:

```
export class MovieItemComponent implements OnInit {
  @Input()
  public movie: Movie;


  ...
}
```

In the HTML template of the preceding component, use the getters of the `Movie` class to get the values of attributes:

```
<div class="card">
    <img class="card-img-top" [src]="movie.getCover()"
alt="{{movie.getName()}}">
    <div class="card-block">
      <h4 class="card-title">{{movie.getName()}}</h4>
```

```
    <p class="card-text">{{movie.getDescription()}}</p>
    <a href="#" class="btn btn-primary">Rent</a>
  </div>
</div>
```

Finally, make the `ListMoviesComponent` nest the `MovieItemComponent` child inside an `*ngFor` repeater, and bind the`movie` instance to the child's `movie` property on each iteration:

```
<div class="row">
  <div class="col-sm-3" *ngFor="let movie of movies">
    <movie-item [movie]="movie"></movie-item>
  </div>
</div>
```

In the browser, you should ensure that the movie's attributes are properly defined:

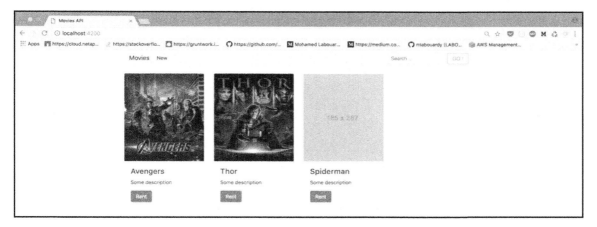

Everything is going well so far. However, the movies list is still static and hardcoded. We will fix that by calling the serverless API to retrieve the list of movies dynamically from the database.

Accessing Rest web services with Angular

In the previous chapters, we created two stages, the `staging` and `production` environments. Therefore, we should create two environment files to point to the right API Gateway deployment stage:

- `environment.ts`: Contains the development HTTP URL:

```
export const environment = {
  api:
'https://51cxzthvma.execute-api.us-east-1.amazonaws.com/staging/mov
ies'
};
```

- `environment.prod.ts`: Contains the production HTTP URL:

```
export const environment = {
  api:
'https://51cxzthvma.execute-api.us-east-1.amazonaws.com/production/
movies'
};
```

The `environment` object will read the values from `environment.ts` if `ng build` or `ng serve` are executed, and read the values from `environment.prod.ts` if you build your application for production mode with the `ng build --prod` command.

To create a service, we need to make use of the command line. The command is as follows:

```
ng generate service services/moviesApi
```

`movies-api.service.ts` will implement the `findAll` function, which will call the API Gateway `findAll` endpoint using the `Http` service. The `map` method will help convert the response to JSON format:

```
import { Injectable } from '@angular/core';
import { Http } from '@angular/http';
import 'rxjs/add/operator/map';
import { environment } from '../../environments/environment';

@Injectable()
  export class MoviesApiService {

    constructor(private http:Http) { }

    findAll(){
      return this.http
      .get(environment.api)
```

```
    .map(res => {
      return res.json()
    })
  }

}
```

Before calling `MoviesApiService`, it needs to be imported in the `app.module.ts` main module in the providers section.

Update `MoviesListComponent` to call the new service. On the browser console, you should have an error message regarding the **Access-Control-Allow-Origin** header not being present in the response returned by the API Gateway.That will be the topic of the upcoming section:

Cross Origin Resource Sharing

For security purposes, the browser will block the flow if the external requests don't match the exact host, protocol, and port of your website. In our example, we have different domain names (localhost and API Gateway URL).

This mechanism is known as the **Same-origin policy**. To solve this problem, you can either use a CORS header, proxy server, or JSON workaround. In this section, I will demonstrate how we can use a CORS header in the response returned by the Lambda function to resolve this issue:

1. Modify the `findAllMovie` function's code to add `Access-Control-Allow-Origin:*` to enable cross-origin requests from anywhere (or specify a domain instead of *):

   1. ```
      return events.APIGatewayProxyResponse{
           StatusCode: 200,
           Headers: map[string]string{
             "Content-Type": "application/json",
             "Access-Control-Allow-Origin": "*",
      ```
      ```

```
    },
    Body: string(response),
}, nil
```

2. Commit your changes; a new build should be triggered. At the end of the CI/CD pipeline, the `FindAllMovies` Lambda function's code will be updated. Test it out; you should have the new key as part of the `headers` attribute:

1. If you refresh the web application page, the JSON objects will be displayed in the console too:

4. Update `list-movies.component.ts` to call the `findAll` function from `MoviesApiService`. The data returned will be stored in the `movies` variable:

```
constructor(private moviesApiService: MoviesApiService) {
  this.movies = []

  this.moviesApiService.findAll().subscribe(res => {
    res.forEach(movie => {
    this.movies.push(new Movie(movie.name, "Some description"))
    })
  })
}
```

5. As a result, the list of movies will be retrieved and displayed:

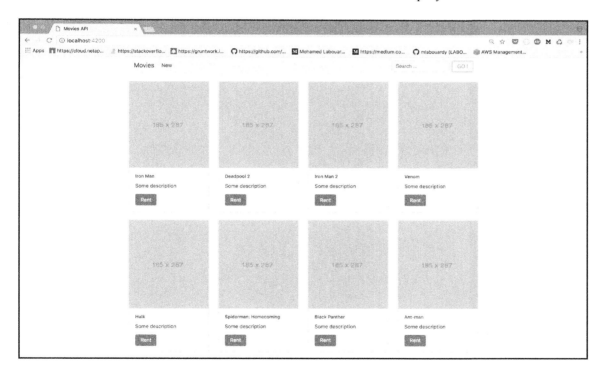

6. We don't have cover images; you can update the DynamoDB `movies` table to add an image and description attributes:

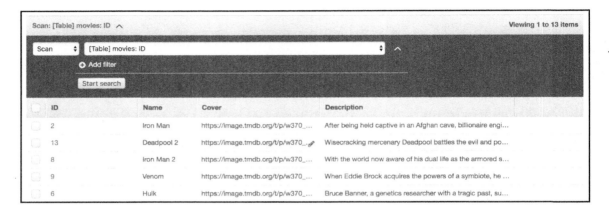

The NoSQL database allows you to alter the table schema at any time without having to first define the structure, while the relational database requires you to use predefined schemas to determine the structure of your data before you work with it.

7. If you refresh the web-application page, you should have the movies with their corresponding description and poster cover:

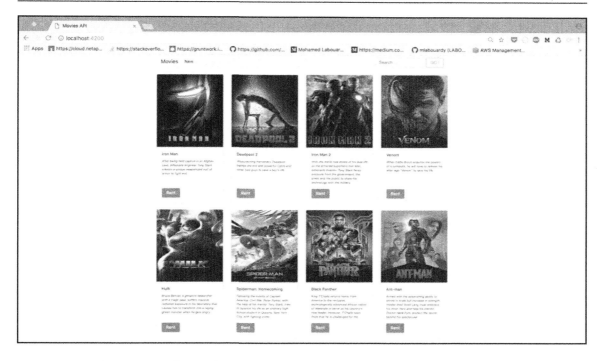

8. Let's improve this web application by implementing a new movie feature. As the user needs to fill in the movie's image cover and description, we need to update the `insert` Lambda function to add a cover and description fields in addition to a random unique ID generated on the backend:

```
svc := dynamodb.New(cfg)
req := svc.PutItemRequest(&dynamodb.PutItemInput{
  TableName: aws.String(os.Getenv("TABLE_NAME")),
  Item: map[string]dynamodb.AttributeValue{
    "ID": dynamodb.AttributeValue{
      S: aws.String(uuid.Must(uuid.NewV4()).String()),
    },
    "Name": dynamodb.AttributeValue{
      S: aws.String(movie.Name),
    },
    "Cover": dynamodb.AttributeValue{
      S: aws.String(movie.Cover),
    },
    "Description": dynamodb.AttributeValue{
      S: aws.String(movie.Description),
    },
  },
})
```

9. Once the new changes are pushed to the code repository and deployed, open your REST client and issue a POST request to add a new movie with the following JSON scheme:

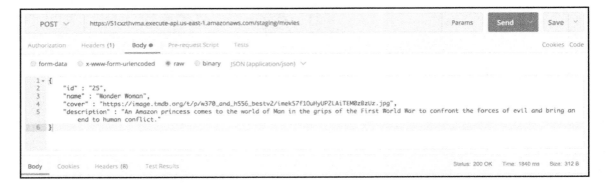

10. A `200` success code should be returned, and in the web application, the new movie should be listed:

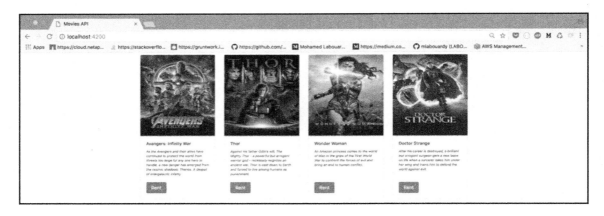

As seen in the *Single Page Application* section, when the user clicks on the **New** button, a modal will pop up with a creation form. In order to build this modal and to avoid using jQuery, we will use another library that provides a set of native Angular directives based on Bootstrap's markup and CSS:

- Install this library with the following command:

  npm install --save @ng-bootstrap/ng-bootstrap@2.0.0

- Once installed, you need to import it into the main `app.module.ts` module, as follows:

```
import {NgbModule} from '@ng-bootstrap/ng-bootstrap';

@NgModule({
  declarations: [AppComponent, ...],
  imports: [NgbModule.forRoot(), ...],
  bootstrap: [AppComponent]
})
export class AppModule {
}
```

- To hold the creation form, we need to create a new component:

  ng generate component components/new-movie

- This component will have two `input` fields for the movie's title and cover link. Plus, a `textarea` element for the movie's description:

```
<div class="modal-header">
 <h4 class="modal-title">New Movie</h4>
 <button type="button" class="close" aria-label="Close"
(click)="d('Cross click')">
 <span aria-hidden="true">&times;</span>
 </button>
</div>
<div class="modal-body">
 <div *ngIf="showMsg" class="alert alert-success" role="alert">
 <b>Well done !</b> You successfully added a new movie.
 </div>
 <div class="form-group">
 <label for="title">Title</label>
 <input type="text" class="form-control" #title>
 </div>
 <div class="form-group">
 <label for="description">Description</label>
```

```
<textarea class="form-control" #description></textarea>
</div>
<div class="form-group">
<label for="cover">Cover</label>
<input type="text" class="form-control" #cover>
</div>
</div>
<div class="modal-footer">
   <button type="button" class="btn btn-success"
(click)="save(title.value, description.value,
cover.value)">Save</button>
</div>
```

- Each time the user clicks on the **Save** button, a `save` function will be invoked in response to the click event. The `insert` function defined in the `MoviesApiService` service calls the `POST` method on the `insert` endpoint of the API Gateway:

```
insert(movie: Movie){
  return this.http
    .post(environment.api, JSON.stringify(movie))
    .map(res => {
    return res
  })
}
```

- Add a click event on the **New** element from the navigation bar:

```
<a class="nav-link" href="#" (click)="newMovie(content)">New <span
class="badge badge-danger">+</span></a>
```

- The click event will call `newMovie` and open the modal by calling the `ModalService` module of the `ng-bootstrap` library:

```
import { Component, OnInit, Input } from '@angular/core';
import { NgbModal } from '@ng-bootstrap/ng-bootstrap';

@Component({
 selector: 'movies-navbar',
 templateUrl: './navbar.component.html',
 styleUrls: ['./navbar.component.css']
})
export class NavbarComponent implements OnInit {

  constructor(private modalService: NgbModal) {}
```

```
ngOnInit() {}

newMovie(content){
this.modalService.open(content);
}

}
```

- Once these changes are compiled, click on the **New** item from the navigation bar, and the modal will pop up. Fill in the required fields and click on the **Save** button:

- The movie will be saved in the database table. If you refresh the page, the movie will be in the list of movies displayed:

S3 static website hosting

Now that our application has been created, let's deploy it to a remote server. Instead of maintaining a web server, such as Apache or Nginx in an EC2 instance, let's keep it serverless and use an S3 bucket with the S3 website-hosting feature enabled.

Setting up an S3 bucket

To get started, create an S3 bucket either from the AWS console or with the following AWS CLI command:

```
aws s3 mb s3://serverlessmovies.com
```

Next, build the web application for production mode:

```
ng build --prod
```

The --prod flag will generate an optimized version of the code and do additional build steps, such as JavaScript and CSS minification, dead code elimination, and bundling:

```
Date:  2018-06-24T17:39:31.482Z
Hash:  4870a3911724918b2466
Time:  20396ms
chunk {0} polyfills.515ed9df1f4876ab6cb6.bundle.js (polyfills) 60 kB [initial] [rendered]
chunk {1} main.ecb96ae2bb4355e70eb4.bundle.js (main) 9.13 kB [initial] [rendered]
chunk {2} styles.5c9d48c2c251b98de238.bundle.css (styles) 137 kB [initial] [rendered]
chunk {3} vendor.334b71a0e16bfb5f7e15.bundle.js (vendor) 1.08 MB [initial] [rendered]
chunk {4} inline.31e1fb380eb7cf3d75b1.bundle.js (inline) 798 bytes [entry] [rendered]
```

This will give you the dist/ directory with index.html and all the bundled js files ready for production. Configure the bucket to host a website:

```
aws s3 website s3://serverlessmovies.com --index-document index.html
```

Copy everything within the *dist/* folder into the S3 bucket we created earlier:

```
aws s3 cp --recursive dist/ s3://serverlessmovies.com/
```

You can verify that the files have been successfully stored from the S3 bucket dashboard or with the `aws s3 ls` command:

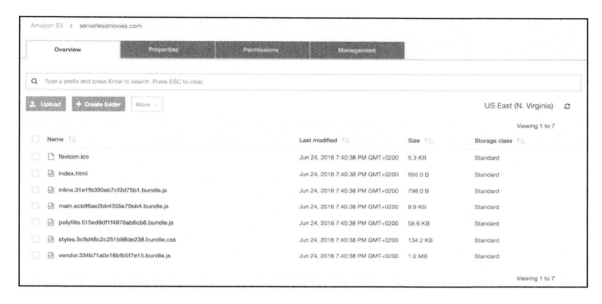

By default, when you create an S3 bucket, it's private. Hence, you should make it publicly accessible with the following bucket policy:

```
{
  "Id": "Policy1529862214606",
  "Version": "2012-10-17",
  "Statement": [
    {
      "Sid": "Stmt1529862213126",
      "Action": [
        "s3:GetObject"
      ],
      "Effect": "Allow",
      "Resource": "arn:aws:s3:::serverlessmovies.com/*",
      "Principal": "*"
    }
  ]
}
```

On the bucket configuration page, click on the **Permissions** tab, then **Bucket Policy**, paste the policy content to the editor, and then **Save** it. A warning message will pop up indicating that the bucket has become public:

To access the web application, point your browser to `http://serverlessmovies.s3-website-us-east-1.amazonaws.com` (replace this with your own bucket name):

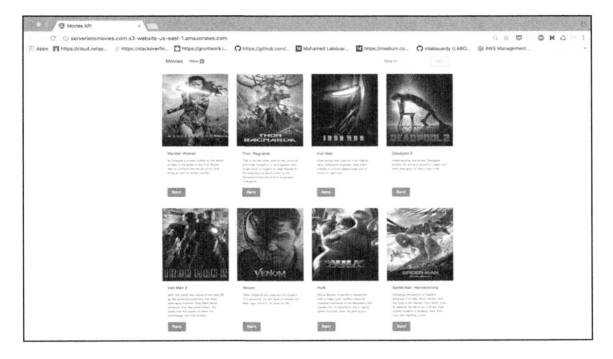

Now that our application is deployed to production, let's create a custom domain name to have a user-friendly link to access the website. To route domain traffic to the S3 bucket, we will use **Amazon Route 53** to create an alias record that points into the bucket.

Setting up Route 53

If you are new to Route 53, create a new hosted zone with the domain name you own, as in the following image. You can either use an existing domain name or buy one from the Amazon registrar or an external DNS registrar, such as GoDaddy. Make sure to choose **Public Hosted Zone**:

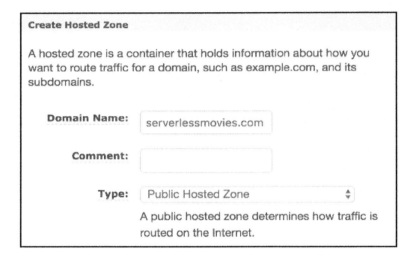

Once created, the NS and SOA records are created automatically for you. If you bought your domain name from AWS, you can skip this section. If not, you must change the nameservers record on the registrar you bought the domain name from. In this example, I bought the `http://serverlessmovies.com/` domain name from GoDaddy, so on the domain name settings page, I have changed the nameservers to point to the NS record values provided by AWS, as follows:

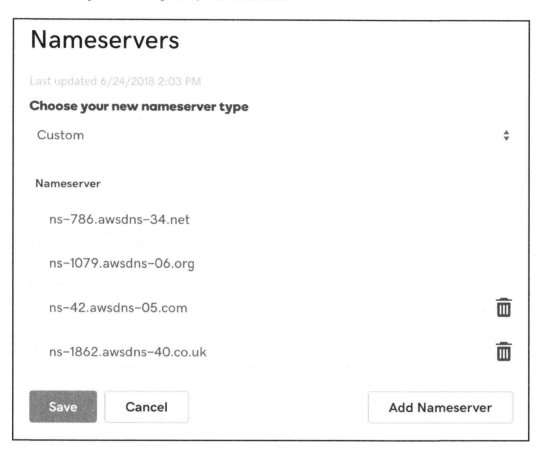

It may take a few minutes for the changes to propagate. Once it's validated by the registrar, hop over to `Route 53` and create a new `A` alias record that points to the S3 website we created earlier by selecting the target S3 bucket from the drop-down list:

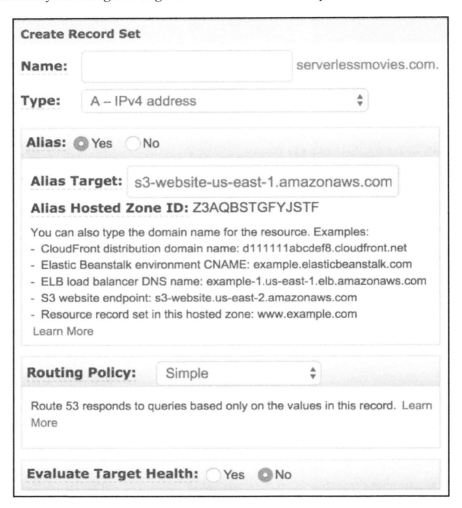

When you're finished, you'll be able to open a browser, enter the name of your domain, and view your web application:

Having a secure website can make a difference and make users trust your web application more, which is why, in the upcoming section, we will use a free SSL provided by AWS to show the content with `HTTPS` at your custom domain name.

Certificate Manager

You can easily get an SSL certificate with **AWS Certificate Manager (ACM)**. Click on the **Request a certificate** button to create a new SSL certificate:

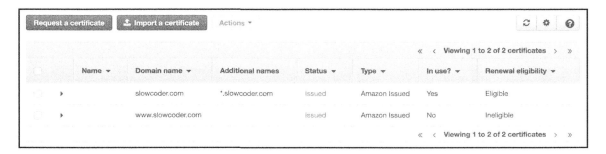

Select **Request a public certificate**and add your domain name. You might also want to secure your subdomains by adding an asterisk:

Under both domain names, click on the **Create record in Route 53** button. This will automatically create a CNAME record set in Route 53 with the given values, which ACM will then check in order to validate that you own those domains:

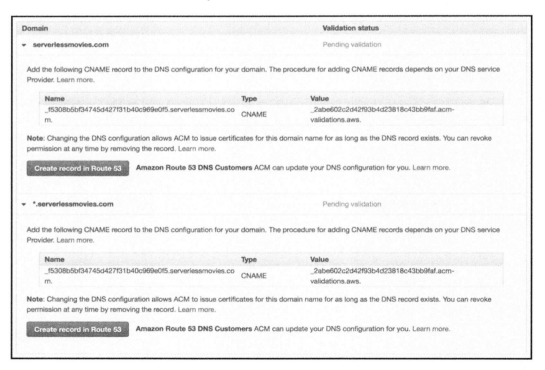

Once Amazon verifies that the domain name is yours, the certificate status will change from **Pending validation** to **Issued**:

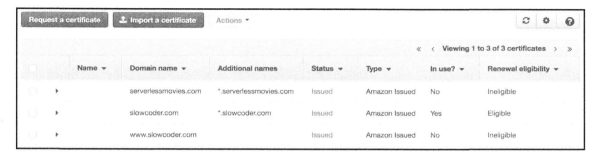

	Name ▾	Domain name ▾	Additional names	Status ▾	Type ▾	In use? ▾	Renewal eligibility ▾
▸		serverlessmovies.com	*.serverlessmovies.com	Issued	Amazon Issued	No	Ineligible
▸		slowcoder.com	*.slowcoder.com	Issued	Amazon Issued	Yes	Eligible
▸		www.slowcoder.com		Issued	Amazon Issued	No	Ineligible

However, we can't configure the S3 bucket to use our SSL to encrypt the traffic. That's why we will use a **CloudFront** distribution, also known as a CDN, in front of the S3 bucket.

CloudFront distribution

In addition to using CloudFront to add SSL termination on the website, CloudFront is mostly used as a **Content Delivery Network (CDN)** to store static assets (such as HTML pages, images, fonts, CSS, and JavaScript) in multiple edge locations around the world, which results in faster downloads and within less response time.

That being said, navigate to CloudFront, and then create a new web distribution. Set the S3 website URL in the **Origin Domain Name** field and leave the other fields as the default. You may want to redirect the HTTP traffic to HTTPS:

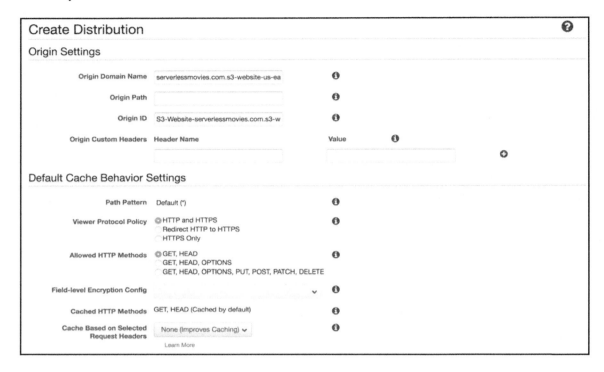

Next, select the SSL certificate we created in the *Certificate Manager* section and add your domain name to the **Alternate Domain Names (CNAMEs)** area:

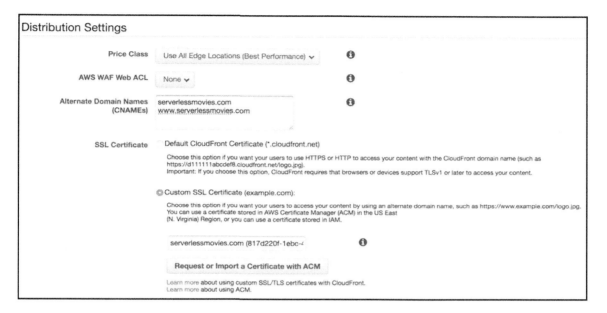

Click on **Save** and wait a few minutes while CloudFront copies all the files to the AWS edge locations:

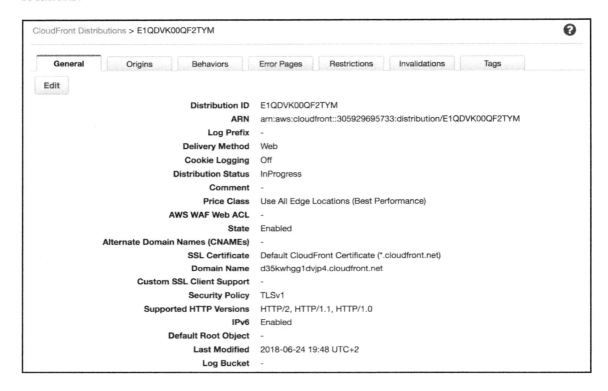

Once the CDN is fully deployed, jump to the domain-name-hosted zone page and update the website record to point to the CloudFront distribution domain:

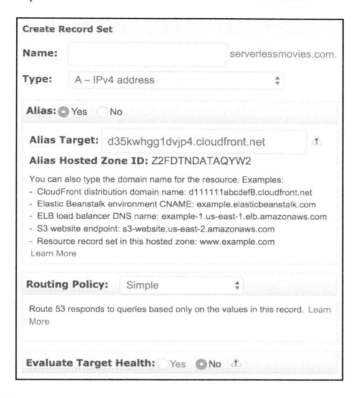

If you go to the URL again, you should be redirected to HTTPS:

 Feel free to create a new CNAME record for the API Gateway URL. The record might be https://api.serverlessmovies.com, which points tohttps://51cxzthvma.execute-api.us-east-1.amazonaws.com/production/movies.

CI/CD workflow

Our serverless application is deployed to production. However, to avoid doing the same steps over and over each time you implement a new functionality, we can create a CI/CD pipeline to automate the workflow described in the previous section. I opt for CircleCI as a CI server. However, you might use Jenkins or CodePipeline—make sure to read the previous chapters for more details.

As seen in the previous chapters, the pipeline should be defined in a template file. The following is an example of the pipeline used to automate the deployment process of the web app:

```
version: 2
jobs:
  build:
    docker:
      - image: node:10.5.0

    working_directory: ~/serverless-movies
    steps:
      - checkout
      - restore_cache:
          key: node-modules-{{checksum "package.json"}}
      - run:
          name: Install dependencies
          command: npm install && npm install -g @angular/cli
      - save_cache:
          key: node-modules-{{checksum "package.json"}}
          paths:
            - node_modules
      - run:
          name: Build assets
          command: ng build --prod --aot false
      - run:
          name: Install AWS CLI
          command: |
            apt-get update
            apt-get install -y awscli
      - run:
          name: Push static files
          command: aws s3 cp --recursive dist/ s3://serverlessmovies.com/
```

The following steps will be executed in order:

- Checking out the changes from the code repository
- Installing the AWS CLI, application npm dependencies, and the Angular CLI
- Building the artifacts with the `ng build` command
- Copying over the artefacts to the S3 bucket

Now, all changes to your web application's code will go through the pipeline and will be deployed automatically to production:

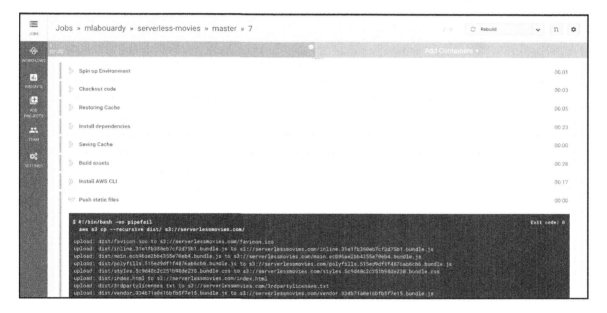

API documentation

Before finishing this chapter, we will go through how to create documentation for the serverless API we've built so far.

On the API Gateway console, select the deployment stage that you're interested in generating documentation for. In the following example, I chose the `production` environment. Then, click on the **Export** tab and click on the **Export as Swagger** section:

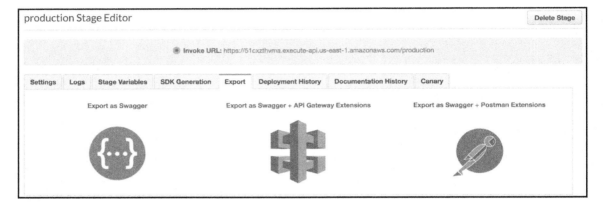

Swagger is an implementation of the **OpenAPI**, which is a standard defined by the Linux Foundation on how to describe and define APIs. This definition is called the **OpenAPI specification document**.

You can save the document in either a JSON or YAML file. Then, navigate to `https://editor.swagger.io/` and paste the content on the website editor, it will be compiled and an HTML page will be generated as follows:

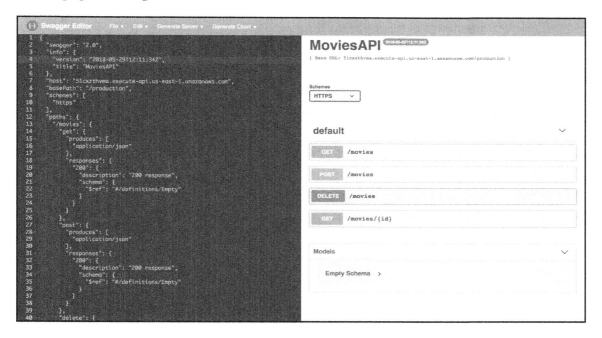

The AWS CLI can also be used to export the API Gateway documentation with the `aws apigateway get-export --rest-api-id API_ID --stage-name STAGE_NAME --export-type swagger swagger.json` command.

API Gateway and Lambda functions are similar to the serverless application. A CI/CD can be written to automate the generation of the documentation automatically each time a new endpoint or resource has been implemented on the API Gateway. The pipeline must implement the following steps:

- Create an S3 bucket
- Enable a static website feature on the bucket
- Download the Swagger UI from `https://github.com/swagger-api/swagger-ui` and copy the source code to S3
- Create a DNS record (`docs.serverlessmovies.com`)
- Run the `aws apigateway export` command to generate the Swagger definition file
- Copy the `spec` file to S3 with the `aws s3 cp` command

Summary

To sum up, we have seen how to build a serverless API from scratch using multiple Lambda functions, as well as how to use API Gateway to create a unified API and dispatch the incoming requests to the right Lambda function. We resolved the Lambda's stateless issue with a DynamoDB datastore and looked at how the use of reserved concurrency can help protect downstream resources. Then, we hosted a serverless web application in an S3 bucket with CloudFront in front of it to optimize the delivery of the web assets. Finally, we learned how to route domain traffic to the web application using Route 53 and how to secure it with SSL termination.

The following figure illustrates the architecture we've implemented so far:

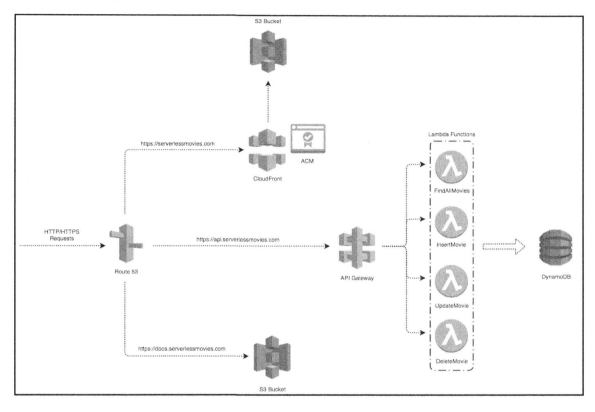

In the next chapter, we will improve the CI/CD workflow to add unit and integration testing to catch bugs and issues before deploying Lambda functions to production.

Questions

1. Implement a Lambda function that takes the movie category as input and returns a list of movies that correspond to that category.
2. Implement a Lambda function that takes a movie's title as input and returns all movies that have the keyword in their title.
3. Implement a delete button on the web application to delete a movie by calling the `DeleteMovie` Lambda function from API Gateway.
4. Implement an edit button on the web application to allow the user to update movie attributes.
5. Implement a CI/CD workflow with either CircleCI, Jenkins, or CodePipeline to automate the generation and deployment of the API Gateway documentation.

10
Testing Your Serverless Application

This chapter will teach you how to test your serverless application locally using the AWS Serverless Application Model. We will also cover Go unit testing and performance testing with third-party tools, and how Lambda itself can be used to perform test harness.

Technical requirements

This chapter is a follow-up to Chapter 7, *Implementing a CI/CD Pipeline*, and hence it's recommended to read that chapter first to follow this one with ease. In addition, experience with test-driven development practices is recommended. The code bundle for this chapter is hosted on GitHub at `https://github.com/PacktPublishing/Hands-On-Serverless-Applications-with-Go`.

Unit testing

Unit testing your Lambda function means testing the function handler in total isolation (as far as possible) from external resources (such as the following events: DynamoDB, S3, Kinesis). These tests allow you to catch bugs before actually deploying your new changes to production and maintain the quality, reliability, and security of your source code.

Before we write our first unit test, some background about testing in Golang might be helpful. To write a new test suite in Go, the filename must end with `_test.go` and contain the functions with a `TestFUNCTIONNAME` prefix. The `Test` prefix helps to identify the test routine. The files that end with the `_test` suffix will be excluded while building the deployment package and will be executed only if the `go test` command is issued. In addition, Go comes with a built-in `testing` package with a lot of helper functions. However, for simplicity, we will use a third-party package called `testify` that you can install with the following command:

```
go get -u github.com/stretchr/testify
```

Here is an example of the Lambda function we built in the previous chapter to list all the movies in the DynamoDB table. The following represents the code we want to test:

```go
func findAll() (events.APIGatewayProxyResponse, error) {
  ...

  svc := dynamodb.New(cfg)
  req := svc.ScanRequest(&dynamodb.ScanInput{
    TableName: aws.String(os.Getenv("TABLE_NAME")),
  })
  res, err := req.Send()
  if err != nil {
    return events.APIGatewayProxyResponse{
      StatusCode: http.StatusInternalServerError,
      Body: "Error while scanning DynamoDB",
    }, nil
  }

  ...

  return events.APIGatewayProxyResponse{
    StatusCode: 200,
    Headers: map[string]string{
      "Content-Type": "application/json",
      "Access-Control-Allow-Origin": "*",
    },
    Body: string(response),
  }, nil
}
```

To cover the code fully, we need to test all the edge cases. Examples of tests we can perform include:

- Testing the behavior without an IAM role assigned to the function.
- Testing with an IAM role assigned to the function.

In order to simulate the Lambda function running without an IAM role, we can remove the credentials file or unset the AWS environment variables if you're using them locally. Then, issue the `aws s3 ls` command to verify the AWS CLI cannot locate the AWS credentials. If you see the following message, you should be good to go:

```
Unable to locate credentials. You can configure credentials by running "aws
configure".
```

Write your unit test in a file called `main_test.go`:

```
package main

import (
  "net/http"
  "testing"

  "github.com/aws/aws-lambda-go/events"
  "github.com/stretchr/testify/assert"
)

func TestFindAll_WithoutIAMRole(t *testing.T) {
  expected := events.APIGatewayProxyResponse{
    StatusCode: http.StatusInternalServerError,
    Body: "Error while scanning DynamoDB",
  }
  response, err := findAll()
  assert.IsType(t, nil, err)
  assert.Equal(t, expected, response)
}
```

The test function starts with the `Test` keyword, followed by the function name and the behavior we want to test. Next, it calls the `findAll` handler and compares the actual result with the expected response. Then, you can follow these steps:

1. Launch the test with the following command. The command will look for any tests in any of the files in the current folder and run them. Make sure to set the TABLE_NAME environment variable:

   TABLE_NAME=movies go test

   Great! Our test works because the expected and actual response body are equal to the **Error while scanning DynamoDB** value:

```
PASS
ok      github.com/mlabouardy/Hands-On-Serverless-Applications-with-Go/ch10/findAll    0.020s
```

2. Write another test function to validate the behavior of the handler if an IAM role is assigned to the Lambda function at runtime:

```
package main

import (
  "testing"

  "github.com/stretchr/testify/assert"
)

func TestFindAll_WithIAMRole(t *testing.T) {
  response, err := findAll()
  assert.IsType(t, nil, err)
  assert.NotNil(t, response.Body)
}
```

Once again, the test should pass as the expected and actual response body is not empty:

```
PASS
ok      github.com/mlabouardy/Hands-On-Serverless-Applications-with-Go/ch10/findAll      0.683s
```

You have now run a unit test in Go; let's write another unit test for the Lambda function that expects an input parameter. Let's take the insert method as an example. The code we want to test is the following (the full code can be found in the GitHub repository):

```
func insert(request events.APIGatewayProxyRequest)
(events.APIGatewayProxyResponse, error) {
  ...
  return events.APIGatewayProxyResponse{
    StatusCode: 200,
    Headers: map[string]string{
      "Content-Type": "application/json",
      "Access-Control-Allow-Origin": "*",
    },
  }, nil
}
```

This scenario is an invalid payload as an input parameter. The function should return a 400 error with an Invalid payload message:

```
func TestInsert_InvalidPayLoad(t *testing.T) {
  input := events.APIGatewayProxyRequest{
    Body: "{'name': 'avengers'}",
  }
```

```
    expected := events.APIGatewayProxyResponse{
      StatusCode: 400,
      Body: "Invalid payload",
    }
    response, _ := insert(input)
    assert.Equal(t, expected, response)
  }
```

Another use case is when given a valid payload; the function should insert the movie into the database and return a 200 success code:

```
func TestInsert_ValidPayload(t *testing.T) {
  input := events.APIGatewayProxyRequest{
    Body: "{\"id\":\"40\", \"name\":\"Thor\", \"description\":\"Marvel
movie\", \"cover\":\"poster url\"}",
  }
  expected := events.APIGatewayProxyResponse{
    StatusCode: 200,
    Headers: map[string]string{
      "Content-Type": "application/json",
      "Access-Control-Allow-Origin": "*",
    },
  }
  response, _ := insert(input)
  assert.Equal(t, expected, response)
}
```

The two tests should successfully pass. This time, we will run the `go test` command in code coverage mode with the `-cover` flag:

TABLE_NAME=movies go test -cover

We have 78% of the code covered by the unit test:

```
PASS
coverage: 78.6% of statements
ok      github.com/mlabouardy/Hands-On-Serverless-Applications-with-Go/ch10/insert      0.711s
```

If you want in-depth details about which statements are covered by the test and which are not, you can generate an HTML coverage report with the following commands:

TABLE_NAME=movies go test -cover -coverprofile=coverage.out
go tool cover -html=coverage.out -o coverage.html

If you open `coverage.html` in the browser, you can see the statements that are not covered by the unit test:

You can improve the unit test by taking advantage of Go's interface to mock the DynamoDB calls. This allows you to mock out the implementation of DynamoDB instead of using the concrete service client directly (for example, `https://aws.amazon.com/blogs/developer/mocking-out-then-aws-sdk-for-go-for-unit-testing/`).

Automated unit tests

Having unit tests is great. Yet, a unit test without automation is not useful, so your CI/CD pipeline should have a testing stage to execute the unit test for every change committed to the code repository. This mechanism has many benefits, such as ensuring your codebase is in a bug-free state and allowing developers to detect and fix integration problems continuously, and thus avoid last-minute chaos on release dates. The following is an example of the pipeline we built in previous chapters to deploy the Lambda function automatically:

```
version: 2
jobs:
  build:
    docker:
      - image: golang:1.8

    working_directory: /go/src/github.com/mlabouardy/lambda-circleci

    environment:
      S3_BUCKET: movies-api-deployment-packages
      TABLE_NAME: movies
      AWS_REGION: us-east-1

    steps:
      - checkout

      - run:
          name: Install AWS CLI & Zip
          command: |
            apt-get update
            apt-get install -y zip python-pip python-dev
            pip install awscli

      - run:
          name: Test
          command: |
            go get -u github.com/golang/lint/golint
            go get -t ./...
            golint -set_exit_status
            go vet .
            go test .

      - run:
          name: Build
          command: |
            GOOS=linux go build -o main main.go
            zip $CIRCLE_SHA1.zip main
      - run:
          name: Push
          command: aws s3 cp $CIRCLE_SHA1.zip s3://$S3_BUCKET

      - run:
          name: Deploy
          command: |
            aws lambda update-function-code --function-name InsertMovie \
                --s3-bucket $S3_BUCKET \
                --s3-key $CIRCLE_SHA1.zip --region us-east-1
```

All changes to the Lambda function's source code will trigger a new build and the unit tests will be re-executed:

If you click on the **Test** stage, you will see the detailed `go test` command results:

Integration testing

Unlike unit testing, which tests a unit of the system, integration testing focuses on testing the Lambda function as a whole. So, how do we test Lambda functions in a local development environment without deploying them to AWS? Read on to find out more.

RPC communications

If you read the code under the hood of the official Go library for AWS Lambda (https://github.com/aws/aws-lambda-go), you will notice that Go-based Lambda functions are invoked using net/rpc over **TCP**. Every Go Lambda function starts a server on a port defined by the _LAMBDA_SERVER_PORT environment variable and waits for incoming requests. To interact with the function, two RPC methods are used:

- Ping: Used to check whether the function is still alive and running
- Invoke: Used to perform a request

With this knowledge in mind, we can simulate a Lambda function's execution, and perform integration testing or pre-deploy tests to reduce the waiting time when deploying the function to AWS but before checking its new behavior. We can also fix the bugs during the early phases of the development life cycle before committing the new changes to the code repository.

The following example is a simple Lambda function that calculates the Fibonacci value of a given number. The Fibonacci series is the sum of the two previous numbers. The following code is an implementation of the Fibonacci series using recursion:

```go
package main

import "github.com/aws/aws-lambda-go/lambda"

func fib(n int64) int64 {
  if n > 2 {
    return fib(n-1) + fib(n-2)
  }
  return 1
}

func handler(n int64) (int64, error) {
  return fib(n), nil
}

func main() {
```

```
    lambda.Start(handler)
}
```

The Lambda function is listening on a port over TCP, so we need to define the port by setting the _LAMBDA_SERVER_PORT environment variable:

_LAMBDA_SERVER_PORT=3000 go run main.go

To invoke the function, you can either use the invoke method from the net/rpc go package or install a Golang library that abstracts the RPC communication into a single method:

go get -u github.com/djhworld/go-lambda-invoke

Then, invoke the function by setting the port on which it's running and the number we want to calculate its Fibonacci number:

```
package main

import (
  "fmt"
  "log"

  "github.com/djhworld/go-lambda-invoke/golambdainvoke"
)

func main() {
  response, err := golambdainvoke.Run(3000, 9)
  if err != nil {
    log.Fatal(err)
  }
  fmt.Println(string(response))
}
```

Invoke the Fibonacci Lambda function with the following command:

go run client.go

As a result, fib(9)=34 is returned as expected:

```
[serverless:fibonacci mlabouardy$ go run client.go
34
serverless:fibonacci mlabouardy$ 
```

Another approach is building an HTTP server using the `net/http` package to simulate the Lambda function running behind an API Gateway, and testing the function the same way you test any HTTP server to validate the handler.

In the next section, we will see how to use AWS Serverless Application Model to test Lambda functions locally in an easier manner.

Serverless Application Model

Serverless Application Model (SAM), is a way to define serverless applications in AWS. It's an extension to **CloudFormation** in the way it allows to define all resources needed to run your functions in AWS in a template file.

 Please see `Chapter 14`, *Infrastructure as Code*, for instructions on how to use SAM to build serverless applications from scratch.

In addition, AWS SAM allows you to create a development environment to test, debug, and deploy your functions locally. Perform the following steps:

1. To get started, install the SAM CLI with the `pip` Python package manager:

   ```
   pip install aws-sam-cli
   ```

    Make sure to install all the prerequisites and ensure that the Docker engine is running. For more details, check out the official documentation at `https://docs.aws.amazon.com/lambda/latest/dg/sam-cli-requirements.html`.

2. Once installed, run `sam --version`. If everything works as expected, it should output the SAM version (*v0.4.0* at the time of writing this book).

3. Create `template.yml` for the SAM CLI, in which we will define the runtime and the required resources to run the function:

   ```
   AWSTemplateFormatVersion : '2010-09-09'
   Transform: AWS::Serverless-2016-10-31
   Description: List all movies.
   Resources:
     FindAllMovies:
       Type: AWS::Serverless::Function
       Properties:
   ```

```
Handler: main
Runtime: go1.x
Events:
  Vote:
    Type: Api
    Properties:
      Path: /movies
      Method: get
```

The SAM file describes the runtime environment and the name of the handler containing the code your Lambda function will execute when invoked. Plus, the template defines the event that will trigger the function; in this case, it's an API Gateway endpoint.

- Build the deployment package for Linux:

```
GOOS=linux go build -o main
```

- Run the function locally using the `sam local` command:

```
sam local start-api
```

An HTTP server will be running and listening on port `3000`:

If you navigate to `http://localhost:3000/movies`, it should take a few minutes before returning a response as it needs to fetch a Docker image:

SAM local leverages the power of containers to run your Lambda function's code in a Docker container. In the preceding screenshot, it's pulling the `lambci/lambda:go1.x` Docker image from DockerHub (an image repository). You can confirm that by running the following command to list all available images on your machine:

```
docker image ls
```

Here is the output of the preceding command:

```
REPOSITORY       TAG      IMAGE ID       CREATED        SIZE
lambci/lambda    go1.x    3f0eaedadec5   29 hours ago   954MB
```

Once the image is pulled, a new container will be created based on your `deployment` package:

In the browser, an error message will be displayed, as we forgot to set the DynamoDB table's name:

We can fix that by creating an `env.json` file, as follows:

```
{
    "FindAllMovies" : {
        "TABLE_NAME" : "movies"
    }
}
```

Run the `sam` command, this time with the `--env-var` argument:

sam local start-api --env-vars env.json

> You can also declare environment variables in the same SAM template file with the `Environment` property.

This time, you should have all the movies in the DynamoDB `movies` table, and the function should work as expected:

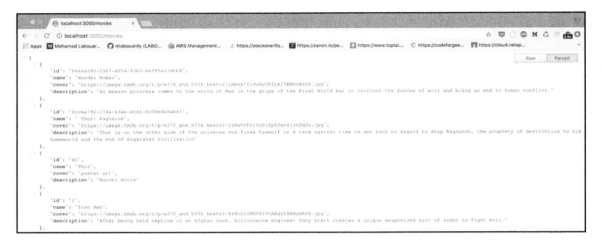

Load testing

We've already seen how to use benchmark tools, such as Apache Benchmark, and how to test harness. In this section, we will look at how to use the Lambda itself as a **serverless testing** test platform.

The idea is simple: we will write a Lambda function that will call the Lambda function we want to test, and write its result to a DynamoDB table for reporting. Fortunately, no coding is required here, as the Lambda function is already available in the **Blueprints** section:

Give the function a name and create a new IAM role, as described in the following schema:

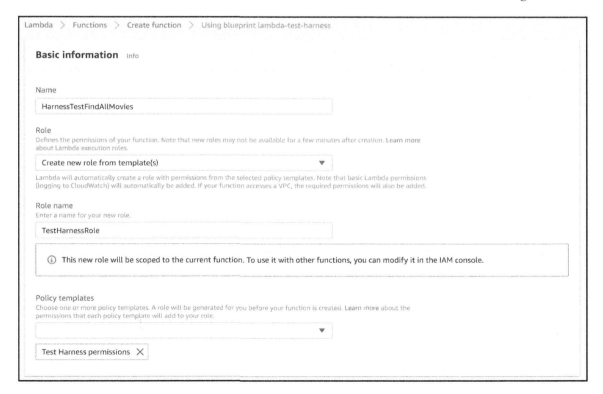

Click on **Create function** and the function should be created with permissions granted to perform the following:

- Push logs to CloudWatch.
- Invoke other Lambda functions.
- Write data to the DynamoDB table.

The following screenshot gives you the glimpse of after the preceding task is completed:

Before launching the load test, we need to create a DynamoDB table in which the Lambda will record the output of the test. This table must have a hash key string of `testId` and a range number of `iteration`:

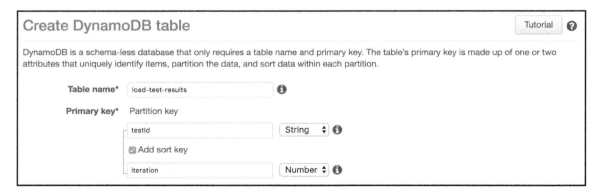

Once created, invoke the Lambda function using the following JSON schema. It will invoke the given function asynchronously 100 times. Specify a unique `event.testId` to differentiate each unit test run:

```
{
    "operation": "load",
    "iterations": 100,
    "function": "HarnessTestFindAllMovies",
    "event": {
      "operation": "unit",
      "function": "FindAllMovies",
      "resultsTable": "load-test-results",
      "testId": "id",
      "event": {
        "options": {
          "host": "https://51cxzthvma.execute-api.us-east-1.amazonaws.com",
          "path": "/production/movies",
          "method": "GET"
        }
      }
    }
}
```

The result will be recorded in the DynamoDB table given in the JSON schema:

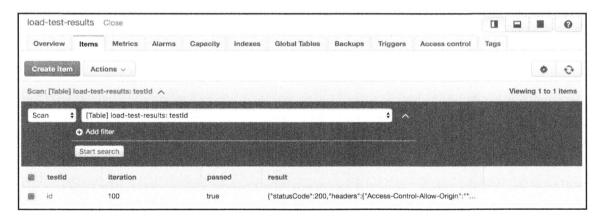

You may want to modify the function's code to save additional information, such as running time, resource usage, and response time.

Summary

In this chapter, we learned how to write unit tests for the Lambda function to cover all the edge cases of the function. We also learned how to use AWS SAM to set up a local development environment to test and deploy the function locally, in order to ensure its behavior is working as expected before deploying it to AWS Lambda.

In the next chapter, we will cover how to troubleshoot and debug serverless applications using AWS-managed services such as CloudWatch and X-Ray.

Questions

1. Write a unit test for the `UpdateMovie` Lambda function.
2. Write a unit test for the `DeleteMovie` Lambda function.
3. Modify the `Jenkinsfile` provided in previous chapters to include the execution of automated unit tests.
4. Modify the `buildspec.yml` definition file to include the execution of unit tests, before pushing the deployment package to S3 using AWS CodeBuild.
5. Write a SAM template file for each Lambda function implemented in previous chapters.

Monitoring and Troubleshooting

11

Lambda monitoring is different from traditional application monitoring, due to the fact that you're not managing the underlying infrastructure on which your code is running. Thus, there is no access to OS metrics. However, you still need function-level monitoring to optimize your function performance and debug in case of failure. In this chapter, you will learn how to achieve that and also how to debug and troubleshoot serverless applications in AWS. You will learn to set up alarms based on metric thresholds in CloudWatch to be notified of potential issues. You will also look at how to use AWS X-Ray to profile the application to detect abnormal behavior.

Monitoring and debugging with AWS CloudWatch

AWS CloudWatch is the easiest and most reliable solution to monitor AWS services, including Lambda functions. It's a centralized monitoring service to gather metrics and logs, and also creates alarms based on them. AWS Lambda automatically monitors Lambda functions on your behalf, reporting metrics through CloudWatch.

CloudWatch metrics

By default, each time you invoke your function through the Lambda console, it reports the key information about the function resource usage, execution duration, and how much time is billed:

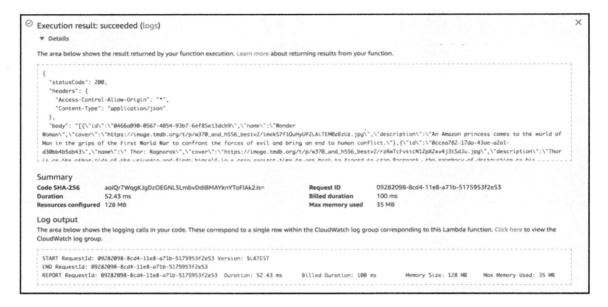

A quick real-time insight can be found by clicking on the **Monitoring** tab. This page will show a graphical representation of multiple CloudWatch metrics. You can control the observable time period in the top-right corner of the graph area:

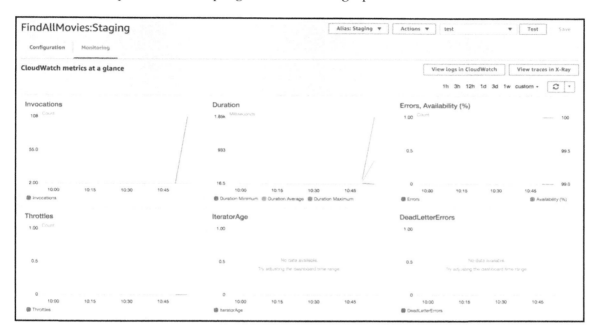

These metrics include:

- Number of times the function has been invoked
- Execution time in milliseconds
- Error rates, and throttle count due to concurrency reservation and unprocessed events (dead letter errors)

 A list of all the available metrics in CloudWatch for AWS Lambda can be found at `https://docs.aws.amazon.com/lambda/latest/dg/monitoring-functions-metrics.html`.

For each metric, you can also click on **View in metrics** to view the CloudWatch metric directly:

The preceding graph represents the number of invocations of the `production` and `staging` aliases of the `FindAllMovies` function in the last 15 minutes. You can take this further and create your own custom graphs. This allows you to construct a custom dashboard for your Lambda functions. It will outline the load (any problems you might face), the cost, and other important metrics.

Moreover, you can also create your own custom metrics and publish them to CloudWatch using the CloudWatch Golang SDK. The following code snippet is of a Lambda function that uses the CloudWatch SDK to publish a custom metric. The metric represents the number of Action movies inserted into DynamoDB (some parts were omitted for brevity):

```
svc := cloudwatch.New(cfg)
req := svc.PutMetricDataRequest(&cloudwatch.PutMetricDataInput{
    Namespace: aws.String("InsertMovie"),
    MetricData: []cloudwatch.MetricDatum{
        cloudwatch.MetricDatum{
            Dimensions: []cloudwatch.Dimension{
                cloudwatch.Dimension{
                    Name: aws.String("Environment"),
                    Value: aws.String("production"),
                },
            },
            MetricName: aws.String("ActionMovies"),
            Value: aws.Float64(1.0),
            Unit: cloudwatch.StandardUnitCount,
        },
    },
})
```

The metric is uniquely defined by a name, a namespace, a list of dimensions (name-value pair), a value, and a unit of measure. After you have published some values to CloudWatch, you can use the CloudWatch console to view statistical graphs:

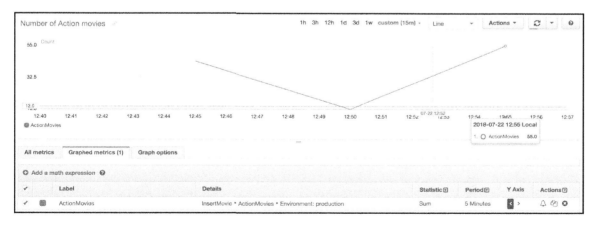

Now we know how to monitor our Lambda functions using out-of-the-box metrics provided by AWS and insert custom metrics into CloudWatch to enrich their observability. Let's look at how to create an alarm based on those metrics to alert us in real time if something goes wrong in our Lambda functions.

CloudWatch alarms

CloudWatch allows you to create alerts-based on the available metrics when unexpected behavior occurs. In the following example, we will create an alarm based on the error rate of the `FindAllMovies` function:

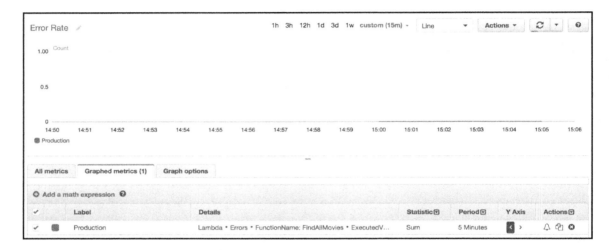

In order to achieve that, click on the ring bell icon from the **Actions** column. Then, fill in the following fields to set up an alarm that will be triggered if the number of errors is more than 10 within five minutes. Once the alarm is triggered, an email will be sent using **Simple Notification Service** (SNS):

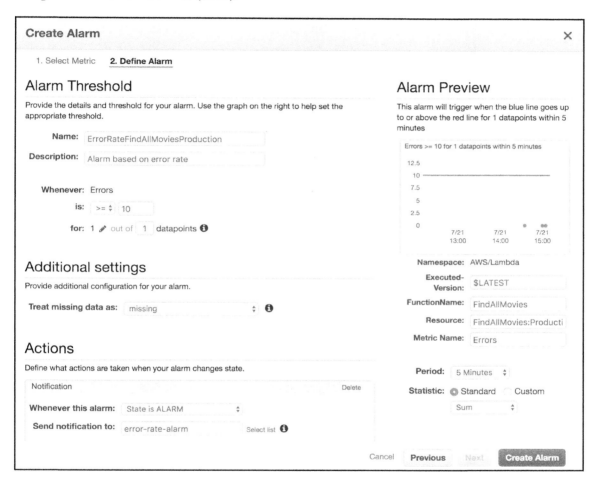

CloudWatch will send a notification through an SNS topic, and you can create as many SNS topic subscriptions as needed to deliver the notifications to where you want (SMS, HTTP, email).

Click on the **Create Alarm** button; you should receive an email to confirm the subscription. You must confirm the subscription before notifications can be sent:

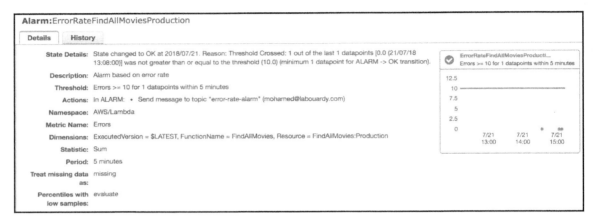

Once confirmed, every time the error rate of the Lambda function crosses the defined threshold, the alert will change its state from **OK** to **ALARM**:

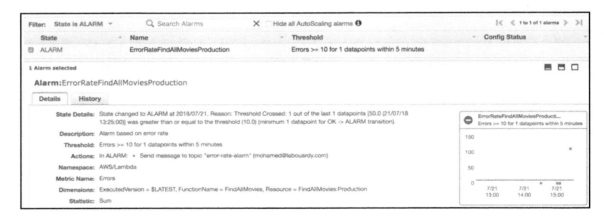

After this, an email will be sent to you in response to the event:

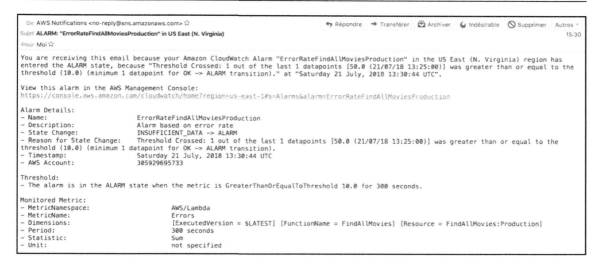

 You can simulate an alarm by changing its state temporarily with this AWS CLI command: `aws cloudwatch set-alarm-state --alarm-name ALARM_NAME --state-value ALARM --state-reason demo`.

CloudWatch logs

While working with AWS Lambda, you might face the following errors when your function is being invoked:

- Application error
- Permissions denied
- Timeout exceeded
- Memory exceeded

Aside from the first use case, the rest can be fixed easily, by granting the right IAM policies and increasing the Lambda function's timeout or memory usage. However, the first error requires more debugging and troubleshooting, which requires adding logging statements into your code to validate that your code is working as expected. Fortunately, each time the Lambda function's code is executed in response to an event, it writes a log entry into the CloudWatch log group associated with a Lambda function, which is `/aws/lambda/FUNCTION_NAME`.

Your Lambda function should be granted the following permissions to achieve that:

```
{
  "Version": "2012-10-17",
  "Statement": [
    {
      "Sid": "1",
      "Effect": "Allow",
      "Action": [
        "logs:CreateLogStream",
        "logs:CreateLogGroup",
        "logs:PutLogEvents"
      ],
      "Resource": "*"
    }
  ]
}
```

That being said, you might use Go's built-in logging library, called the `log` package. The following is an example of how to use the `log` package:

```
package main

import (
  "log"

  "github.com/aws/aws-lambda-go/lambda"
)

func reverse(s string) string {
  runes := []rune(s)
  for i, j := 0, len(runes)-1; i < j; i, j = i+1, j-1 {
    runes[i], runes[j] = runes[j], runes[i]
  }
  return string(runes)
}

func handler(input string) (string, error) {
  log.Println("Before:", input)
  output := reverse(input)
  log.Println("After:", output)
  return output, nil
}

func main() {
  lambda.Start(handler)
}
```

The code is self-explanatory, it performs a reverse operation on a given string. I have added logging statements around various parts of the code using the `log.Println` method.

You can then deploy the function to AWS Lambda, and invoke it either from the AWS console or with the `invoke` command. Lambda automatically integrates with Amazon CloudWatch logs and pushes all logs from your code to a CloudWatch logs, group associated with a Lambda function:

So far, we've learned how to troubleshoot and analyze each invocation with log and runtime data. In the upcoming section, we will cover how to track all upstream and downstream calls to external services in the Lambda function's code to troubleshoot errors quickly and easily. To track all these calls, using AWS X-Ray, we will add code instrumentation in different code segments where the actual work is performed.

There are many third-party tools you might use to monitor serverless applications, which rely on CloudWatch. Therefore, they are failing too on the real-time issue. We expect this to be resolved in the future as AWS is launching new services and features at a rapid pace.

Tracing with AWS X-Ray

AWS X-Ray is an AWS-managed service that allows you to track incoming and outgoing requests that your Lambda functions are issuing. It collects that information in segments and uses metadata to record additional data to help you debug, analyze, and optimize your function.

Overall, X-Ray can help you identify performance bottlenecks. However, it might require additional network calls that need to be made during the function's execution, adding to user-facing latency.

To get started, enable active tracing from the Lambda function's configuration page:

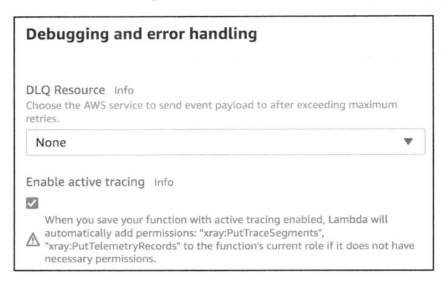

The following IAM policy is required to make the Lambda function publish the trace segments to X-Ray:

```
{
  "Version": "2012-10-17",
  "Statement": {
    "Effect": "Allow",
    "Action": [
      "xray:PutTraceSegments",
      "xray:PutTelemetryRecords"
    ],
    "Resource": [
      "*"
    ]
  }
}
```

Next, navigate to AWS X-Ray console, click on **Traces**, invoke the Lambda function a few times, and refresh the page. New rows will be added to the trace list. For each trace, you will be given the code response and execution time:

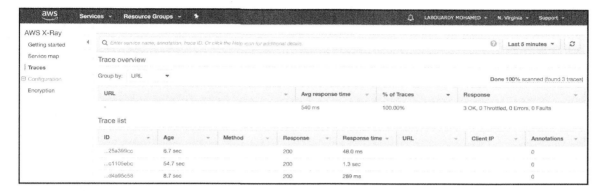

Here is a trace of the `FindAllMovies` function; it includes the time it takes for Lambda to initialize the function:

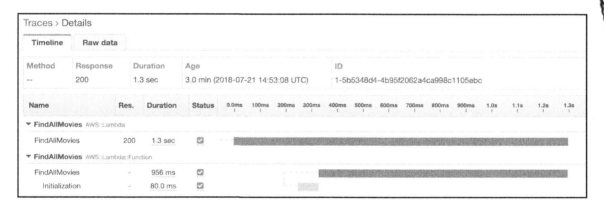

You can also visualize this information in graph format, by clicking on the **Service map** item:

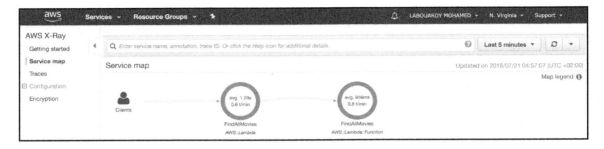

For each traced invocation, Lambda will emit the Lambda service segment and all of its subsegments. In addition, Lambda will emit the Lambda function segment and the init subsegment. These segments will be emitted regardless of the function's runtime, and without any code changes or additional libraries required. If you want your Lambda function's X-Ray traces to include custom segments, annotations, or subsegments for downstream calls, you might need to install the following X-Ray Golang SDK:

```
go get -u github.com/aws/aws-xray-sdk-go/...
```

Update the `FindAllMovies` function's code to configure X-Ray using the `Configure` method:

```
xray.Configure(xray.Config{
  LogLevel: "info",
  ServiceVersion: "1.2.3",
})
```

We will track the call to DynamoDB in a subsegment by wrapping the DynamoDB client with the `xray.AWS` call, as shown in the following code:

```
func findAll(ctx context.Context) (events.APIGatewayProxyResponse, error) {
  xray.Configure(xray.Config{
    LogLevel: "info",
    ServiceVersion: "1.2.3",
  })

  sess := session.Must(session.NewSession())
  dynamo := dynamodb.New(sess)
  xray.AWS(dynamo.Client)

  res, err := dynamo.ScanWithContext(ctx, &dynamodb.ScanInput{
    TableName: aws.String(os.Getenv("TABLE_NAME")),
  })
```

```
    . . .
}
```

Once again, invoke the Lambda function on the X-Ray `Traces` page; a new subsegment will be added with the time it spent scanning the `movies` table:

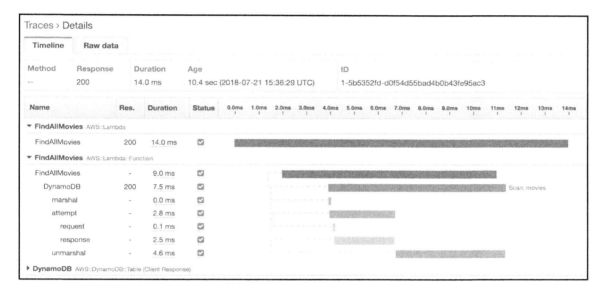

The DynamoDB call will also appear as a downstream node on the service map in the X-Ray console:

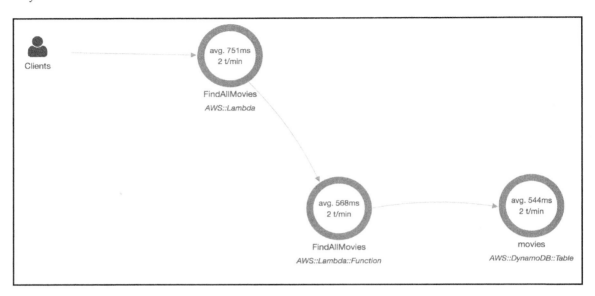

Now that we are familiar how X-Ray works, let's create something complex. Consider a simple Lambda function, which takes the URL of a movie poster page as input. It parses the HTML page, scraps the data, and saves it to a DynamoDB table. This function will do a GET method on the given URL:

```
res, err := http.Get(url)
if err != nil {
  log.Fatal(err)
}
defer res.Body.Close()
```

Then, it uses the `goquery` library (**JQuery** Go-based implementation) to scrap the data from the HTML page, using CSS selectors:

```
doc, err := goquery.NewDocumentFromReader(res.Body)
if err != nil {
  log.Fatal(err)
}

title := doc.Find(".header .title span a h2").Text()
description := doc.Find(".overview p").Text()
cover, _ := doc.Find(".poster .image_content img").Attr("src")

movie := Movie{
  ID: uuid.Must(uuid.NewV4()).String(),
  Name: title,
  Description: description,
  Cover: cover,
}
```

Once the movie object is created, it uses the `PutItem` method to save the movie to a DynamoDB table:

```
sess := session.Must(session.NewSession())
dynamo := dynamodb.New(sess)
req, _ := dynamo.PutItemRequest(&dynamodb.PutItemInput{
  TableName: aws.String(os.Getenv("TABLE_NAME")),
  Item: map[string]*dynamodb.AttributeValue{
    "ID": &dynamodb.AttributeValue{
      S: aws.String(movie.ID),
    },
    "Name": &dynamodb.AttributeValue{
      S: aws.String(movie.Name),
    },
    "Cover": &dynamodb.AttributeValue{
      S: aws.String(movie.Cover),
    },
    "Description": &dynamodb.AttributeValue{
      S: aws.String(movie.Description),
    },
  },
})
err = req.Send()
if err != nil {
  log.Fatal(err)
}
```

Now that our function handler is defined, deploy it to AWS Lambda, and test it out by giving it a URL as an input parameter. As a result, the movie information will be displayed in a JSON format:

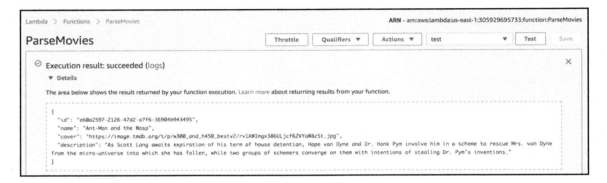

If you point your browser to the frontend built in previous chapters, the new movie should be part of the movies listed in the page:

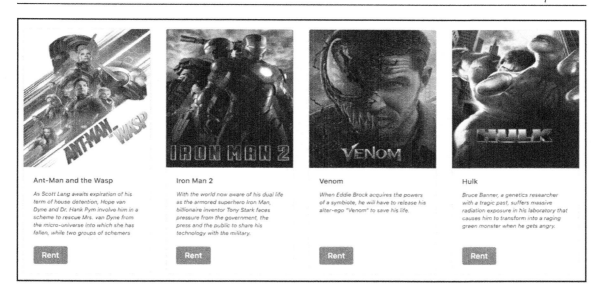

Now our Lambda function is working as expected; let's add tracing calls to downstream services. First, configure the X-Ray and use the `ctxhttp.Get` method to instrument the `GET` call as a subsegment:

```
xray.Configure(xray.Config{
  LogLevel: "info",
  ServiceVersion: "1.2.3",
})

// Get html page
res, err := ctxhttp.Get(ctx, xray.Client(nil), url)
if err != nil {
  log.Fatal(err)
}
defer res.Body.Close()
```

Next, create a subsegment around the parsing logic. The subsegment is called `Parsing` and the `AddMetaData` method has been used to record additional information about the subsegment in order to troubleshoot:

```go
xray.Capture(ctx, "Parsing", func(ctx1 context.Context) error {
  doc, err := goquery.NewDocumentFromReader(res.Body)
  if err != nil {
    return err
  }

  title := doc.Find(".header .title span a h2").Text()
  description := doc.Find(".overview p").Text()
  cover, _ := doc.Find(".poster .image_content img").Attr("src")

  movie := Movie{
    ID: uuid.Must(uuid.NewV4()).String(),
    Name: title,
    Description: description,
    Cover: cover,
  }

  xray.AddMetadata(ctx1, "movie.title", title)
  xray.AddMetadata(ctx1, "movie.description", description)
  xray.AddMetadata(ctx1, "movie.cover", cover)

  return nil
})
```

Finally, wrap the DynamoDB client with the `xray.AWS()` call:

```go
sess := session.Must(session.NewSession())
dynamo := dynamodb.New(sess)
xray.AWS(dynamo.Client)
```

As a result, the following subsegment will appear in **traces** for the `ParseMovies` Lambda function:

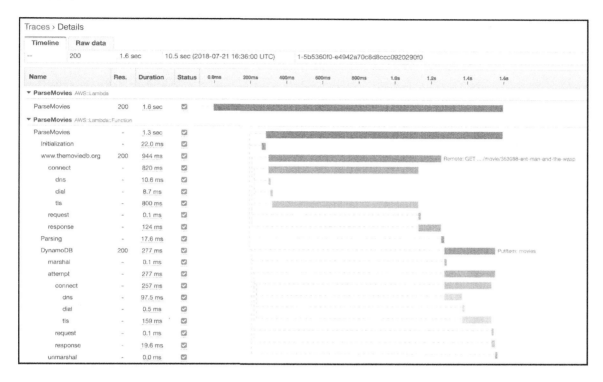

If you click on the **Subsegments – Parsing** on the **Metadata** tab, the movie attributes will be displayed as follows:

On the service map, the downstream call to DynamoDB and outgoing HTTP call will also be displayed:

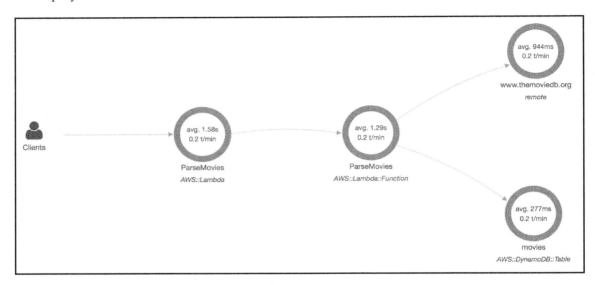

By now, you should have a clear idea of how to easily troubleshoot performance bottlenecks, latency spikes, and other issues that impact the performance of your Lambda-based application.

 When you trace your Lambda function, an X-Ray daemon will automatically run in the Lambda environment to gather trace data and send it to X-Ray. The X-Ray daemon can be run locally if you want to test your function before deploying it to Lambda. A step-by-step installation guide can be found here: https://docs.aws.amazon.com/xray/latest/devguide/xray-daemon-local.html.

Summary

In this chapter, you learned how to monitor your Lambda function in near real time using AWS CloudWatch metrics. You also learned how to publish custom metrics and detect problems with alerts and reporting. In addition, we covered how to stream a function's code logs to CloudWatch. Finally, we saw how to use AWS X-Ray to debug, how to trace upstream and downstream calls, and how to integrate the X-Ray SDK with Lambda in Golang.

In the next chapter, you will learn about securing your serverless application.

12
Securing Your Serverless Application

AWS Lambda is the ultimate pay-as-you-go cloud computing service. Customers just need to upload their Lambda function code to the cloud and it will be up and running with no underlying infrastructure to secure or patch. However, according to AWS's Shared Responsibility model, you're still responsible for securing your Lambda function's code. This chapter is dedicated to the best practices and recommendations one can follow in AWS Lambda to make applications resilient and secure according to the AWS Well-Architected Framework. We will cover the following topics in this chapter:

- Authentication and user control access
- Encrypted environment variables
- Logging AWS Lambda API calls with CloudTrail
- Vulnerability scanning for your dependencies

Technical requirements

In order to follow this chapter, you can either follow the API Gateway setup chapter or prepare a serverless RESTful API based on Lambda and the API Gateway. The code bundle for this chapter is hosted on GitHub at `https://github.com/PacktPublishing/Hands-On-Serverless-Applications-with-Go`.

Authentication and user control access

The serverless application that we have built so far works like a charm, and is open to the public. Anyone can invoke Lambda functions if he/she has the API Gateway invocation URL. Luckily, AWS offers a managed service called Cognito.

Amazon Cognito is an authentication provider and management service at scale that allows you to add user sign up and sign in easily to your applications. The users are stored in a scalable directory called the user pool. In the upcoming section, Amazon Cognito will be used to authenticate users before allowing them to request the RESTful API.

To get started, create a new user pool in Amazon Cognito and give it a name:

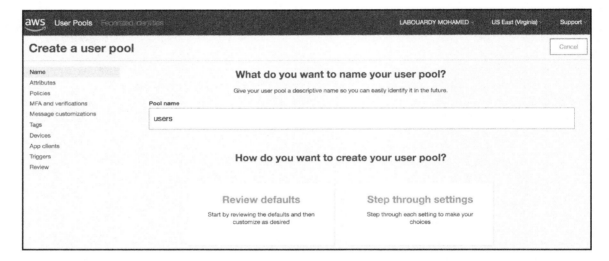

Click on the **Review defaults** option to create a pool with the default settings:

Click on **Attributes** from the navigation pane and tick the **Allow email addresses** option under **Email address or phone number** to allow users to sign in with an email address:

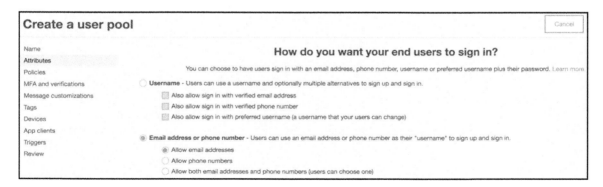

Go back to **Review** and click on **Create pool**. A success message should be displayed at the end of the creation process:

After creating your first user pool, register your serverless API from **App clients** under **General settings** and select **Add an app client**. Give the application a name and uncheck the **Generate client secret** option as follows: the authentication will be done on the client side. Hence, the client secret should not be passed on the URL for security purposes:

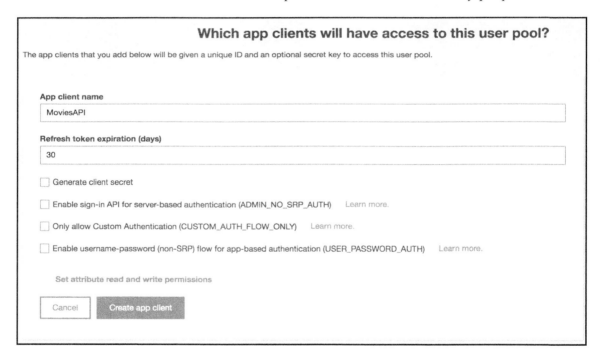

Choose **Create app client** to register the application and copy the **App client id** to the clipboard:

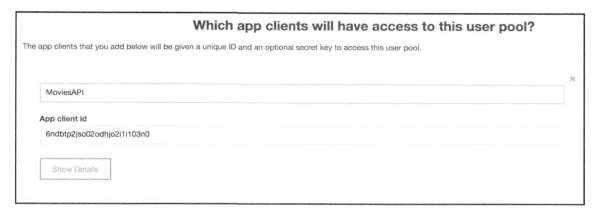

Now that the user pool has been created, we can configure the API Gateway to validate access tokens from a successful user pool authentication before granting access to Lambda functions.

Securing API access

To begin securing API access, go to API Gateway console, choose the RESTful API that we built in the previous chapters, and click on **Authorizers** from the navigation bar:

Authorizers

Authorizers enable you to control access to your APIs using Amazon Cognito User Pools or a Lambda function.

+ Create New Authorizer

Click on the **Create New Authorizer** button and select **Cognito**. Then, select the user pool that we created earlier and set the token source field to Authorization. This defines the name of the incoming request header containing the API caller's identity token for Authorization:

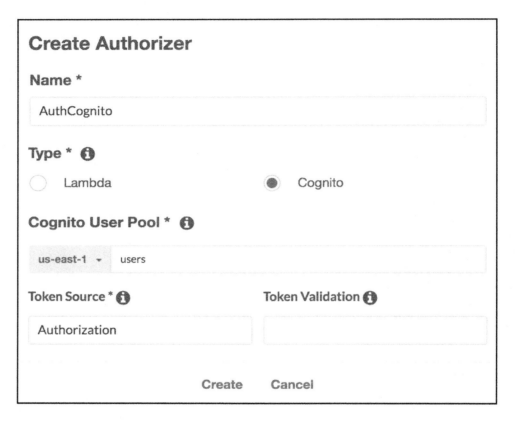

Once the form has been filled in, click on **Create** to integrate the **Cognito User Pool** with the API Gateway:

You can now secure all of the endpoints, for example, in order to secure the endpoint responsible for listing all `movies`. Click on the corresponding `GET` method under the `/movies` resource:

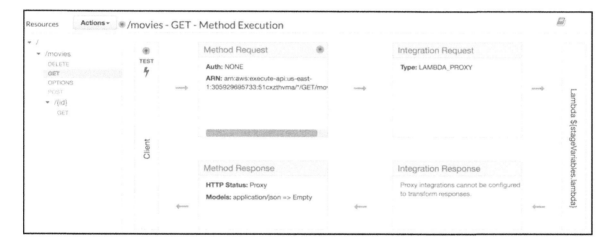

Click on the **Method Request** box, then on **Authorization**, and select the user pool we created previously:

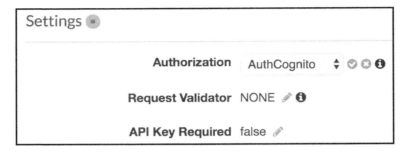

Leave the **OAuth Scopes** option as None, and repeat the preceding procedure for the remaining methods to secure them:

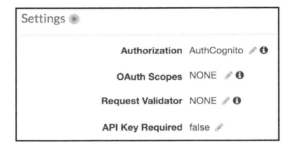

Once done, redeploy the API and point your browser to the API Gateway invocation URL:

```
{
    "message": "Unauthorized"
}
```

This time, the endpoint is secured and requires authentication. You can confirm the behavior by checking the frontend we built previously. If you inspect the network requests, the API Gateway request should return a 401 Unauthorised error:

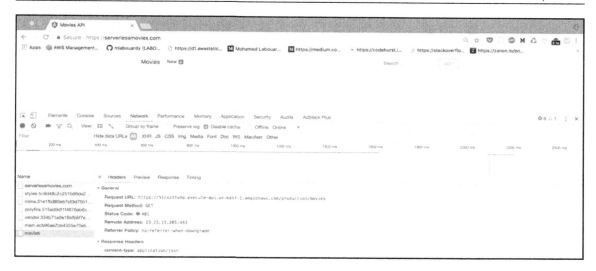

In order to fix this error, we will need to update the client (web application) to do the following:

- Sign in to the user pool using the Cognito JavaScript SDK
- Obtain an identity token for the signed-in user from the the user pool
- Include the identity token in the `Authorization` header for the API Gateway requests

 The identity token returned has an expiration date of 1 hour. Once expired, you need to use a refresh token to refresh the session.

User management with AWS Cognito

Before making changes on the client side, we need to create a test user in Amazon Cognito. To achieve this, you can either use the AWS Management Console or complete this programmatically with the AWS Golang SDK.

Setting up a test user via the AWS Management Console

Click on **Users and groups** and click on the **Create user** button:

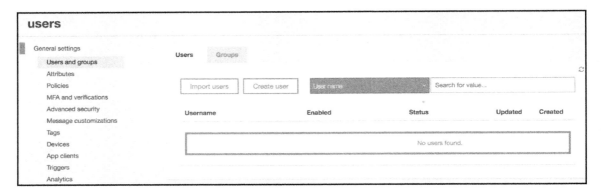

Set a username and a password. If you want to receive a confirmation email, you can untick the **Mark email as verified?** box:

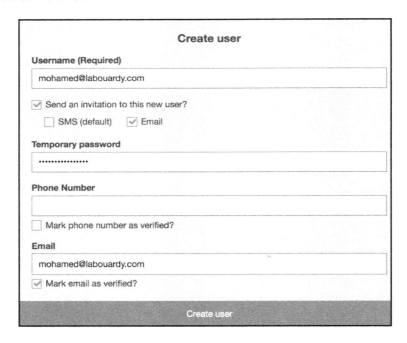

Setup using Cognito Golang SDK

Create a `main.go` file with the below content. The code uses the `SignUpRequest` method from the `cognitoidentityprovider` package to create a new user. As a parameter, it takes a struct with the client ID, username, and password:

```go
package main

import (
  "log"
  "os"

  "github.com/aws/aws-sdk-go-v2/aws/external"
  "github.com/aws/aws-sdk-go-v2/service/cognitoidentityprovider"
  "github.com/aws/aws-sdk-go/aws"
)

func main() {
  cfg, err := external.LoadDefaultAWSConfig()
  if err != nil {
    log.Fatal(err)
  }

  cognito := cognitoidentityprovider.New(cfg)
  req := cognito.SignUpRequest(&cognitoidentityprovider.SignUpInput{
    ClientId: aws.String(os.Getenv("COGNITO_CLIENT_ID")),
    Username: aws.String("EMAIL"),
    Password: aws.String("PASSWORD"),
  })
  _, err = req.Send()
  if err != nil {
    log.Fatal(err)
  }
}
```

Run the preceding command using the `go run main.go` command. You will receive an email with a temporary password:

After signing up, the user must confirm the sign up by entering a code that is sent via email. To confirm the sign up process, you must collect the code received by the user and use it as follows:

```
cognito := cognitoidentityprovider.New(cfg)
req :=
cognito.ConfirmSignUpRequest(&cognitoidentityprovider.ConfirmSignUpInput{
  ClientId: aws.String(os.Getenv("COGNITO_CLIENT_ID")),
  Username: aws.String("EMAIL"),
  ConfirmationCode: aws.String("CONFIRMATION_CODE"),
})
_, err = req.Send()
if err != nil {
  log.Fatal(err)
}
```

Now that a user has been created in the Cognito User Pool, we are ready to update the client side. Start by creating a sign in form as follows:

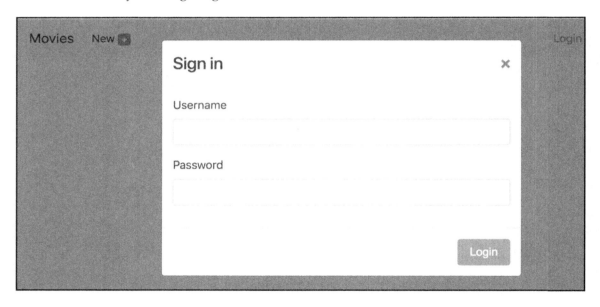

Next, install the Cognito SDK for Javascript using the Node.js package manager. This package contains the Angular module and the providers you might need to interact with Cognito:

```
npm install --save amazon-cognito-identity-js
```

Furthermore, we have to create an Angular service with an `auth` method that creates a `CognitoUserPool` object by providing a `UserPoolId` object and a `ClientId`, which authenticate a user based on the username and password given in the parameters. If the sign in is successful, the `onSuccess` callback is called. If the sign in fails, the `onFailure` callback is called:

```
import { Injectable } from '@angular/core';
import { CognitoUserPool, CognitoUser, AuthenticationDetails} from 'amazon-
cognito-identity-js';
import { environment } from '../../environments/environment';

@Injectable()
export class CognitoService {

  public static CONFIG = {
    UserPoolId: environment.userPoolId,
    ClientId: environment.clientId
  }

  auth(username, password, callback){
    let user = new CognitoUser({
      Username: username,
      Pool: this.getUserPool()
    })

    let authDetails = new AuthenticationDetails({
      Username: username,
      Password: password
    })

    user.authenticateUser(authDetails, {
      onSuccess: res => {
        callback(null, res.getIdToken().getJwtToken())
      },
      onFailure: err => {
        callback(err, null)
      }
    })
  }

  getUserPool() {
    return new CognitoUserPool(CognitoService.CONFIG);
  }

  getCurrentUser() {
    return this.getUserPool().getCurrentUser();
  }
```

```
}
```

The `auth` method will be invoked each time the login button is clicked. If the user enters the right credentials, a user session will be established with the Amazon Cognito service, and a user identity token will be saved in the local storage of the browser. If the right credentials aren't entered, an error message will be displayed to the user:

```
signin(username, password){
    this.cognitoService.auth(username, password, (err, token) => {
      if(err){
        this.loginError = true
      }else{
        this.loginError = false
        this.storage.set("COGNITO_TOKEN", token)
        this.loginModal.close()
      }
    })
  }
```

Finally, the `MoviesAPI` service should be updated to include the user identity token (called the JWT token – https://docs.aws.amazon.com/cognito/latest/developerguide/amazon-cognito-user-pools-using-tokens-with-identity-providers.html#amazon-cognito-user-pools-using-the-id-token) in the `Authorization` header of each API Gateway request call, as follows:

```
@Injectable()
export class MoviesApiService {

  constructor(private http: Http,
    @Inject(LOCAL_STORAGE) private storage: WebStorageService) {}

    findAll() {
      return this.http
          .get(environment.api, {
              headers: this.getHeaders()
          })
          .map(res => {
              return res.json()
          })
    }

    getHeaders() {
      let headers = new Headers()
      headers.append('Authorization', this.storage.get("COGNITO_TOKEN"))
      return headers
    }
```

```
}
```

The preceding code samples have been tested with Angular 5. In addition, make sure that you adopt the code into your own web framework accordingly.

To test it out, head back to the browser. The sign in form should pop up; fill the fields with the user credentials we created earlier. Then, click on the **Login** button:

The user identity will be returned and the RESTful API will be called with the token that's included in the request header. The API Gateway will verify the token and will invoke the `FindAllMovies` Lambda function, which will return movies from the DynamoDB table:

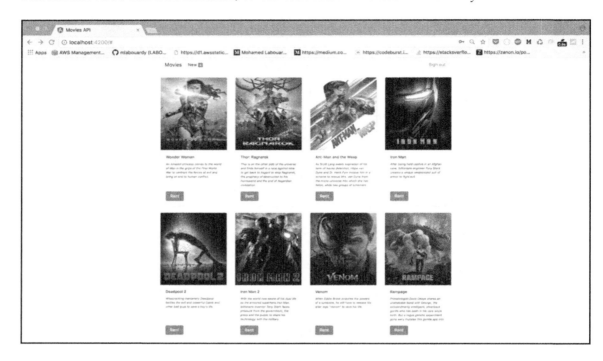

For web developers, Cognito's `getSession` method can be used to retrieve the current user from local storage since the JavaScript SDK is configured to automatically store the tokens after authenticating properly, as you can see in the following screenshot:

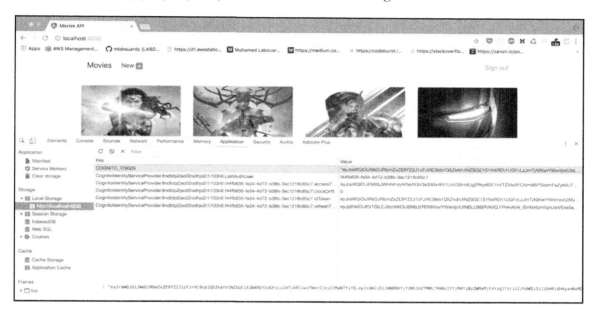

To sum up, so far we have done the following:

- Built multiple Lambda functions to manage a store of movies
- Managed Lambda data persistency in a DynamoDB table
- Exposed those Lambda functions through the API Gateway
- Built a web client for testing the built stack in S3
- Sped up web client assets with the CloudFront distribution
- Set up custom domain names in Route 53
- Secured the API with AWS Cognito

The following schema illustrates the serverless architecture that we have built so far:

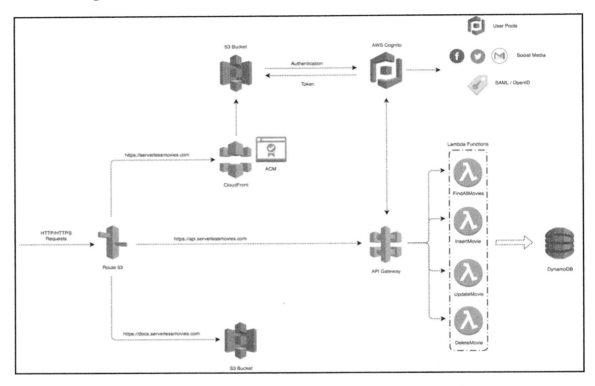

 Amazon Cognito can be configured with multiple identity providers such as Facebook, Twitter, Google, or developer authenticated identities.

Encrypted environment variables

In previous chapters, we saw how to use environment variables with AWS Lambda to dynamically pass data to the function code without changing any code. According to the **Twelve Factor App** methodology (https://12factor.net/), you should always separate your configuration from your code to avoid checking sensitive credentials to a repository and to be able to define multiple releases of your Lambda functions (staging, production, and sandbox) with the same source code. Moreover, environment variables can be used to change the function behavior based on different settings **(A/B testing)**.

> If you want to share secrets across multiple Lambda functions, you can use AWS's **System Manager Parameter Store**.

The following example illustrates how environment variables can be used to pass MySQL credentials to the function's code:

```go
func handler() error {
  MYSQL_USERNAME := os.Getenv("MYSQL_USERNAME")
  MYSQL_PASSWORD := os.Getenv("MYSQL_PASSWORD")
  MYSQL_DATABASE := os.Getenv("MYSQL_DATABASE")
  MYSQL_PORT := os.Getenv("MYSQL_PORT")
  MYSQL_HOST := os.Getenv("MYSQL_HOST")

  uri := fmt.Sprintf("%s:%s@tcp(%s:%s)/%s", MYSQL_USERNAME, MYSQL_PASSWORD,
MYSQL_HOST, MYSQL_PORT, MYSQL_DATABASE)
  db, err := sql.Open("mysql", uri)
  if err != nil {
    return err
  }
  defer db.Close()

  _, err = db.Query(`CREATE TABLE IF NOT EXISTS movies(id INT PRIMARY KEY
AUTO_INCREMENT, name VARCHAR(50) NOT NULL)`)
  if err != nil {
    return err
  }

  for _, movie := range []string{"Iron Man", "Thor", "Avengers", "Wonder
Woman"} {
    _, err := db.Query("INSERT INTO movies(name) VALUES(?)", movie)
    if err != nil {
      return err
    }
  }
}
```

```
movies, err := db.Query("SELECT id, name FROM movies")
if err != nil {
  return err
}

for movies.Next() {
  var name string
  var id int
  err = movies.Scan(&id, &name)
  if err != nil {
    return err
  }

  log.Printf("ID=%d\tName=%s\n", id, name)
}
return nil
}
```

Once the function is deployed to AWS Lambda and the environment variables are set, you can invoke the function. It will output a list of movies that were inserted into the database:

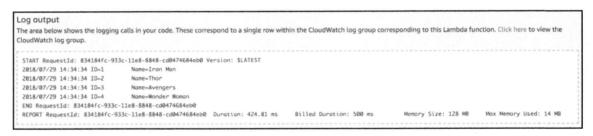

So far, so good. However, the database credentials are in plain text!

Fortunately, AWS Lambda provides encryption at two levels: in transit and at rest, using the AWS Key Management Service.

Data encryption at rest

AWS Lambda encrypts all environment variables while your function is being deployed and decrypts them when the function is invoked (on-the-fly).

If you expand the **Encryption configuration** section, you will notice that by default AWS Lambda encrypts, at rest, environment variables using a default Lambda service key. This key is created automatically the first time you create a Lambda function in a specific region:

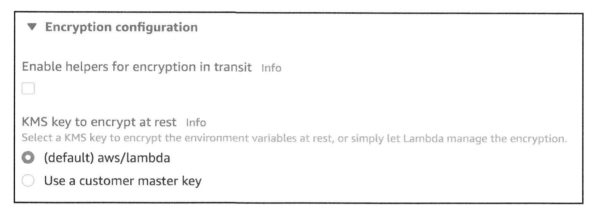

You can change the key and use your own by navigating to the Identity and Access Management Console. Then, click on **Encryption keys**:

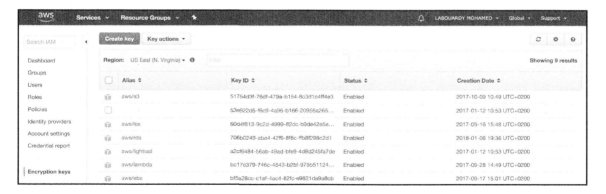

Click on the **Create key** button to create a new customer master key:

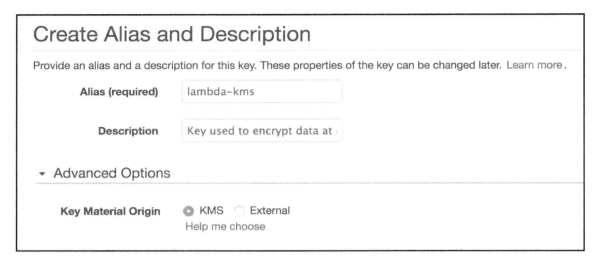

Select an IAM role and account to manage the key through the **Key Management Service (KMS)** API. Then, select the IAM role you used while creating your Lambda function. This allows the Lambda function to use the **customer master key (CMK)** and successfully request the encrypt and decrypt methods:

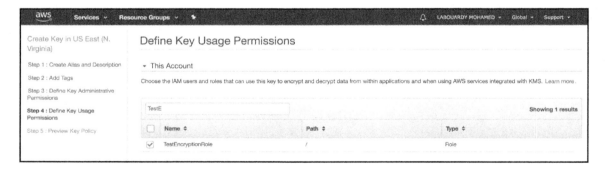

Once the key is created, head back to the Lambda function configuration page and change the key to the one you just created:

Now, AWS Lambda will use your own key to encrypt environment variables at rest when stored in Amazon.

Data encryption in transit

It's recommended you encrypt environment variables (sensitive information) before the function is deployed. AWS Lambda provides encryption helpers on the console to make this process easy to follow.

In order to encrypt in transit (by using the KMS we used earlier), you will need to enable this by checking the **Enable helpers for encryption in transit** checkbox:

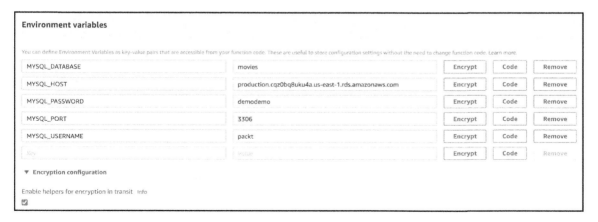

Encrypt `MYSQL_USERNAME` and `MYSQL_PASSWORD` by clicking on the appropriate **Encrypt** buttons:

The credentials will be encrypted and you'll see them in the console as `CipherText`. Next, you need to update the function's handler to decrypt environment variables using the KMS SDK:

```go
var encryptedMysqlUsername string = os.Getenv("MYSQL_USERNAME")
var encryptedMysqlPassword string = os.Getenv("MYSQL_PASSWORD")
var mysqlDatabase string = os.Getenv("MYSQL_DATABASE")
var mysqlPort string = os.Getenv("MYSQL_PORT")
var mysqlHost string = os.Getenv("MYSQL_HOST")
var decryptedMysqlUsername, decryptedMysqlPassword string

func decrypt(encrypted string) (string, error) {
  kmsClient := kms.New(session.New())
  decodedBytes, err := base64.StdEncoding.DecodeString(encrypted)
  if err != nil {
    return "", err
  }
  input := &kms.DecryptInput{
    CiphertextBlob: decodedBytes,
  }
  response, err := kmsClient.Decrypt(input)
  if err != nil {
    return "", err
  }
  return string(response.Plaintext[:]), nil
}
```

```
func init() {
  decryptedMysqlUsername, _ = decrypt(encryptedMysqlUsername)
  decryptedMysqlPassword, _ = decrypt(encryptedMysqlPassword)
}

func handler() error {
  uri := fmt.Sprintf("%s:%s@tcp(%s:%s)/%s", decryptedMysqlUsername,
decryptedMysqlPassword, mysqlHost, mysqlPort, mysqlDatabase)
  db, err := sql.Open("mysql", uri)
  if err != nil {
    return err
  }
  ...
}
```

 In the event you used your own KMS key, you will need to grant
kms:Decrypt permissions to the execution role (IAM role) that's attached
to the Lambda function. Also, make sure you increase the default
execution timeout to allow enough time for the function's code to be
completed.

Logging AWS Lambda API calls with CloudTrail

Capturing all calls made by your Lambda functions is important for auditing, security, and compliance. It gives you a global overview of the AWS services they interact with. One service that leverages this feature is **CloudTrail**.

CloudTrail records API calls made by your Lambda functions. It's straightforward and easy to use. All you need to do is navigate to CloudTrail from the AWS Management Console and filter events by the event source, which should be lambda.amazonaws.com.

There, you should have all of the calls that have been made by each Lambda function, as shown in the following screenshot:

In addition to exposing event history, you can create a trail in each AWS region to record your Lambda function's events in a single S3 bucket, then implement a log analysis pipeline using the **ELK (Elasticsearch, Logstash, and Kibana)** stack to process your logs as follows:

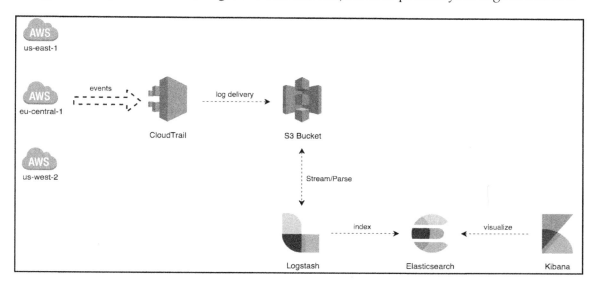

Finally, you can create interactive and dynamic widgets to construct a dashboard in **kibana** to view your Lambda function events:

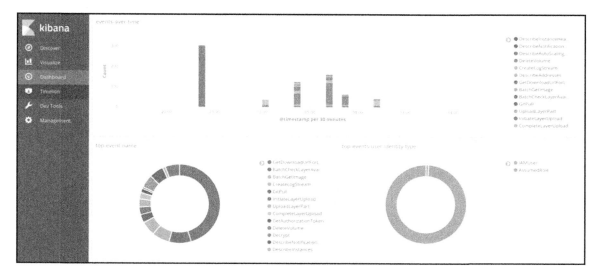

Vulnerability scanning for your dependencies

Since most Lambda function code contains multiple third-party Go dependencies (remember the `go get` commands), it's important to carry out audits for all of these. Hence, vulnerability scanning your Golang dependencies should be part of your CI/CD. You must automate the security analysis using a third-party tool such as **Snyk** (`https://snyk.io/`) to continuously scan for known security vulnerabilities in dependencies. The following screenshot describe a complete end-to-end deployment process that you might choose to implement for your Lambda functions:

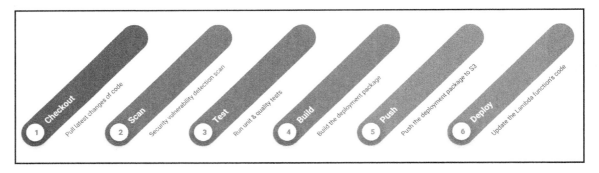

By making vulnerability scanning part of your workflow, you will be capable of finding and fixing known vulnerabilities in packages which could potentially cause data loss, service outages, and unauthorised access to sensitive information.

In addition, application best practices can still apply in serverless architectures, software engineering practices such as code review and git branches, and security safety checks as input validation or sanitization to avoid SQL injection.

Summary

In this chapter, you learned a few best practices and recommendations for building a secure serverless application based on Lambda functions. We covered how Amazon Cognito can be used as an authentication provider and how it can be integrated with API Gateway to secure API endpoints. Then, we looked at Lambda function code practices such as encrypting sensitive data using AWS KMS and input validation. Moreover, other practices can be useful and life saving, such as applying quotas and throttling to prevent a consumer from consuming all of your Lambda function capacity and use of one IAM role per function to leverage the principle of least privilege.

In the next chapter, we will discuss the Lambda pricing model and how to estimate pricing based on the expected load.

Questions

1. Integrate a user in a user pool with an identity pool to allow users to log in with their Facebook account.
2. Integrate a user in a user pool with an identity pool to allow users to log in with their Twitter account.
3. Integrate a user in a user pool with an identity pool to allow users to log in with their Google account.
4. Implement a form to allow users to create an account on a web application so that they are able to log in.
5. Implement a forgotten password flow for an unauthenticated user.

13
Designing Cost-Effective Applications

In this chapter, we will discuss the pricing model of AWS Lambda and learn how to estimate this pricing based on the expected load. We will also cover some tips to optimize and reduce your serverless application cost while maintaining resiliency and availability. We will cover the following topics in this chapter:

- Lambda pricing model
- Optimal memory size
- Code optimization
- Lambda cost and memory tracking

Lambda pricing model

AWS Lambda shifted in the way Ops teams provision and manage their organization's infrastructure. Customers can now run their code without worrying about the underlying infrastructure while paying a low price. The first 1 million requests per month are free, and it's $0.20 per 1 million requests thereafter, so you might use Lambda's free tier indefinitely. However, intensive use cases and huge workload applications can unnecessarily cost you thousands of dollars if you don't pay extra attention to your function's resource usage and code optimization.

In order to keep your Lambda costs under control, you must understand how the Lambda pricing model works. There are three factors that determine the cost of your function:

- **Number of executions**: Number of invocations; you pay $0.0000002 per request.
- **Allocated memory**: The amount of RAM provisioned for your function (ranges between 128 MB and 3,008 MB).
- **Execution time**: The duration is calculated from the time your code begins executing until it returns a response or otherwise terminates. The time is rounded up to the nearest 100 ms (Lambda is billed in 100 ms increments), and the maximum timeout you can set is 5 minutes.
- **Data transfer**: If your Lambda function initiates external data transfers, they will be charged at the EC2 data transfer rate (`https://aws.amazon.com/ec2/pricing`).

Lambda cost calculator

Now that you're familiar with the pricing model, let's see how you can calculate the cost of your Lambda function in advance.

In the previous chapters, we allocated 128 MB of memory to the `FindAllMovies` function, and we set the execution timeout to be 3 seconds. Let's suppose the function will be executed 10 times per second (25 million times in one month). Your charges would be calculated as follows:

- **Monthly compute charges**: The monthly compute price is $0.00001667 per GB/s and the free tier provides 400,000 GB/s. Total compute (seconds) = 25 M * (1s) = 25,000,000 seconds. Total compute (GB/s) = 25,000,000 * 128 MB/1,024 =3,125,000 GB/s.

  Total compute – Free tier compute = Monthly billable compute GB/s

  3,125,000 GB/s – 400,000 free tier GB/s = 2,725,000 GB/s

  Monthly compute charges = 2,725,000 GB/s * $0.00001667 = $45.42

- **Monthly request charges**: The monthly request price is $0.20 per 1 million requests and the free tier provides 1 million requests per month.

  Total requests – Free tier requests = Monthly billable requests

  25 M requests – 1 M free tier requests = 24 M monthly billable requests

  Monthly request charges = 24 M * $0.2/M = $4.8

  Hence, the total monthly charges is the sum of the compute and request charges, as follows:

  Total charges = Compute charges + Request charges = $45.24 + $4.8 = $50.04

Optimal memory size

As we saw in the previous section, the amount of allocated RAM impacts billing. Furthermore, it impacts the amount of CPU and network bandwidth your function receives. Hence, you need to choose the optimal memory size. In order to find the right balance and optimal level of price and performance for your function, you must test your Lambda function with different memory settings and analyze the actual memory used by your function. Fortunately, AWS Lambda writes a log entry in the associated log group. The logs contains, for each request, the amount of memory allocated and used by the function. The following is an example of a log output:

```
Log output
The area below shows the logging calls in your code. These correspond to a single row within the CloudWatch log group corresponding to this Lambda function. Click here to view the
CloudWatch log group.

START RequestId: b9852dc2-9754-11e8-b867-71ba032220cf Version: $LATEST
END RequestId: b9852dc2-9754-11e8-b867-71ba032220cf
REPORT RequestId: b9852dc2-9754-11e8-b867-71ba032220cf   Duration: 1852.83 ms    Billed Duration: 1900 ms        Memory Size: 128 MB     Max Memory Used: 45 MB
```

By comparing the **Memory Size** and **Max Memory Used** fields, you can determine whether your function needs more memory or if you over-provisioned your function's memory size. In case your function needs more memory, you can always give it more memory from the **Basic settings** section, as follows:

Basic settings

Description

[   ]

Memory (MB) Info
Your function is allocated CPU proportional to the memory configured.

●━━━━━━━━━━━━

256 MB

Timeout Info

| 0 | min | 3 | sec |

Click on **Save** and then invoke the function once again. In the log's output, you will notice that the memory size impacts the execution time:

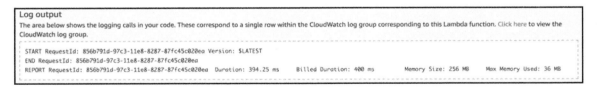

```
Log output
The area below shows the logging calls in your code. These correspond to a single row within the CloudWatch log group corresponding to this Lambda function. Click here to view the
CloudWatch log group.

START RequestId: 856b791d-97c3-11e8-8287-87fc45c020ea Version: $LATEST
END RequestId: 856b791d-97c3-11e8-8287-87fc45c020ea
REPORT RequestId: 856b791d-97c3-11e8-8287-87fc45c020ea  Duration: 394.25 ms    Billed Duration: 400 ms    Memory Size: 256 MB    Max Memory Used: 36 MB
```

While increasing the function memory settings will provide substantial performance gains. The cost will increase linearly as the memory settings increase in Lambda. Similarly, decreasing the function memory setting might help reduce costs, but this will also increase your execution time, and, in the worst case scenario, lead to timeouts or memory exceeded errors.

Provisioning the smallest memory settings to your Lambda function won't always provide the lowest total cost. The function will fail and timeout due to insufficient memory. Also, it might take longer time to complete. By consequence, you will pay more.

Code optimization

In the previous section, we saw how testing your function at scale with different memory settings results in more CPU capacity allocated, which could impact your Lambda function's performance and cost. However, before optimizing the resource usage, you need to optimize your function's code first to help reduce the amount of memory and CPU it needs in order to be executed. Contrary to traditional applications, AWS Lambda manages and patches the infrastructure for you, which allows developers to focus on writing good quality, efficient, and world-class code that executes fast.

Allocating more resources to your function can result in faster executions until a certain threshold, where adding more memory will no longer provide better performance.

The following are some points you should keep in mind when designing your function with AWS Lambda in a cost-effective manner:

- Warm containers can be used for certain requests. Having this knowledge in mind, we can improve the Lambda function's performance by implementing the following:
    - Avoid the reinitialization of variables on every invocation by using global variables and the singleton pattern.
    - Keep alive and reuse databases and HTTP connections that were established during a previous invocation. In Go, you can use the `init` function to set up the required state and run one-time computations when your function handler is loaded.
- Design your architecture to be asynchronous; a decoupled component might take less compute time to finish its work than a tightly coupled component. Also, avoid spending CPU cycles awaiting responses to synchronous requests.
- Use monitoring and debugging tools like AWS X-Ray to analyze and troubleshoot performance bottlenecks, latency spikes, and other issues that impact the performance of your Lambda application.

- Set limits using concurrency reservation to prevent unlimited autoscaling, cold starts, and to protect your downstream services. You can also throttle and limit the number of executions by placing a **Simple Queue Service (SQS)** between the Lambda trigger and the function to adjust how frequently your Lambda function should be triggered.

Lambda cost and memory tracking

The key behind designing cost-effective serverless applications in AWS Lambda is by monitoring your cost and resource usage. Unfortunately, CloudWatch doesn't provide out of the box metrics about the resource usage or the Lambda function cost. Luckily, for each execution, the Lambda function writes an execution log to CloudWatch that looks like the following:

```
REPORT RequestId: 147e72f8-5143-11e8-bba3-b5140c3dea53 Duration: 12.00 ms
Billed Duration: 100 ms  Memory Size: 128 MB Max Memory Used: 21 MB
```

The preceding log shows the memory that's allocated and used for a given request. Those values can be extracted with a simple CloudWatch log metric filter. This feature enables you to search for specific keywords in your logs.

Open the AWS **CloudWatch** console and select **Log Groups** from the navigation pane. Next, search for the log group associated with your Lambda function. It should be named as follows: /aws/lambda/FUNCTION_NAME:

Next, click on the **Create Metric Filter** button:

Step 1: Define Pattern

Step 2: Assign Metric

Define Logs Metric Filter

Filter for Log Group: /aws/lambda/FindAllMovies

You can use metric filters to monitor events in a log group as they are sent to CloudWatch Logs. You can monitor and count specific terms or extract values from log events and associate the results with a metric. Learn more about pattern syntax.

Filter Pattern

Show examples

Select Log Data to Test

2018/05/06/[$LATEST]5749b1b4851b4db59111896312513446

Clear

Test Pattern

START RequestId: 147e72f8-5143-11e8-bba3-b5140c3dea53 Version: $LATEST
END RequestId: 147e72f8-5143-11e8-bba3-b5140c3dea53
REPORT RequestId: 147e72f8-5143-11e8-bba3-b5140c3dea53 Duration: 12.00 ms Billed Duration: 100 ms M
START RequestId: 1b06659e-5144-11e8-a048-553aea51eeb2 Version: $LATEST
END RequestId: 1b06659e-5144-11e8-a048-553aea51eeb2
REPORT RequestId: 1b06659e-5144-11e8-a048-553aea51eeb2 Duration: 38.61 ms Billed Duration: 100 ms M
START RequestId: fbbd8e49-5144-11e8-8f21-0d80cc70ac80 Version: $LATEST

Results

Found **15** matches out of 15 event(s) in the sample log.

Show test results

Cancel   **Assign Metric**

Define a metric filter pattern that parses space-delimited terms. The metric filter pattern has to specify the fields with a name, separated by commas, with the entire pattern enclosed in square brackets, for example, [a,b,c]. Then, click on **Test Pattern** to test the results of your filter pattern against the existing data in the logs. The following records will be printed:

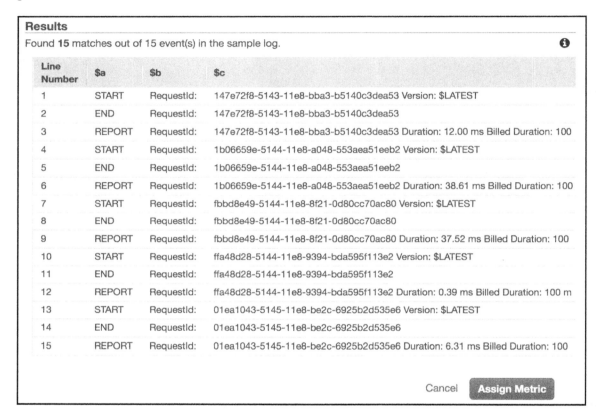

Results

Found **15** matches out of 15 event(s) in the sample log.

Line Number	$a	$b	$c
1	START	RequestId:	147e72f8-5143-11e8-bba3-b5140c3dea53 Version: $LATEST
2	END	RequestId:	147e72f8-5143-11e8-bba3-b5140c3dea53
3	REPORT	RequestId:	147e72f8-5143-11e8-bba3-b5140c3dea53 Duration: 12.00 ms Billed Duration: 100
4	START	RequestId:	1b06659e-5144-11e8-a048-553aea51eeb2 Version: $LATEST
5	END	RequestId:	1b06659e-5144-11e8-a048-553aea51eeb2
6	REPORT	RequestId:	1b06659e-5144-11e8-a048-553aea51eeb2 Duration: 38.61 ms Billed Duration: 100
7	START	RequestId:	fbbd8e49-5144-11e8-8f21-0d80cc70ac80 Version: $LATEST
8	END	RequestId:	fbbd8e49-5144-11e8-8f21-0d80cc70ac80
9	REPORT	RequestId:	fbbd8e49-5144-11e8-8f21-0d80cc70ac80 Duration: 37.52 ms Billed Duration: 100
10	START	RequestId:	ffa48d28-5144-11e8-9394-bda595f113e2 Version: $LATEST
11	END	RequestId:	ffa48d28-5144-11e8-9394-bda595f113e2
12	REPORT	RequestId:	ffa48d28-5144-11e8-9394-bda595f113e2 Duration: 0.39 ms Billed Duration: 100 m
13	START	RequestId:	01ea1043-5145-11e8-be2c-6925b2d535e6 Version: $LATEST
14	END	RequestId:	01ea1043-5145-11e8-be2c-6925b2d535e6
15	REPORT	RequestId:	01ea1043-5145-11e8-be2c-6925b2d535e6 Duration: 6.31 ms Billed Duration: 100

Cancel   **Assign Metric**

If you don't know the number of fields that you have, you can use an ellipsis enclosed in square brackets:

Results

Found **15** matches out of 15 event(s) in the sample log.   ❶

$6	$7	$8	$9	$10	$11	$12	$13	$14	$15	$16	$17	$18	$19
ms	Billed	Duration:	100	ms	Memory	Size:	128	MB	Max	Memory	Used:	21	MB
ms	Billed	Duration:	100	ms	Memory	Size:	128	MB	Max	Memory	Used:	22	MB
ms	Billed	Duration:	100	ms	Memory	Size:	128	MB	Max	Memory	Used:	22	MB
ms	Billed	Duration:	100	ms	Memory	Size:	128	MB	Max	Memory	Used:	22	MB
ms	Billed	Duration:	100	ms	Memory	Size:	128	MB	Max	Memory	Used:	22	MB

Cancel   **Assign Metric**

Column $13 will be storing the memory allocated to the function and $18 represents the actual memory used. Next, click on **Assign Metric** to create a metric for the memory that's been allocated:

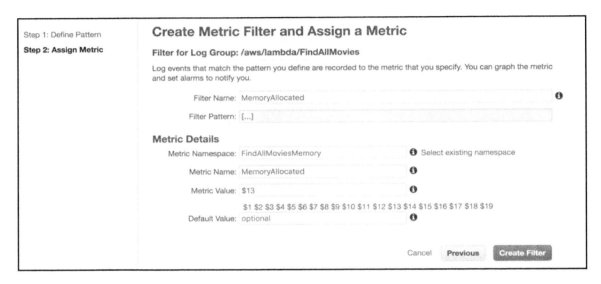

Click on the **Create Filter** button to save it. You should now see the newly created filter:

Apply the same steps to create another filter for the memory usage:

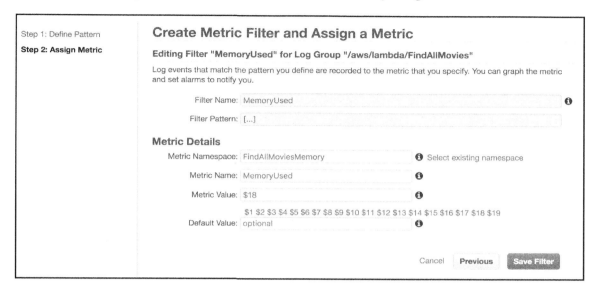

Once the two filters are defined, make sure your Lambda function is running and wait a few seconds while the function is populating the new CloudWatch metrics with some values:

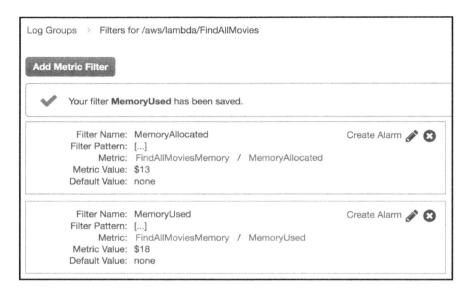

Back in CloudWatch, create a new chart based on the two metrics that we created previously:

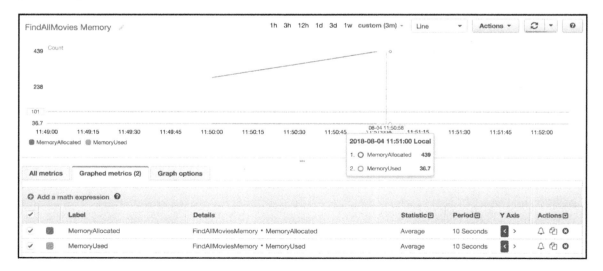

You can take this further and create a near real-time CloudWatch alarm if the memory used exceeds a certain threshold (for instance, 80% relative to the memory that you allocated). Moreover, it's important to keep an eye on the function's duration. You can follow the same procedure that was described in this section to extract the billed duration from Lambda execution logs and set up an alarm based on the extracted value so that you're notified if your function is taking a suspiciously long time to complete.

Summary

Getting started with AWS Lambda is easy – you don't have to provision and manage any underlying infrastructure and it's very cheap to get something useful up and running in a few seconds. Plus, a great advantage of AWS Lambda over EC2 is that you don't have to pay for idle resources. This is extremely powerful, but it's also one of Lambda's biggest risks. It's very common to forget about cost during development, but once you start running heavy workloads and multiple functions in production, cost can be significant. Hence, it's very important to keep track of Lambda cost and usage before this becomes an issue.

The final chapter will introduce the concept of **Infrastructure as Code (IaC)** to help you design and deploy your N-tier serverless application in an automated way, in order to avoid human errors and repeatable tasks.

Infrastructure as Code

14

A typical Lambda-based application consists of multiple functions triggered by events, such as a new object in the S3 bucket, incoming HTTP requests, or a new SQS message. Those functions can stand alone or leverage other resources, such as DynamoDB tables, Amazon S3 buckets, and other Lambda functions. So far, we have seen how to create those resources from the AWS Management Console or with the AWS CLI. In a real-world scenario, you want to spend less time provisioning the required resources and focus more on your application logic. In the end, that's the serverless approach.

This last chapter will introduce the concept of Infrastructure as Code to help you design and deploy your N-Tier serverless application in an automated way, in order to avoid human error and repeatable tasks.

Technical requirements

This book assumes some basic familiarity with the AWS Serverless Application Model. If you're new to SAM itself, refer to Chapter 1, *Go Serverless* through Chapter 10, *Testing Your Serverless Application*. You will get a step-by-step guide on how to get started with SAM. The code bundle for this chapter is hosted on GitHub at https://github.com/ PacktPublishing/Hands-On-serverless-Applications-with-Go.

Deploying AWS Lambda with Terraform

Terraform is an open source automation tool built by HashiCorp. It is used to create, manage, and update infrastructure resources through declarative configuration files. It supports the following providers:

- **Cloud providers**: AWS, Azure, Oracle Cloud, and GCP
- **Infrastructure software**:
    - **Consul**: It is a distributed, highly available service-discovery and configuration system.
    - **Docker**: It is a tool designed to make it easier to create, deploy, and run applications by using containers.
    - **Nomad**: It is an easy-to-use enterprise-grade cluster scheduler.
    - **Vault**: It is a tool that provides a secure, reliable way to store and distribute secrets.
- Other **SaaS** and **PaaS**

 Terraform is not a configuration-management tool (such as Ansible, Chef, and Puppet & Salt). It was created to spawn and destroy infrastructure, while configuration-management tools were used to install things on top of existing infrastructure. However, Terraform can do a bit of provisioning (https://www.terraform.io/docs/provisioners/index.html).

This guide will show you how to deploy AWS Lambda using Terraform, so you will need to have Terraform installed. You can find the appropriate package for your system and download it (https://www.terraform.io/downloads.html). Once downloaded, make sure that the `terraform` binary is available on the `PATH` variable. Configure your credentials so that Terraform is able to act on your behalf. The following are four ways to provide credentials for authentication:

- Provide AWS `access_key` and `secret_key` directly through the provider.
- AWS environment variables.
- Shared credentials file.
- EC2 IAM role.

If you followed Chapter 2, *Getting Started with AWS Lambda*, you should have installed and configured the AWS CLI. Therefore, no action is required on your part.

Creating the Lambda function

To begin creating the Lambda function, follow the given steps:

1. Create a new project with the following structure:

```
.
├── assume-role-policy.json
├── function
│   └── main.go
├── main.tf
└── policy.json
```

2. We will use the easiest Hello world example. The function folder contains a Go-based Lambda function that displays a simple message:

```
package main

import "github.com/aws/aws-lambda-go/lambda"

func handler() (string, error) {
  return "First Lambda function with Terraform", nil
}
func main() {
  lambda.Start(handler)
}
```

3. You can build a Linux-based binary and generate a deployment package with the following commands:

```
GOOS=linux go build -o main main.go
zip deployment.zip main
```

4. Now that the function code is defined, let's create our first Lambda function with Terraform. Copy the following content to the main.tf file:

```
provider "aws" {
  region = "us-east-1"
}
```

```
resource "aws_iam_role" "role" {
  name = "PushCloudWatchLogsRole"
  assume_role_policy = "${file("assume-role-policy.json")}"
}

resource "aws_iam_policy" "policy" {
  name = "PushCloudWatchLogsPolicy"
  policy = "${file("policy.json")}"
}

resource "aws_iam_policy_attachment" "profile" {
  name = "cloudwatch-lambda-attachment"
  roles = ["${aws_iam_role.role.name}"]
  policy_arn = "${aws_iam_policy.policy.arn}"
}

resource "aws_lambda_function" "demo" {
  filename = "function/deployment.zip"
  function_name = "HelloWorld"
  role = "${aws_iam_role.role.arn}"
  handler = "main"
  runtime = "go1.x"
}
```

5. This is telling Terraform that we're going to be using the AWS provider and to default to the us-east-1 region for creating our resources:

- **IAM role** is an execution role that will be assumed by the Lambda function during execution. It defines the resources our Lambda function has access to:

```
{
  "Version": "2012-10-17",
  "Statement": [
    {
      "Action": "sts:AssumeRole",
      "Principal": {
        "Service": "lambda.amazonaws.com"
      },
      "Effect": "Allow",
      "Sid": ""
    }
  ]
}
```

- **IAM policy** is a list of permissions to grant our Lambda function the right to stream its logs to CloudWatch. The following policy will be attached to the IAM role:

```
{
  "Version": "2012-10-17",
  "Statement": [
    {
      "Sid": "1",
      "Effect": "Allow",
      "Action": [
        "logs:CreateLogStream",
        "logs:CreateLogGroup",
        "logs:PutLogEvents"
      ],
      "Resource": "*"
    }
  ]
}
```

- **Lambda function** is a Go-based Lambda function. The deployment package can be specified either directly as a local file (using the `filename` attribute) or via Amazon S3 bucket. For in-depth details on how to deploy the Lambda function to AWS, refer to `Chapter 6`, *Deploying Your Serverless Application*.

6. On the terminal, run the `terraform init` command to download and install the AWS provider, shown as follows:

```
Initializing provider plugins...
- Checking for available provider plugins on https://releases.hashicorp.com...
- Downloading plugin for provider "aws" (1.31.0)...

The following providers do not have any version constraints in configuration,
so the latest version was installed.

To prevent automatic upgrades to new major versions that may contain breaking
changes, it is recommended to add version = "..." constraints to the
corresponding provider blocks in configuration, with the constraint strings
suggested below.

* provider.aws: version = "~> 1.31"

Terraform has been successfully initialized!

You may now begin working with Terraform. Try running "terraform plan" to see
any changes that are required for your infrastructure. All Terraform commands
should now work.

If you ever set or change modules or backend configuration for Terraform,
rerun this command to reinitialize your working directory. If you forget, other
commands will detect it and remind you to do so if necessary.
```

7. Create an execution plan (dry run) with the `terraform plan` command. It shows you things that will be created in advance, which is good for debugging and ensuring that you're not doing anything wrong, as shown in the next screenshot:

```
Refreshing Terraform state in-memory prior to plan...
The refreshed state will be used to calculate this plan, but will not be
persisted to local or remote state storage.


------------------------------------------------------------------------


An execution plan has been generated and is shown below.
Resource actions are indicated with the following symbols:
  + create

Terraform will perform the following actions:

  + aws_iam_policy.policy
      id:                        <computed>
      arn:                       <computed>
      name:                      "PushCloudWatchLogsPolicy"
      path:                      "/"
      policy:                    "{\n    \"Version\": \"2012-10-17\",\n    \"Statement\": [\n        {\n
          \"logs:CreateLogGroup\",\n                        \"logs:PutLogEvents\"\n              ],\n

  + aws_iam_policy_attachment.profile
      id:                        <computed>
      name:                      "cloudwatch-lambda-attachment"
      policy_arn:                "${aws_iam_policy.policy.arn}"
      roles.#:                   "1"
      roles.3875647699:          "PushCloudWatchLogsRole"

  + aws_iam_role.role
      id:                        <computed>
      arn:                       <computed>
      assume_role_policy:        "{\n    \"Version\": \"2012-10-17\",\n    \"Statement\": [\n        {\n
fect\": \"Allow\",\n           \"Sid\": \"\"\n        }\n    ]\n  }"
      create_date:               <computed>
      force_detach_policies:     "false"
      max_session_duration:      "3600"
      name:                      "PushCloudWatchLogsRole"
      path:                      "/"
      unique_id:                 <computed>

  + aws_lambda_function.demo
      id:                        <computed>
      arn:                       <computed>
      filename:                  "function/deployment.zip"
      function_name:             "DemoTerraform"
      handler:                   "main"
      invoke_arn:                <computed>
      last_modified:             <computed>
      memory_size:               "128"
      publish:                   "false"
      qualified_arn:             <computed>
      role:                      "PushCloudWatchLogsRole"
      runtime:                   "go1.x"
      source_code_hash:          <computed>
      source_code_size:          <computed>
      timeout:                   "3"
      tracing_config.#:          <computed>
      version:                   <computed>


Plan: 4 to add, 0 to change, 0 to destroy.

------------------------------------------------------------------------

Note: You didn't specify an "-out" parameter to save this plan, so Terraform
can't guarantee that exactly these actions will be performed if
"terraform apply" is subsequently run.
```

8. You will be able to examine Terraform's execution plan before you deploy it to AWS. When you're ready, go ahead and apply the changes by issuing the following command:

```
terraform apply
```

9. Confirm the configuration by typing `yes`. The following output will be displayed (some parts were cropped for brevity):

```
Do you want to perform these actions?
  Terraform will perform the actions described above.
  Only 'yes' will be accepted to approve.

  Enter a value: yes

aws_lambda_function.demo: Creating...
  arn:                "" => "<computed>"
  filename:           "" => "function/deployment.zip"
  function_name:      "" => "DemoTerraform"
  handler:            "" => "main"
  invoke_arn:         "" => "<computed>"
  last_modified:      "" => "<computed>"
  memory_size:        "" => "128"
  publish:            "" => "false"
  qualified_arn:      "" => "<computed>"
  role:               "" => "arn:aws:iam::305929695733:role/PushCloudWatchLogsRole"
  runtime:            "" => "go1.x"
  source_code_hash:   "" => "<computed>"
  source_code_size:   "" => "<computed>"
  timeout:            "" => "3"
  tracing_config.#:   "" => "<computed>"
  version:            "" => "<computed>"
aws_iam_policy_attachment.profile: Creation complete after 2s (ID: cloudwatch-lambda-attachment)
aws_lambda_function.demo: Still creating... (10s elapsed)
aws_lambda_function.demo: Still creating... (20s elapsed)
aws_lambda_function.demo: Still creating... (30s elapsed)
aws_lambda_function.demo: Still creating... (40s elapsed)
aws_lambda_function.demo: Creation complete after 42s (ID: DemoTerraform)

Apply complete! Resources: 4 added, 0 changed, 0 destroyed.
```

 Make sure the IAM user used to execute these commands has permissions to perform IAM and Lambda operations.

10. If you head back to AWS Lambda Console, a new Lambda function should be created. If you try to invoke it, it should return the expected message, as shown in the next screenshot:

11. So far, we defined the AWS region and function name in the template file. However, one of the reasons we use infrastructure-as-code tools is usability and automation. Hence, you should always use variables and avoid hardcoding values. Luckily, Terraform allows you to define your own variables. To do so, create a `variables.tf` file as follows:

```
variable "aws_region" {
  default = "us-east-1"
  description = "AWS region"
}

variable "lambda_function_name" {
  default = "DemoFunction"
  description = "Lambda function's name"
}
```

12. Update `main.tf` to use the variables instead of hardcoded values. Note the usage of the `${var.variable_name}` keyword:

```
provider "aws" {
  region = "${var.aws_region}"
```

```
}

resource "aws_lambda_function" "demo" {
  filename = "function/deployment.zip"
  function_name = "${var.lambda_function_name}"
  role = "${aws_iam_role.role.arn}"
  handler = "main"
  runtime = "go1.x"
}
```

13. With the function working as expected, create the serverless API we built so far with Terraform.

14. In a new directory, create a file named `main.tf` that contains the following configuration:

```
resource "aws_iam_role" "role" {
 name = "FindAllMoviesRole"
 assume_role_policy = "${file("assume-role-policy.json")}"
}

resource "aws_iam_policy" "cloudwatch_policy" {
 name = "PushCloudWatchLogsPolicy"
 policy = "${file("cloudwatch-policy.json")}"
}

resource "aws_iam_policy" "dynamodb_policy" {
 name = "ScanDynamoDBPolicy"
 policy = "${file("dynamodb-policy.json")}"
}

resource "aws_iam_policy_attachment" "cloudwatch-attachment" {
 name = "cloudwatch-lambda-attchment"
 roles = ["${aws_iam_role.role.name}"]
 policy_arn = "${aws_iam_policy.cloudwatch_policy.arn}"
}

resource "aws_iam_policy_attachment" "dynamodb-attachment" {
 name = "dynamodb-lambda-attchment"
 roles = ["${aws_iam_role.role.name}"]
 policy_arn = "${aws_iam_policy.dynamodb_policy.arn}"
}
```

15. The preceding code snippet creates an IAM role with permissions to scan a DynamoDB table and writes the log entry to CloudWatch. Configure a Go-based Lambda function with the DynamoDB table name as an environment variable:

```
resource "aws_lambda_function" "findall" {
```

```
function_name = "FindAllMovies"
handler = "main"
filename = "function/deployment.zip"
runtime = "go1.x"
role = "${aws_iam_role.role.arn}"

environment {
  variables {
    TABLE_NAME = "movies"
  }
}
}
```

Setting up DynamoDB table

Next, we have to set up the DynamoDB table. Perform the following steps:

1. Create a DynamoDB table with an ID as the partition key for the table:

```
resource "aws_dynamodb_table" "movies" {
  name = "movies"
  read_capacity = 5
  write_capacity = 5
  hash_key = "ID"

  attribute {
    name = "ID"
    type = "S"
  }
}
```

2. Initialize the `movies` table with a new item:

```
resource "aws_dynamodb_table_item" "items" {
  table_name = "${aws_dynamodb_table.movies.name}"
  hash_key = "${aws_dynamodb_table.movies.hash_key}"
  item = "${file("movie.json")}"
}
```

3. The item attributes are defined in the `movie.json` file:

```
{
  "ID": {"S": "1"},
  "Name": {"S": "Ant-Man and the Wasp"},
  "Description": {"S": "A Marvel's movie"},
  "Cover": {"S": http://COVER_URL.jpg"}
}
```

Configuring API Gateway

Finally, we need to trigger the function with API Gateway:

1. Create a `movies` resource on the REST API and expose a `GET` method on it. If the incoming requests match the resource defined, it will call the Lambda function defined earlier:

```
resource "aws_api_gateway_rest_api" "api" {
  name = "MoviesAPI"
}

resource "aws_api_gateway_resource" "proxy" {
  rest_api_id = "${aws_api_gateway_rest_api.api.id}"
  parent_id   = "${aws_api_gateway_rest_api.api.root_resource_id}"
  path_part   = "movies"
}

resource "aws_api_gateway_method" "proxy" {
  rest_api_id   = "${aws_api_gateway_rest_api.api.id}"
  resource_id   = "${aws_api_gateway_resource.proxy.id}"
  http_method   = "GET"
  authorization = "NONE"
}

resource "aws_api_gateway_integration" "lambda" {
  rest_api_id = "${aws_api_gateway_rest_api.api.id}"
  resource_id = "${aws_api_gateway_method.proxy.resource_id}"
  http_method = "${aws_api_gateway_method.proxy.http_method}"

  integration_http_method = "POST"
  type = "AWS_PROXY"
  uri = "${aws_lambda_function.findall.invoke_arn}"
}
```

2. Issue the following commands to install the AWS plugin, generate an execution plan, and apply the changes:

```
terraform init
terraform plan
terraform apply
```

3. It should take a few seconds to create the whole infrastructure. After the creation steps are complete, the Lambda function should be created and properly configured, as shown in the following screenshot:

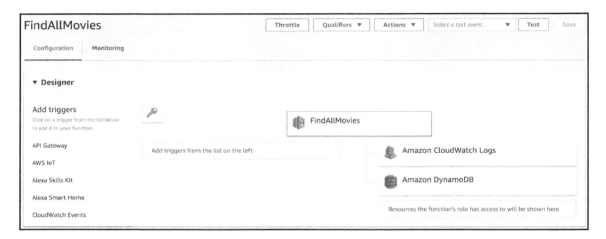

4. The same goes for API Gateway, a new REST API should be defined with a GET method on /movies resource, shown as follows:

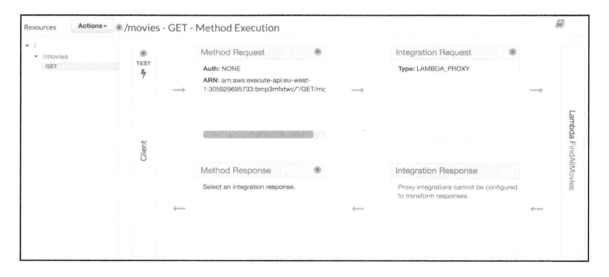

5. In DynamoDB Console, a new table should be created with a movie item, as shown in the next screenshot:

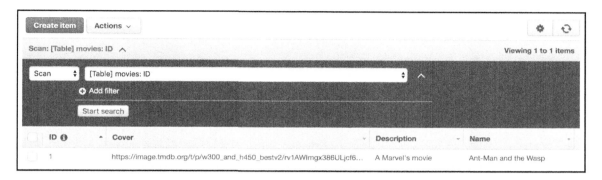

6. In order to invoke our API Gateway, we need to deploy it. Create a deployment stage, let's call it `staging`:

```
resource "aws_api_gateway_deployment" "staging" {
  depends_on = ["aws_api_gateway_integration.lambda"]

  rest_api_id = "${aws_api_gateway_rest_api.api.id}"
  stage_name = "staging"
}
```

7. We will use Terraform's output feature to expose the API URL; create an `outputs.tf` file with the following content:

```
output "API Invocation URL" {
  value = "${aws_api_gateway_deployment.staging.invoke_url}"
}
```

8. Run `terraform apply` again to create these new objects, it will detect the changes and ask you to confirm it should perform the actions, shown as follows:

```
aws_dynamodb_table.movies: Refreshing state... (ID: movies)
aws_api_gateway_rest_api.api: Refreshing state... (ID: bmp3mfxtwc)
aws_iam_policy.dynamodb_policy: Refreshing state... (ID: arn:aws:iam::305929695733:policy/ScanDynamoDBPolicy)
aws_iam_policy.cloudwatch_policy: Refreshing state... (ID: arn:aws:iam::305929695733:policy/PushCloudWatchLogsPolicy)
aws_iam_role.role: Refreshing state... (ID: FindAllMovies2Role)
aws_api_gateway_resource.proxy: Refreshing state... (ID: o4w8px)
aws_lambda_function.findall: Refreshing state... (ID: FindAllMovies)
aws_api_gateway_method.proxy: Refreshing state... (ID: agm-bmp3mfxtwc-o4w8px-GET)
aws_dynamodb_table_item.items: Refreshing state... (ID: movies|ID||1|)
aws_iam_policy_attachment.cloudwatch-attachment: Refreshing state... (ID: cloudwatch-lambda-attchment)
aws_iam_policy_attachment.dynamodb-attachment: Refreshing state... (ID: dynamodb-lambda-attchment)
aws_api_gateway_integration.lambda: Refreshing state... (ID: agi-bmp3mfxtwc-o4w8px-GET)

An execution plan has been generated and is shown below.
Resource actions are indicated with the following symbols:
  + create

Terraform will perform the following actions:

  + aws_api_gateway_deployment.staging
      id:             <computed>
      created_date:   <computed>
      execution_arn:  <computed>
      invoke_url:     <computed>
      rest_api_id:    "bmp3mfxtwc"
      stage_name:     "staging"

Plan: 1 to add, 0 to change, 0 to destroy.

Do you want to perform these actions?
  Terraform will perform the actions described above.
  Only 'yes' will be accepted to approve.

  Enter a value:
```

9. The API Gateway URL will be displayed in the **Outputs** section; copy it to the clipboard:

```
aws_api_gateway_deployment.staging: Creating...
  created_date:    "" => "<computed>"
  execution_arn:   "" => "<computed>"
  invoke_url:      "" => "<computed>"
  rest_api_id:     "" => "bmp3mfxtwc"
  stage_name:      "" => "staging"
aws_api_gateway_deployment.staging: Creation complete after 1s (ID: ezk9r4)

Apply complete! Resources: 1 added, 0 changed, 0 destroyed.

Outputs:

API Invocation URL = https://bmp3mfxtwc.execute-api.eu-west-1.amazonaws.com/staging
```

10. If you point your favorite browser to the API Invocation URL, an error message should be displayed, as shown in the next screenshot:

11. We will fix that, by granting execution permission to API Gateway to invoke the Lambda function. Update the `main.tf` file to create a `aws_lambda_permission` resource:

```
resource "aws_lambda_permission" "apigw" {
  statement_id = "AllowAPIGatewayInvoke"
  action = "lambda:InvokeFunction"
  function_name = "${aws_lambda_function.findall.arn}"
  principal = "apigateway.amazonaws.com"

  source_arn =
"${aws_api_gateway_deployment.staging.execution_arn}/*/*"
}
```

12. Apply the latest changes with the `terraform apply` command. On the Lambda Console, the API Gateway trigger should be displayed, shown as follows:

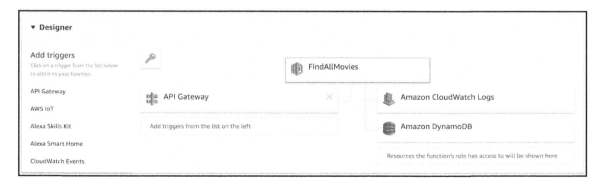

13. Load the URL given in the output from your run in your favorite web browser. If everything has worked, you will see the movie stored in the DynamoDB table in a JSON format, as shown in the next screenshot:

```
https://bmp3mfxtwc.execute- ×

←  →  C    🔒 Secure   https://bmp3mfxtwc.execute-api.eu-west-1.amazonaws.com/staging/movies

⋮⋮⋮ Apps  ◯ mlabouardy (LABO...    AWS Management...   M Mohamed Labouar...    https://aws.amazon...   https://d1.awsstatic...

[
  {
    "id": "1",
    "name": "Ant-Man and the Wasp",
    "cover": "https://image.tmdb.org/t/p/w300_and_h450_bestv2/rv1AWImgx386ULjcf62VYaW8zSt.jpg",
    "description": "A Marvel's movie"
  }
]
```

Terraform stores the state of the infrastructure in a state file (`.tfstate`). The state contains resource IDs and all the resource attributes. If you're using Terraform to create a RDS instance, the database credentials will be in plaintext in the state file. Hence, you should keep your file in a remote backend, such as S3 bucket.

Cleaning up

Finally, to delete all the resources (Lambda function, IAM role, IAM policies, DynamoDB table, and API Gateway), you can issue the `terraform destroy` command, shown as follows:

```
Terraform will perform the following actions:

  - aws_api_gateway_deployment.staging

  - aws_api_gateway_integration.lambda

  - aws_api_gateway_method.proxy

  - aws_api_gateway_resource.proxy

  - aws_api_gateway_rest_api.api

  - aws_dynamodb_table.movies

  - aws_dynamodb_table_item.items

  - aws_iam_policy.cloudwatch_policy

  - aws_iam_policy.dynamodb_policy

  - aws_iam_policy_attachment.cloudwatch-attachment

  - aws_iam_policy_attachment.dynamodb-attachment

  - aws_iam_role.role

  - aws_lambda_function.findall

  - aws_lambda_permission.apigw


Plan: 0 to add, 0 to change, 14 to destroy.

Do you really want to destroy?
  Terraform will destroy all your managed infrastructure, as shown above.
  There is no undo. Only 'yes' will be accepted to confirm.

  Enter a value: yes
```

If you want to delete a specific resource, you can use the `--target` option as follows: `terraform destroy --target=RESOURCE_NAME`. The operation will be limited to the resource and its dependencies.

So far, we have defined the AWS Lambda function and its dependencies using a template file. Hence, we can version it just like any other code. The whole serverless infrastructure we use and configure is treated as a source code, allowing us to share it among team members, replicate it in other AWS regions, and rollback in case of failure.

Deploying AWS Lambda with CloudFormation

AWS CloudFormation is an infrastructure-as-code tool for specifying resources in a declarative way. You model all the resources you want AWS to spin up in a blueprint document (template) and AWS creates the defined resources for you. Thus, you spend less time managing those resources and more time focusing on your applications that run in AWS.

 Terraform covers almost all services and features by AWS and supports third-party providers (platform-agnostic) while CloudFormation is AWS specific (vendor lock-in).

You can use AWS CloudFormation to specify, deploy, and configure serverless applications. You create a template that describes your serverless application dependencies (Lambda functions, DynamoDB tables, API Gateway, IAM roles, and so on), and AWS CloudFormation takes care of provisioning and configuring those resources for you. You don't need to individually create and configure AWS resources and figure out what depends on what.

Before we dive into CloudFormation, we need to understand the template structure:

- **AWSTemplateFormatVersion**: CloudFormation template version.
- **Description**: A brief description of the template.
- **Mappings**: A mapping of keys and associated values that you can use to specify conditional parameter values.
- **Parameters**: Values to pass to your template at runtime.
- **Resources**: AWS resources and their properties (Lambda, DynamoDB, S3, and so on).
- **Outputs**: Describe the values that are returned whenever you view your stack's properties.

After you understand the different parts of the AWS CloudFormation template, you can put them together and define a minimal template in a `template.yml` file, as follows:

```yaml
AWSTemplateFormatVersion: "2010-09-09"
Description: "Simple Lambda Function"
Parameters:
  FunctionName:
    Description: "Function name"
    Type: "String"
    Default: "HelloWorld"
  BucketName:
    Description: "S3 Bucket name"
    Type: "String"
Resources:
  ExecutionRole:
    Type: "AWS::IAM::Role"
    Properties:
      AssumeRolePolicyDocument:
        Version: "2012-10-17"
        Statement:
          - Effect: "Allow"
            Principal:
              Service:
                - "lambda.amazonaws.com"
            Action:
              - "sts:AssumeRole"
      Policies:
        - PolicyName: "PushCloudWatchLogsPolicy"
          PolicyDocument:
            Version: "2012-10-17"
            Statement:
              - Effect: "Allow"
              - Action:
                - logs:CreateLogGroup
                - logs:CreateLogStream
                - logs:PutLogEvents
              - Resource: "*"
  HelloWorldFunction:
    Type: "AWS::Lambda::Function"
    Properties:
      Code:
        S3Bucket: !Ref BucketName
        S3Key: deployment.zip
      FunctionName: !Ref FunctionName
      Handler: "main"
      Runtime: "go1.x"
      Role: !GetAtt ExecutionRole.Arn
```

The preceding file defines two resources:

- `ExecutionRole`: The IAM role assigned to the Lambda function, it defines what entitlements the code invoked by the Lambda runtime has.
- `HelloWorldFunction`: The AWS Lambda definition, we have set the runtime property to use Go and set the function's code to be stored in a ZIP file on S3. The function references the IAM role using CloudFormation's built-in `GetAtt` function; it also uses the `Ref` keyword to reference variables defined in the parameters section.

 The JSON format can be used also; a JSON version can be found on the GitHub repository (`https://github.com/PacktPublishing/Hands-On-serverless-Applications-with-Go`).

Perform the following steps to begin:

1. Create an S3 bucket on which you store the deployment package after building it with the following commands:

```
aws s3 mb s3://hands-on-serverless-go-packt/
GOOS=linux go build -o main main.go
zip deployment.zip main
aws s3 cp deployment.zip s3://hands-on-serverless-go-packt/
```

2. Navigate to AWS CloudFormation Console, and choose **Create Stack**, as shown in the next screenshot:

3. On the **Select Template** page, select the template file, and it will be uploaded to the Amazon S3 bucket, shown as follows:

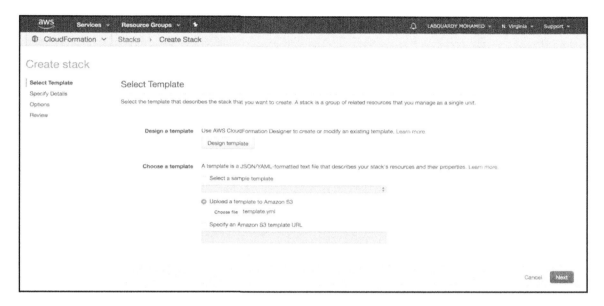

4. Click on **Next**, define the stack name, and override the default parameters if needed, as shown in the next screenshot:

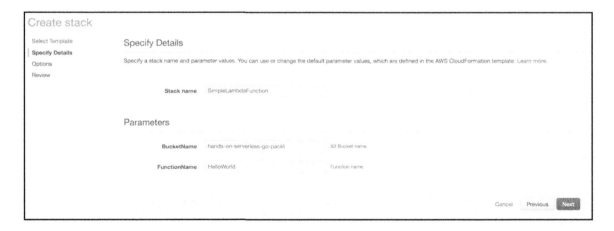

5. Click on **Next**, leave the options as default, and click on **Create**, as shown in the next screenshot:

6. The stack will start creating all the resources defined in the template file. Once created, the stack status will change from **CREATE_IN_PROGRESS** to **CREATE_COMPLETE** (in case something went wrong, a rollback will be executed automatically), shown as follows:

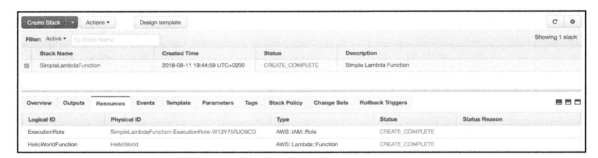

7. As a result, our Lambda function should be created as illustrated in the following screenshot:

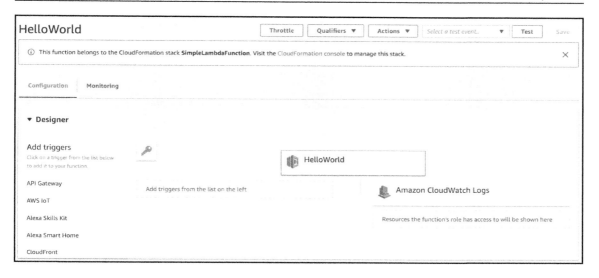

8. You can always update your CloudFormation template file. For example, let's create a new DynamoDB table:

```
AWSTemplateFormatVersion: "2010-09-09"
Description: "Simple Lambda Function"
Parameters:
  FunctionName:
    Description: "Function name"
    Type: "String"
    Default: "HelloWorld"
  BucketName:
    Description: "S3 Bucket name"
    Type: "String"
  TableName:
    Description: "DynamoDB Table Name"
    Type: "String"
    Default: "movies"
Resources:
  ExecutionRole:
    Type: "AWS::IAM::Role"
    Properties:
      AssumeRolePolicyDocument:
        Version: "2012-10-17"
        Statement:
          -
            Effect: "Allow"
            Principal:
              Service:
                - "lambda.amazonaws.com"
```

```
                    Action:
                      - "sts:AssumeRole"
              Policies:
                -
                  PolicyName: "PushCloudWatchLogsPolicy"
                  PolicyDocument:
                    Version: "2012-10-17"
                    Statement:
                      - Effect: Allow
                        Action:
                        - logs:CreateLogGroup
                        - logs:CreateLogStream
                        - logs:PutLogEvents
                        Resource: "*"
                -
                  PolicyName: "ScanDynamoDBTablePolicy"
                  PolicyDocument:
                    Version: "2012-10-17"
                    Statement:
                      - Effect: Allow
                        Action:
                        - dynamodb:Scan
                        Resource: "*"
      HelloWorldFunction:
        Type: "AWS::Lambda::Function"
        Properties:
          Code:
            S3Bucket: !Ref BucketName
            S3Key: deployment.zip
          FunctionName: !Ref FunctionName
          Handler: "main"
          Runtime: "go1.x"
          Role: !GetAtt ExecutionRole.Arn
          Environment:
            Variables:
              TABLE_NAME: !Ref TableName
      DynamoDBTable:
        Type: "AWS::DynamoDB::Table"
        Properties:
          TableName: !Ref TableName
          AttributeDefinitions:
            -
              AttributeName: "ID"
              AttributeType: "S"
          KeySchema:
            -
              AttributeName: "ID"
              KeyType: "HASH"
```

```
ProvisionedThroughput:
    ReadCapacityUnits: 5
    WriteCapacityUnits: 5
```

9. On the CloudFormation Console, select the stack we created earlier and click on **Update Stack** from the menu, shown as follows:

10. Upload the updated template file, shown as follows:

11. Similar to Terraform, AWS CloudFormation will detect the changes and display the resources that will be changed in advance, shown as follows:

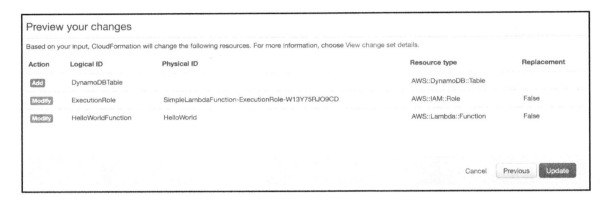

12. Click on the **Update** button to apply the changes. The stack status will change to **UPDATE_IN_PROGRESS**, as shown in the next screenshot:

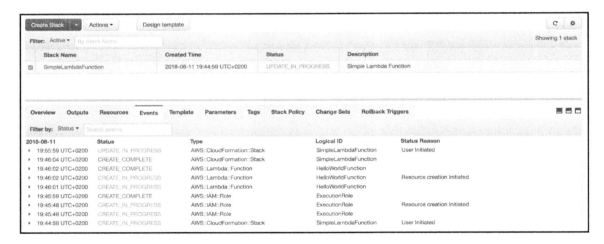

13. After the changes have been applied, a new DynamoDB table will be created and DynamoDB permissions will be granted to the Lambda function, shown as follows:

The `--capabilities CAPABILITY_IAM` option is required whenever the CloudFormation has to define IAM roles, policies, or related resources.

14. The AWS CLI can also be used to create your CloudFormation stack with the following command:

```
aws cloudformation create-stack --stack-name=SimpleLambdaFunction \
    --template-body=file://template.yml \
    --capabilities CAPABILITY_IAM \
 --parameters ParameterKey=BucketName,ParameterValue=hands-on-
serverless-go-packt
 ParameterKey=FunctionName,ParameterValue=HelloWorld \
 ParameterKey=TableName,ParameterValue=movies
```

CloudFormation designer

In addition to writing your own template from scratch, you can use the CloudFormation design template feature to create your stack easily. The following screenshot shows how to view the design of the stack we've created so far:

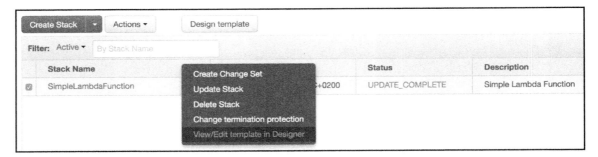

If all has gone well, you should see the following components:

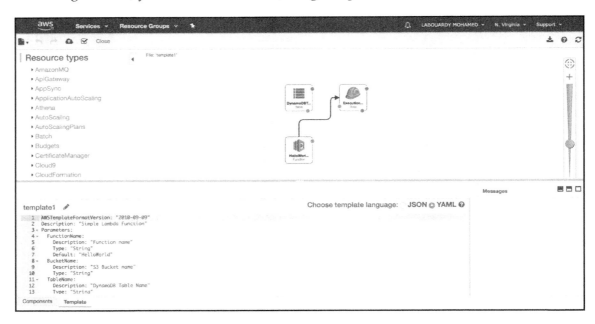

You can now create a complex CloudFormation template by dragging and dropping components from the left menu.

Deploying AWS Lambda with SAM

The **AWS Serverless Application Model (AWS SAM)** is a model to define serverless applications. AWS SAM is natively supported by AWS CloudFormation and defines a simplified syntax for expressing serverless resources. You simply define the resources you need as part of your application in the template file and create a CloudFormation stack with the SAM deploy command.

Previously, we saw how AWS SAM can be used to locally test your Lambda function. In addition, SAM can be used to design and deploy your function to AWS Lambda. You can initialize a quick Go-based serverless project (a boilerplate) with the following command:

```
sam init --name api --runtime go1.x
```

The preceding command will create a folder with the following structure:

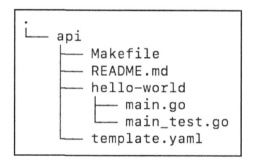

The `sam init` command provides a quick way to create a serverless application. It generates a simple Lambda function in Go with an associated unit test. In addition, a **Makefile** will be generated with a list of steps to build and generate the deployment package. Finally, a template file, called a SAM file, will be created which describes all the AWS resources needed to deploy the function to AWS Lambda.

Now that we know how to generate a boilerplate with SAM, let's write our own template from scratch. Create a folder called `findall`, and inside it, create a `main.go` file with the content of the `FindAllMovies` function's code:

```
// Movie entity
type Movie struct {
  ID string `json:"id"`
```

```
    Name string `json:"name"`
    Cover string `json:"cover"`
    Description string `json:"description"`
}

func findAll() (events.APIGatewayProxyResponse, error) {
  ...
  svc := dynamodb.New(cfg)
  req := svc.ScanRequest(&dynamodb.ScanInput{
    TableName: aws.String(os.Getenv("TABLE_NAME")),
  })
  res, err := req.Send()
  if err != nil {
    return events.APIGatewayProxyResponse{
      StatusCode: http.StatusInternalServerError,
      Body: "Error while scanning DynamoDB",
    }, nil
  }

  movies := make([]Movie, 0)
  for _, item := range res.Items {
    movies = append(movies, Movie{
      ID: *item["ID"].S,
      Name: *item["Name"].S,
      Cover: *item["Cover"].S,
      Description: *item["Description"].S,
    })
  }
  ...
  return events.APIGatewayProxyResponse{
    StatusCode: 200,
    Headers: map[string]string{
      "Content-Type": "application/json",
      "Access-Control-Allow-Origin": "*",
    },
    Body: string(response),
  }, nil
}

func main() {
  lambda.Start(findAll)
}
```

Next, create a serverless app definition in a `template.yaml` file. The following example illustrates how to create a Lambda function with a DynamoDB table:

```
AWSTemplateFormatVersion: '2010-09-09'
Transform: AWS::serverless-2016-10-31
```

```
Resources:
  FindAllFunction:
    Type: AWS::serverless::Function
    Properties:
      Handler: main
      Runtime: go1.x
      Policies: AmazonDynamoDBFullAccess
      Environment:
        Variables:
          TABLE_NAME: !Ref MoviesTable
  MoviesTable:
    Type: AWS::serverless::SimpleTable
    Properties:
      PrimaryKey:
        Name: ID
        Type: String
      ProvisionedThroughput:
        ReadCapacityUnits: 5
        WriteCapacityUnits: 5
```

The template is similar to the CloudFormation template we wrote earlier. SAM extends CloudFormation and simplifies the syntax for expressing serverless resources.

Use the `package` command to upload the deployment package to the S3 bucket created in the *CloudFormation* section:

```
sam package --template-file template.yaml --output-template-file
serverless.yaml \
    --s3-bucket hands-on-serverless-go-packt
```

The preceding command will upload the deployment page to the S3 bucket, as shown in the following screenshot:

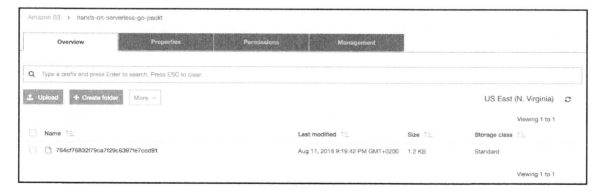

In addition, a SAM template file called `serverless.yaml` will be generated based on the definition file you provided. It should contain the `CodeUri` property that points to the `deployment` ZIP in the Amazon S3 bucket that you specified:

```
AWSTemplateFormatVersion: '2010-09-09'
Resources:
  FindAllFunction:
    Properties:
      CodeUri: s3://hands-on-serverless-go-
packt/764cf76832f79ca7f29c6397fe7ccd91
      Environment:
        Variables:
          TABLE_NAME:
            Ref: MoviesTable
      Handler: main
      Policies: AmazonDynamoDBFullAccess
      Runtime: go1.x
    Type: AWS::serverless::Function
  MoviesTable:
    Properties:
      PrimaryKey:
        Name: ID
        Type: String
      ProvisionedThroughput:
        ReadCapacityUnits: 5
        WriteCapacityUnits: 5
    Type: AWS::serverless::SimpleTable
Transform: AWS::serverless-2016-10-31
```

Finally, deploy the function to AWS Lambda with the following command:

```
sam deploy --template-file serverless.yaml --stack-name APIStack \
    --capabilities CAPABILITY_IAM
```

CAPABILITY_IAM is used to explicitly acknowledge that AWS CloudFormation is allowed to create an IAM role for the Lambda function on your behalf.

When you run the `sam deploy` command, it creates an AWS CloudFormation stack called **APIStack**, as shown in the next screenshot:

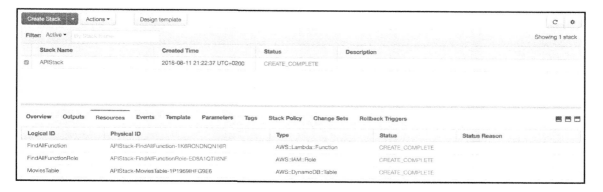

Once the resources are created, the function should be deployed to AWS Lambda, shown as follows:

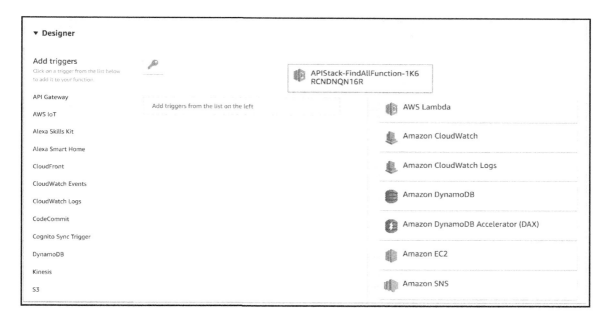

> The SAM scope is limited to serverless resources (a list of supported AWS services is available at: `https://docs.aws.amazon.com/serverlessrepo/latest/devguide/using-aws-sam.html`).

Exporting a serverless application

AWS Lambda allows you to export SAM template files for existing functions. Select the target function and click on **Export function** from the **Actions** menu, shown as follows:

Click on **Download AWS SAM file** to download the template file, shown as follows:

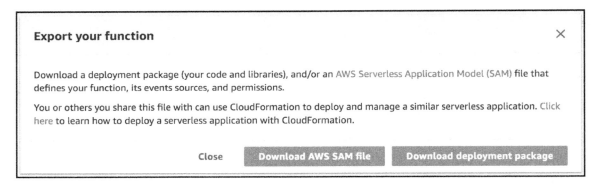

The template will contain the definition of your function, necessary permissions, and triggers:

```
AWSTemplateFormatVersion: '2010-09-09'
Transform: 'AWS::serverless-2016-10-31'
Description: An AWS serverless Specification template describing your
function.
Resources:
  FindAllMovies:
    Type: 'AWS::serverless::Function'
    Properties:
```

```
Handler: main
Runtime: go1.x
CodeUri: .
Description: ''
MemorySize: 128
Timeout: 3
Role: 'arn:aws:iam::ACCOUNT_ID:role/FindAllMoviesRole'
Events:
  Api1:
    Type: Api
    Properties:
      Path: /MyResource
      Method: ANY
  Api2:
    Type: Api
    Properties:
      Path: /movies
      Method: GET
Environment:
  Variables:
    TABLE_NAME: movies
Tracing: Active
ReservedConcurrentExecutions: 10
```

You can now use the `sam package` and `sam deploy` commands to import the function into a different AWS region or AWS account.

Summary

Managing serverless application resources can be either very manual, or you can automate the workflow. Automating the process can be tricky, though, if you have a complex infrastructure. This is where tools such as AWS CloudFormation, SAM, and Terraform come in.

In this chapter, we learned how to use infrastructure-as-code tools to automate the creation of the serverless application resources and dependencies in AWS. We saw tools that are cloud-specific, and loosely coupled ones that work on multiple platforms. Then, we saw how these tools can be used to deploy Lambda-based applications to AWS.

By now, you can write your serverless infrastructure code once and then use it many times. The code that defines the infrastructure can be versioned, forked, rolled back (going back in time), and used for auditing the infrastructure changes, just like any other code. Moreover, it can be discovered and addressed in a programmatic fashion. In other words, if the infrastructure has been manually modified, you destroy that infrastructure and respawn a clean copy—the Immutable Infrastructure.

Questions

1. Write a Terraform template to create the `InsertMovie` Lambda function resources.
2. Update the CloudFormation template to trigger the defined Lambda function with API Gateway in response to incoming HTTP requests.
3. Write a SAM file to model and define all the resources needed to build the serverless API we built throughout this book.
4. Configure Terraform to store the generated state file in a remote S3 backend.
5. Create a CloudFormation template for the serverless API we built throughout this book.
6. Create a Terraform template for the serverless API we built throughout this book.

Assessments

Chapter 1: Go Serverless

1. What are the advantages of using the serverless approach?

   Answer:

   - NoOps: no management or configuration overhead and faster time to market.
   - Autoscaling and HA: enhanced scalability and elasticity based on load.
   - Cost-optimization: pay only for the compute time your consume.
   - Polygot: leverage the power of nanoservices architecture.

2. What makes Lambda a time-saving approach?

   Answer: You pay per execution and you don't pay for idle resources, while with EC2 instances, you pay also for unused resources.

3. How does serverless architecture enable microservices?

   Answer: Microservices is the approach of breaking down a monolithic application into a collection of smaller and modular services. Serverless computing is a key enabled for microservices-based applications. It makes infrastructure even-driven and completely controlled by the needs of each service that makes up an application. Moreover, serverless means functions, and a microservice is a set of functions.

4. What is the maximum time limit for an AWS Lambda function?

   Answer: By default, each Lambda function has a 3 seconds timeout; the maximum duration you can set, is 5 minutes.

5. Which of the following are supported event-sources for AWS Lambda?
    - Amazon Kinesis Data Streams
    - Amazon RDS
    - AWS CodeCommit
    - AWS CloudFormation

    Answer: Amazon Kinesis Data Streams, AWS CodeCommit and CloudFormation are supported event-sources for AWS Lambda. The list of all supported event sources can be found on the following url: `https://docs.aws.amazon.com/lambda/latest/dg/invoking-lambda-function.html`

6. Explain what a goroutine is in Go. How can you stop goroutines?

    Answer: A goroutine is lightweight thread; it uses a resource called **channel** to communicate. Channels, by design, prevent race conditions from happening when accessing shared memory using goroutines. To stop a goroutine, we pass signal channel. That signal channel is used to push a value. The goroutine polls that channel regularly. As soon as it detects a signal, it quits.

7. What's Lambda@Edge in AWS?

    Answer: Lambda@Edge allows you to run Lambda functions at the edge locations of CloudFront in order to customize the content returned to your end users at the lowest latency.

8. What's the difference between Function as a Service and Platform as a Service?

    Answer: Both PaaS and FaaS allow you to easily deploy an application and scale it without worrying about the underlying infrastructure. However, FaaS saves you money because you pay only for the compute time used to handle the incoming requests.

9. What's an AWS Lambda cold start?

    Answer: Cold start happens when a new event is triggered; AWS Lambda creates and initialize a new instance or container to handle the request, which takes longer (Startup latency) compared to warm starts, where the container is reused from a previous event.

10. Can AWS Lambda functions be stateless or stateful?

    Answer: Lambda functions must be stateless to leverage the power of autoscaling due to increasing rate of incoming events.

Chapter 2: Getting Started with AWS Lambda

1. Which format is not supported by the AWS CLI?
    *   JSON
    *   Table
    *   XML
    *   Text

    Answer: The support values are JSON, table, and text. The default output is JSON.

2. Is it recommended to use the AWS root account for everyday interaction with AWS? If yes, why?

    Answer: AWS root account has the ultimate authority to create and delete AWS resources, change the billing, and even close the AWS account. Hence, it is strongly recommended to create an IAM user for everyday tasks with only the needed permissions.

3. What environment variables do you need to set to use the AWS CLI?

    Answer: The following are the required environment variables to configure the AWS CLI:

    *   AWS_ACCESS_KEY_ID
    *   AWS_SECRET_ACCESS_KEY
    *   AWS_DEFAULT_REGION

4. How do you use the AWS CLI with named profiles?

    Answer: AWS_PROFILE can be used to set the CLI profile to use. The profile is stored in the credentials file. By default, AWS CLI uses the default profile.

5. Explain the GOPATH environment variable.

    Answer: The GOPATH environment variable specifies the location of your Go workspace. Default value is $HOME/go.

6. Which command-line command compiles a program in Go?
    - `go build`
    - `go run`
    - `go fmt`
    - `go doc`

    Answer: The as-mentioned commands do the following:

    - `build`: It is a compile package and dependencies and generate a single binary.
    - `run`: It is a compile and run Go program.
    - `fmt`: It is a reformat package resources.
    - `doc`: It is a show documentation for a package or function.

7. What's the Go workspace?

    Answer: A Go workspace is a directory where you will load and work with Go code. The directory must have the following hierarchy:

    - `src`: It contains Go source files.
    - `bin`: It contains executable files.
    - `pkg`: It contains package objects.

Chapter 3: Developing a Serverless Function with Lambda

1. What's the command-line command to create an IAM role for an AWS Lambda function?

    Answer: Create an IAM role with the below command; it allows Lambda function to call AWS services under your account:

    ```
    aws iam create-role ROLE_NAME --assume-role-policy-document
    file://assume-role-lambda.json
    ```

The `assume-role-lambda.json` file contains the following:

```
{
  "Version":"2012-10-17",
  "Statement":[
   {
   "Effect":"Allow",
   "Principal":{
    "AWS":"*"
   },
   "Action":"sts:AssumeRole"
   }
  ]
}
```

3. What's the command-line command to create a new S3 bucket in the Virginia region (`us-east-1`) and upload a Lambda deployment package to it?

Answer: The following command can be used to create an S3 bucket:

```
aws s3 mb s3://BUCKET_NAME --region us-east-1
```

To upload the deployment package to the bucket, issue the following command:

```
aws s3 cp deployment.zip s3://BUCKET_NAME --region us-east-1
```

3. What are the Lambda package size limits?
   - 10 MB
   - 50 MB
   - 250 MB

Answer: AWS Lambda deployment package has a total maximum of 50MB zipped and 250MB uncompressed.

4. AWS Lambda Console supports editing Go source code.
   - True
   - False

Answer: False; Go is a recently added language, and the developers behind it haven't added the capability for an inline editor yet. Hence, you must provide an executable binary in a ZIP file format or reference an S3 bucket and object key where you have uploaded the deployment package.

5. What's the underlying AWS Lambda execution environment?
   - Amazon Linux Image
   - Microsoft Windows Server

Answer: AWS Lambda execution environment is based on Amazon Linux AMI.

6. How are events represented in AWS Lambda?

Answer: Events in AWS Lambda are represented in a JSON format.

Chapter 5: Managing Data Persistence with DynamoDB

1. Implement an update handler to update an existing movie item.

Answer: The handler expects a movie item in a JSON format; the input will be encoded to a `Movie` struct. The `PutItem` method is used to insert the movie to the table as follows:

```
func update(request events.APIGatewayProxyRequest)
(events.APIGatewayProxyResponse, error) {
  var movie Movie
  err := json.Unmarshal([]byte(request.Body), &movie)
  if err != nil {
    return events.APIGatewayProxyResponse{
      StatusCode: 400,
      Body: "Invalid payload",
    }, nil
  }

  ...

  svc := dynamodb.New(cfg)
  req := svc.PutItemRequest(&dynamodb.PutItemInput{
    TableName: aws.String(os.Getenv("TABLE_NAME")),
    Item: map[string]dynamodb.AttributeValue{
      "ID": dynamodb.AttributeValue{
        S: aws.String(movie.ID),
      },
      "Name": dynamodb.AttributeValue{
        S: aws.String(movie.Name),
      },
    },
  })
```

```
_, err = req.Send()
if err != nil {
  return events.APIGatewayProxyResponse{
    StatusCode: http.StatusInternalServerError,
    Body: "Error while updating the movie",
  }, nil
}

response, err := json.Marshal(movie)
...

return events.APIGatewayProxyResponse{
  StatusCode: 200,
  Body: string(response),
  Headers: map[string]string{
    "Content-Type": "application/json",
  },
}, nil
}
```

2. Create a new PUT method in API Gateway to trigger the update Lambda function.

   Answer: Expose a PUT method on the /movies resource and configure the target to be the Lambda function defined earlier. The following screenshot illustrates the results:

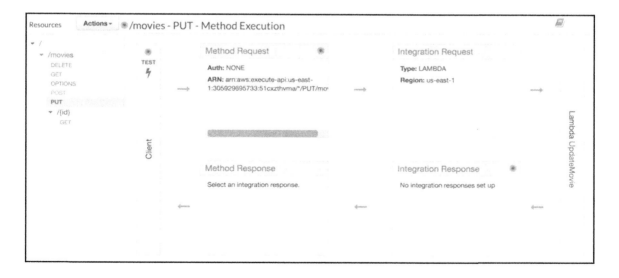

3. Implement a single Lambda function to handle all type of events (GET, POST, DELETE, PUT).

    Answer:

    ```
    func handler(request events.APIGatewayProxyRequest)
    (events.APIGatewayProxyResponse, error) {
    switch request.HTTPMethod {
    case http.MethodGet:
    // get all movies handler
    break
    case http.MethodPost:
    // insert movie handler
    break
    case http.MethodDelete:
    // delete movie handler
    break
    case http.MethodPut:
    // update movie handler
    break
    default:
    return events.APIGatewayProxyResponse{
    StatusCode: http.StatusMethodNotAllowed,
    Body: "Unsupported HTTP method",
    }, nil
    }
    }
    ```

4. Update the findOne handler to return a proper response code for a valid request but an empty data (for example, no movie for the ID requested).

    Answer: When handling input of a user (movie ID in our case), validation is mandatory. Hence, you need to write a regular expression to ensure the ID given in parameter is properly formed. The following are examples of regular expressions to validate an ID:

    - Pattern for alphanumeric ID: [a-zA-Z0-9]+
    - Pattern for digits only ID: [0-9]+

5. Implement a pagination system on the findAll endpoint using a Range header and using a Query string.

Answer: Use the Limit option in the `ScanRequest` method to limit number of returned items:

```
dynamodbClient := dynamodb.New(cfg)
req := dynamodbClient.ScanRequest(&dynamodb.ScanInput{
    TableName: aws.String(os.Getenv("TABLE_NAME")),
    Limit: aws.Int64(int64(size)),
})
```

The number of items to return can be read from the request headers:

```
size, err := strconv.Atoi(request.Headers["Size"])
```

Chapter 7: Implementing a CI/CD Pipeline

1. Implement a CI/CD pipeline for other Lambda functions with CodeBuild and CodePipeline.

Answer: The CI/CD pipeline for `FindAllMovies` Lambda function can be implemented as follows:

```
version: 0.2
env:
  variables:
    S3_BUCKET: "movies-api-deployment-packages"
    PACKAGE: "github.com/mlabouardy/lambda-codepipeline"

phases:
  install:
    commands:
      - mkdir -p "/go/src/$(dirname ${PACKAGE})"
      - ln -s "${CODEBUILD_SRC_DIR}" "/go/src/${PACKAGE}"
      - go get -u github.com/golang/lint/golint

  pre_build:
    commands:
      - cd "/go/src/${PACKAGE}"
      - go get -t ./...
      - golint -set_exit_status
      - go vet .
      - go test .

  build:
    commands:
      - GOOS=linux go build -o main
      - zip $CODEBUILD_RESOLVED_SOURCE_VERSION.zip main
```

```
         - aws s3 cp $CODEBUILD_RESOLVED_SOURCE_VERSION.zip
s3://$S3_BUCKET/

   post_build:
      commands:
         - aws lambda update-function-code --function-name
FindAllMovies --s3-bucket $S3_BUCKET --s3-key
$CODEBUILD_RESOLVED_SOURCE_VERSION.zip
```

The CI/CD pipeline for `InsertMovie` **Lambda function can be implemented as** follows:

```
version: 0.2
env:
   variables:
      S3_BUCKET: "movies-api-deployment-packages"
      PACKAGE: "github.com/mlabouardy/lambda-codepipeline"

phases:
   install:
      commands:
         - mkdir -p "/go/src/$(dirname ${PACKAGE})"
         - ln -s "${CODEBUILD_SRC_DIR}" "/go/src/${PACKAGE}"
         - go get -u github.com/golang/lint/golint

   pre_build:
      commands:
         - cd "/go/src/${PACKAGE}"
         - go get -t ./...
         - golint -set_exit_status
         - go vet .
         - go test .

   build:
      commands:
         - GOOS=linux go build -o main
         - zip $CODEBUILD_RESOLVED_SOURCE_VERSION.zip main
         - aws s3 cp $CODEBUILD_RESOLVED_SOURCE_VERSION.zip
s3://$S3_BUCKET/

   post_build:
      commands:
         - aws lambda update-function-code --function-name
InsertMovie --s3-bucket $S3_BUCKET --s3-key
$CODEBUILD_RESOLVED_SOURCE_VERSION.zip
```

The CI/CD pipeline for `Updatemovie` Lambda function can be implemented as follows:

```
version: 0.2
env:
  variables:
    S3_BUCKET: "movies-api-deployment-packages"
    PACKAGE: "github.com/mlabouardy/lambda-codepipeline"

phases:
  install:
    commands:
      - mkdir -p "/go/src/$(dirname ${PACKAGE})"
      - ln -s "${CODEBUILD_SRC_DIR}" "/go/src/${PACKAGE}"
      - go get -u github.com/golang/lint/golint

  pre_build:
    commands:
      - cd "/go/src/${PACKAGE}"
      - go get -t ./...
      - golint -set_exit_status
      - go vet .
      - go test .

  build:
    commands:
      - GOOS=linux go build -o main
      - zip $CODEBUILD_RESOLVED_SOURCE_VERSION.zip main
      - aws s3 cp $CODEBUILD_RESOLVED_SOURCE_VERSION.zip
s3://$S3_BUCKET/

  post_build:
    commands:
      - aws lambda update-function-code --function-name
UpdateMovie --s3-bucket $S3_BUCKET --s3-key
$CODEBUILD_RESOLVED_SOURCE_VERSION.zip
```

The CI/CD pipeline for `DeleteMovie` Lambda function can be implemented as follows:

```
version: 0.2
env:
  variables:
    S3_BUCKET: "movies-api-deployment-packages"
    PACKAGE: "github.com/mlabouardy/lambda-codepipeline"

phases:
  install:
```

```
              commands:
                - mkdir -p "/go/src/$(dirname ${PACKAGE})"
                - ln -s "${CODEBUILD_SRC_DIR}" "/go/src/${PACKAGE}"
                - go get -u github.com/golang/lint/golint

          pre_build:
              commands:
                - cd "/go/src/${PACKAGE}"
                - go get -t ./...
                - golint -set_exit_status
                - go vet .
                - go test .

          build:
              commands:
                - GOOS=linux go build -o main
                - zip $CODEBUILD_RESOLVED_SOURCE_VERSION.zip main
                - aws s3 cp $CODEBUILD_RESOLVED_SOURCE_VERSION.zip
s3://$S3_BUCKET/

          post_build:
              commands:
                - aws lambda update-function-code --function-name
DeleteMovie --s3-bucket $S3_BUCKET --s3-key
$CODEBUILD_RESOLVED_SOURCE_VERSION.zip
```

2. Implement a similar workflow using Jenkins Pipeline.

   Answer: We can use Jenkins parallel stages feature to run chunks of code in parallel as follows:

```
def bucket = 'movies-api-deployment-packages'

node('slave-golang'){
    stage('Checkout'){
        checkout scm
        sh 'go get -u github.com/golang/lint/golint'
        sh 'go get -t ./...'
    }

    stage('Test'){
        parallel {
            stage('FindAllMovies') {
                sh 'cd findAll'
                sh 'golint -set_exit_status'
                sh 'go vet .'
                sh 'go test .'
            }
```

```
                    stage('DeleteMovie') {
                        sh 'cd delete'
                        sh 'golint -set_exit_status'
                        sh 'go vet .'
                        sh 'go test .'
                    }
                    stage('UpdateMovie') {
                        sh 'cd update'
                        sh 'golint -set_exit_status'
                        sh 'go vet .'
                        sh 'go test .'
                    }
                    stage('InsertMovie') {
                        sh 'cd insert'
                        sh 'golint -set_exit_status'
                        sh 'go vet .'
                        sh 'go test .'
                    }
                }
            }

            stage('Build'){
                parallel {
                    stage('FindAllMovies') {
                        sh 'cd findAll'
                        sh 'GOOS=linux go build -o main main.go'
                        sh "zip findAll-${commitID()}.zip main"
                    }
                    stage('DeleteMovie') {
                        sh 'cd delete'
                        sh 'GOOS=linux go build -o main main.go'
                        sh "zip delete-${commitID()}.zip main"
                    }
                    stage('UpdateMovie') {
                        sh 'cd update'
                        sh 'GOOS=linux go build -o main main.go'
                        sh "zip update-${commitID()}.zip main"
                    }
                    stage('InsertMovie') {
                        sh 'cd insert'
                        sh 'GOOS=linux go build -o main main.go'
                        sh "zip insert-${commitID()}.zip main"
                    }
                }
            }

            stage('Push'){
                parallel {
```

```
                    stage('FindAllMovies') {
                        sh 'cd findAll'
                        sh "aws s3 cp findAll-${commitID()}.zip
s3://${bucket}"
                    }
                    stage('DeleteMovie') {
                        sh 'cd delete'
                        sh "aws s3 cp delete-${commitID()}.zip
s3://${bucket}"
                    }
                    stage('UpdateMovie') {
                        sh 'cd update'
                        sh "aws s3 cp update-${commitID()}.zip
s3://${bucket}"
                    }
                    stage('InsertMovie') {
                        sh 'cd insert'
                        sh "aws s3 cp insert-${commitID()}.zip
s3://${bucket}"
                    }
                }
            }

        stage('Deploy'){
            parallel {
                stage('FindAllMovies') {
                    sh 'cd findAll'
                    sh "aws lambda update-function-code --function-
name FindAllMovies \
                    --s3-bucket ${bucket} \
                    --s3-key findAll-${commitID()}.zip \
                    --region us-east-1"
                }
                stage('DeleteMovie') {
                    sh 'cd delete'
                    sh "aws lambda update-function-code --function-
name DeleteMovie \
                    --s3-bucket ${bucket} \
                    --s3-key delete-${commitID()}.zip \
                    --region us-east-1"
                }
                stage('UpdateMovie') {
                    sh 'cd update'
                    sh "aws lambda update-function-code --function-
name UpdateMovie \
                    --s3-bucket ${bucket} \
                    --s3-key update-${commitID()}.zip \
                    --region us-east-1"
```

```
                }
                stage('InsertMovie') {
                    sh 'cd insert'
                    sh "aws lambda update-function-code --function-
name InsertMovie \
                    --s3-bucket ${bucket} \
                    --s3-key insert-${commitID()}.zip \
                    --region us-east-1"
                }
            }
        }
    }

    def commitID() {
        sh 'git rev-parse HEAD > .git/commitID'
        def commitID = readFile('.git/commitID').trim()
        sh 'rm .git/commitID'
        commitID
    }
```

3. Implement the same pipeline with CircleCI.

   Answer: CircleCI workflow option can be used to define a collection of build jobs:

```
version: 2
jobs:
  build_findall:
    docker:
      - image: golang:1.8

    working_directory: /go/src/github.com/mlabouardy/lambda-
circleci

    build_dir: findAll

    environment:
        S3_BUCKET: movies-api-deployment-packages

    steps:
      - checkout

      - run:
         name: Install AWS CLI & Zip
         command: |
          apt-get update
          apt-get install -y zip python-pip python-dev
          pip install awscli
```

```
        - run:
            name: Test
            command: |
             go get -u github.com/golang/lint/golint
             go get -t ./...
             golint -set_exit_status
             go vet .
             go test .

        - run:
           name: Build
           command: |
            GOOS=linux go build -o main main.go
            zip $CIRCLE_SHA1.zip main
        - run:
            name: Push
            command: aws s3 cp $CIRCLE_SHA1.zip s3://$S3_BUCKET

        - run:
            name: Deploy
            command: |
              aws lambda update-function-code --function-name
FindAllMovies \
                --s3-bucket $S3_BUCKET \
                --s3-key $CIRCLE_SHA1.zip --region us-east-1
   build_insert:
     docker:
       - image: golang:1.8

     working_directory: /go/src/github.com/mlabouardy/lambda-
circleci

     build_dir: insert

     environment:
         S3_BUCKET: movies-api-deployment-packages

     steps:
       - checkout

       - run:
           name: Install AWS CLI & Zip
           command: |
            apt-get update
            apt-get install -y zip python-pip python-dev
            pip install awscli

       - run:
```

```
            name: Test
            command: |
             go get -u github.com/golang/lint/golint
             go get -t ./...
             golint -set_exit_status
             go vet .
             go test .

       - run:
          name: Build
          command: |
           GOOS=linux go build -o main main.go
           zip $CIRCLE_SHA1.zip main
       - run:
          name: Push
          command: aws s3 cp $CIRCLE_SHA1.zip s3://$S3_BUCKET

       - run:
          name: Deploy
          command: |
             aws lambda update-function-code --function-name
InsertMovie \
             --s3-bucket $S3_BUCKET \
             --s3-key $CIRCLE_SHA1.zip --region us-east-1

   build_update:
     ...
   build_delete:
     ...

workflows:
  version: 2
  build_api:
    jobs:
      - build_findall
      - build_insert
      - build_update
      - build_delete
```

4. Add a new stage to the existing pipeline to publish a new version if the current git branch is the master.

Answer:

```
version: 2
jobs:
  build:
    docker:
```

```
        - image: golang:1.8

      working_directory: /go/src/github.com/mlabouardy/lambda-
  circleci

      environment:
          S3_BUCKET: movies-api-deployment-packages

      steps:
        - checkout

        - run:
          name: Install AWS CLI & Zip
          ...

        - run:
           name: Test
           ...

        - run:
          name: Build
          ...
        - run:
          name: Push
          ...

        - run:
          name: Deploy
          ...
        - run:
          name: Publish
          command: |
            if [ $CIRCLE_BRANCH = 'master' ]; then
              aws lambda publish-version --function-name
  FindAllMovies \
                --description $GIT_COMMIT_DESC --region us-
  east-1
            fi
          environment:
            GIT_COMMIT_DESC: git log --format=%B -n 1
  $CIRCLE_SHA1
```

5. Configure the pipeline to send a notification on a Slack channel every time a new Lambda function is deployed or updated.

Answer: You can use the Slack API to post a message to a Slack channel at the end of the deployment step:

```
- run:
    name: Deploy
    command: |
      aws lambda update-function-code --function-name
FindAllMovies \
        --s3-bucket $S3_BUCKET \
        --s3-key $CIRCLE_SHA1.zip --region us-east-1
      curl -X POST -d '{"token":"$TOKEN", "channel":"$CHANNEL",
"text":"FindAllMovies has been updated"}' \
        http://slack.com/api/chat.postMessage
```

Chapter 9: Building the Frontend with S3

1. Implement a Lambda function that takes the movie category as input and returns a list of movies that corresponds to that category.
   Answer:

```
func filter(category string)(events.APIGatewayProxyResponse, error)
{
    ...

    filter: =
expression.Name("category").Equal(expression.Value(category))
    projection: = expression.NamesList(expression.Name("id"),
expression.Name("name"), expression.Name("description"))
    expr, err: =
expression.NewBuilder().WithFilter(filter).WithProjection(projectio
n).Build()
    if err != nil {
        return events.APIGatewayProxyResponse {
            StatusCode: http.StatusInternalServerError,
            Body: "Error while building DynamoDB expression",
        }, nil
    }

    svc: = dynamodb.New(cfg)
    req: = svc.ScanRequest( & dynamodb.ScanInput {
        TableName: aws.String(os.Getenv("TABLE_NAME")),
        ExpressionAttributeNames: expr.Names(),
        ExpressionAttributeValues: expr.Values(),
        FilterExpression: expr.Filter(),
        ProjectionExpression: expr.Projection(),
    })
```

```
    . . .
}
```

2. Implement a Lambda function that takes a movie's title as input and returns all movies that have the keyword in their title.
   Answer:

```
func filter(keyword string) (events.APIGatewayProxyResponse, error)
{
  . . .

  filter := expression.Name("name").Contains(keyword)
  projection := expression.NamesList(expression.Name("id"),
expression.Name("name"), expression.Name("description"))
  expr, err :=
expression.NewBuilder().WithFilter(filter).WithProjection(projectio
n).Build()
  if err != nil {
    return events.APIGatewayProxyResponse{
      StatusCode: http.StatusInternalServerError,
      Body: "Error while building DynamoDB expression",
    }, nil
  }

  svc := dynamodb.New(cfg)
  req := svc.ScanRequest(&dynamodb.ScanInput{
    TableName: aws.String(os.Getenv("TABLE_NAME")),
    ExpressionAttributeNames: expr.Names(),
    ExpressionAttributeValues: expr.Values(),
    FilterExpression: expr.Filter(),
    ProjectionExpression: expr.Projection(),
  })
  . . .
}
```

3. Implement a delete button on the web application to delete a movie by calling the `DeleteMovie` Lambda function from API Gateway.

   Answer: Update the MoviesAPI service to include the following function:

```
delete(id: string){
    return this.http
      .delete(`${environment.api}/${id}`, {headers:
this.getHeaders()})
        .map(res => {
          return res
        })
}
```

4. Implement an edit button on the web application to allow the user to update movie attributes.
   Answer:

```
update(movie: Movie){
    return this.http
        .put(environment.api, JSON.stringify(movie), {headers:
this.getHeaders()})
        .map(res => {
          return res
        })
}
```

5. Implement a CI/CD workflow with either CircleCI, Jenkins, or CodePipeline to automate the generation and deployment of the API Gateway documentation.
   Answer:

```
def bucket = 'movies-api-documentation'
def api_id = ''

node('slaves'){
  stage('Generate'){
    if (env.BRANCH_NAME == 'master') {
      sh "aws apigateway get-export --rest-api-id ${api_id} \
        --stage-name production \
        --export-type swagger swagger.json"
    }
    else if (env.BRANCH_NAME == 'preprod') {
      sh "aws apigateway get-export --rest-api-id ${api_id} \
        --stage-name staging \
        --export-type swagger swagger.json"
    } else {
      sh "aws apigateway get-export --rest-api-id ${api_id} \
        --stage-name sandbox \
        --export-type swagger swagger.json"
    }
  }

  stage('Publish'){
    sh "aws s3 cp swagger.json s3://${bucket}"
  }
}
```

Chapter 10: Testing Your Serverless Application

1. Write a unit test for the `UpdateMovie` Lambda function.
   Answer:

```go
package main

import (
  "testing"

  "github.com/stretchr/testify/assert"

  "github.com/aws/aws-lambda-go/events"
)

func TestUpdate_InvalidPayLoad(t *testing.T) {
  input := events.APIGatewayProxyRequest{
    Body: "{'name': 'avengers'}",
  }
  expected := events.APIGatewayProxyResponse{
    StatusCode: 400,
    Body: "Invalid payload",
  }
  response, _ := update(input)
  assert.Equal(t, expected, response)
}

func TestUpdate_ValidPayload(t *testing.T) {
  input := events.APIGatewayProxyRequest{
    Body: "{\"id\":\"40\", \"name\":\"Thor\",
\"description\":\"Marvel movie\", \"cover\":\"poster url\"}",
  }
  expected := events.APIGatewayProxyResponse{
    Body: "{\"id\":\"40\", \"name\":\"Thor\",
\"description\":\"Marvel movie\", \"cover\":\"poster url\"}",
    StatusCode: 200,
    Headers: map[string]string{
      "Content-Type": "application/json",
      "Access-Control-Allow-Origin": "*",
    },
  }
  response, _ := update(input)
  assert.Equal(t, expected, response)
}
```

2. Write a unit test for the `DeleteMovie` Lambda function.
   Answer:

```
package main

import (
  "testing"

  "github.com/stretchr/testify/assert"

  "github.com/aws/aws-lambda-go/events"
)

func TestDelete_InvalidPayLoad(t *testing.T) {
  input := events.APIGatewayProxyRequest{
    Body: "{'name': 'avengers'}",
  }
  expected := events.APIGatewayProxyResponse{
    StatusCode: 400,
    Body: "Invalid payload",
  }
  response, _ := delete(input)
  assert.Equal(t, expected, response)
}

func TestDelete_ValidPayload(t *testing.T) {
  input := events.APIGatewayProxyRequest{
    Body: "{\"id\":\"40\", \"name\":\"Thor\",
\"description\":\"Marvel movie\", \"cover\":\"poster url\"}",
  }
  expected := events.APIGatewayProxyResponse{
    StatusCode: 200,
    Headers: map[string]string{
      "Content-Type": "application/json",
      "Access-Control-Allow-Origin": "*",
    },
  }
  response, _ := delete(input)
  assert.Equal(t, expected, response)
}
```

3. Modify the `Jenkinsfile` provided in previous chapters to include the execution of automated unit tests.

   Answer: Note the usage of `go test` command in the **Test** stage:

```
def bucket = 'movies-api-deployment-packages'
```

```
node('slave-golang'){
  stage('Checkout'){
    checkout scm
  }

  stage('Test'){
    sh 'go get -u github.com/golang/lint/golint'
    sh 'go get -t ./...'
    sh 'golint -set_exit_status'
    sh 'go vet .'
    sh 'go test .'
  }

  stage('Build'){
    sh 'GOOS=linux go build -o main main.go'
    sh "zip ${commitID()}.zip main"
  }

  stage('Push'){
    sh "aws s3 cp ${commitID()}.zip s3://${bucket}"
  }

  stage('Deploy'){
    sh "aws lambda update-function-code --function-name
FindAllMovies \
      --s3-bucket ${bucket} \
      --s3-key ${commitID()}.zip \
      --region us-east-1"
  }
}

def commitID() {
  sh 'git rev-parse HEAD > .git/commitID'
  def commitID = readFile('.git/commitID').trim()
  sh 'rm .git/commitID'
  commitID
}
```

4. Modify the `buildspec.yml` definition file to include the execution of unit tests, before pushing the deployment package to S3 using AWS CodeBuild.
   Answer:

```
version: 0.2
env:
  variables:
    S3_BUCKET: "movies-api-deployment-packages"
    PACKAGE: "github.com/mlabouardy/lambda-codepipeline"
```

```
phases:
  install:
    commands:
      - mkdir -p "/go/src/$(dirname ${PACKAGE})"
      - ln -s "${CODEBUILD_SRC_DIR}" "/go/src/${PACKAGE}"
      - go get -u github.com/golang/lint/golint

  pre_build:
    commands:
      - cd "/go/src/${PACKAGE}"
      - go get -t ./...
      - golint -set_exit_status
      - go vet .
      - go test .

  build:
    commands:
      - GOOS=linux go build -o main
      - zip $CODEBUILD_RESOLVED_SOURCE_VERSION.zip main
      - aws s3 cp $CODEBUILD_RESOLVED_SOURCE_VERSION.zip
s3://$S3_BUCKET/

  post_build:
    commands:
      - aws lambda update-function-code --function-name
FindAllMovies --s3-bucket $S3_BUCKET --s3-key
$CODEBUILD_RESOLVED_SOURCE_VERSION.zip
```

5. Write a SAM template file for each Lambda function implemented in previous chapters.

   Answer: The following is a SAM template file for the `FindAllMovies` Lambda function; the same resources can be used to create other functions:

```
AWSTemplateFormatVersion: '2010-09-09'
Transform: AWS::Serverless-2016-10-31

Parameters:
  StageName:
    Type: String
    Default: staging
    Description: The API Gateway deployment stage

Resources:
  FindAllMovies:
    Type: AWS::Serverless::Function
    Properties:
      Handler: main
```

```
            Runtime: go1.x
            Role: !GetAtt FindAllMoviesRole.Arn
            CodeUri: ./findall/deployment.zip
            Environment:
              Variables:
                TABLE_NAME: !Ref MoviesTable
            Events:
              AnyRequest:
                Type: Api
                Properties:
                  Path: /movies
                  Method: GET
                  RestApiId:
                    Ref: MoviesAPI
      FindAllMoviesRole:
        Type: "AWS::IAM::Role"
        Properties:
          Path: "/"
          ManagedPolicyArns:
            - "arn:aws:iam::aws:policy/service-
      role/AWSLambdaBasicExecutionRole"
          AssumeRolePolicyDocument:
            Version: "2012-10-17"
            Statement:
              -
                Effect: "Allow"
                Action:
                  - "sts:AssumeRole"
                Principal:
                  Service:
                    - "lambda.amazonaws.com"
          Policies:
            -
              PolicyName: "PushCloudWatchLogsPolicy"
              PolicyDocument:
                Version: "2012-10-17"
                Statement:
                  - Effect: Allow
                    Action:
                      - logs:CreateLogGroup
                      - logs:CreateLogStream
                      - logs:PutLogEvents
                    Resource: "*"
              -
              PolicyName: "ScanDynamoDBTablePolicy"
              PolicyDocument:
                Version: "2012-10-17"
                Statement:
```

```
                - Effect: Allow
                  Action:
                  - dynamodb:Scan
                  Resource: "*"

      MoviesTable:
        Type: AWS::Serverless::SimpleTable
        Properties:
          PrimaryKey:
            Name: ID
            Type: String
          ProvisionedThroughput:
            ReadCapacityUnits: 5
            WriteCapacityUnits: 5

      MoviesAPI:
        Type: 'AWS::Serverless::Api'
        Properties:
          StageName: !Ref StageName
          DefinitionBody:
            swagger: 2.0
            info:
              title: !Sub API-${StageName}
            paths:
              /movies:
                x-amazon-apigateway-any-method:
                  produces:
                    - application/json
                  x-amazon-apigateway-integration:
                    uri:
                      !Sub
"arn:aws:apigateway:${AWS::Region}:lambda:path/2015-03-31/funct
ions/${FindAllMovies.Arn}:current/invocations"
                    passthroughBehavior: when_no_match
                    httpMethod: POST
                    type: aws_proxy
```

Chapter 12: Securing Your Serverless Application

1. Integrate a user in a user pool with an identity pool to allow users to log in with their Facebook account.

Answer: In order to integrate Facebook with Amazon Cognito identity pools, you must follow the given procedure:

- Create a Facebook Application from the Facebook Developers portal (`https://developers.facebook.com/`).
- Copy the App ID and secret.
- Configure Facebook as a provider in Amazon Cognito Console:

- Follow the Facebook Guide (`https://developers.facebook.com/docs/facebook-login/login-flow-for-web/v2.3`) to add the Facebook login button to the web application.
- Once the user is authenticated, a Facebook session token will be returned; this token must be added to the Amazon Cognito credentials provider to fetch a JWT token.
- Finally, add the JWT token to the API Gateway request `Authorization` header.

2. Integrate a user in a user pool with an identity pool to allow users to log in with their Twitter account.

Answer: Amazon Cognito doesnot support Twitter as an authentication provider out of the box. Hence, you will need to use **OpenID Connect** to extend Amazon Cognito:

3. Integrate a user in a user pool with an identity pool to allow users to log in with their Google account.

- To enable Google Sign in, you will need to create a new project from Google Developers Console (`https://console.developers.google.com/`)
- Enable the Google API under APIs and auth, and then create an OAuth 2.0 client ID.
- Configure Google in the Amazon Cognito Console:

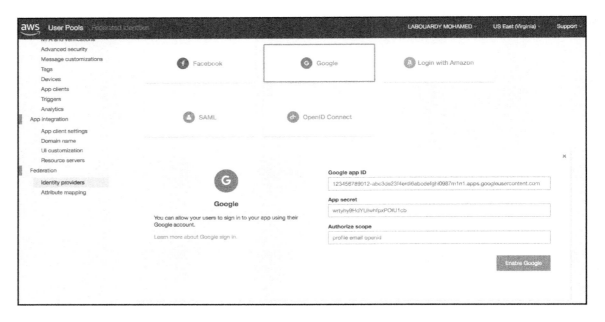

- Follow the Google documentation for Web (`https://developers.google.com/identity/sign-in/web/sign-in`) to add the Google sign in button.
- Once the user is authenticated, an authentication token will be generated, which can be used to retrieve the JWT token.

4. Implement a form to allow users to create an account on a web application so that they are able to log in.

   Answer: A Go based Lambda function might be created to handle the account creation workflow. The function's entry point is given as follows:

```go
package main

import (
  "os"

  "github.com/aws/aws-lambda-go/lambda"
  "github.com/aws/aws-sdk-go-v2/aws"
  "github.com/aws/aws-sdk-go-v2/aws/external"
  "github.com/aws/aws-sdk-go-
v2/service/cognitoidentityprovider"
)

type Account struct {
  Username string `json:"username"`
  Password string `json:"password"`
}

func signUp(account Account) error {
  cfg, err := external.LoadDefaultAWSConfig()
  if err != nil {
    return err
  }

  cognito := cognitoidentityprovider.New(cfg)
  req :=
cognito.SignUpRequest(&cognitoidentityprovider.SignUpInput{
    ClientId: aws.String(os.Getenv("COGNITO_CLIENT_ID")),
    Username: aws.String(account.Username),
    Password: aws.String(account.Password),
  })
  _, err = req.Send()
  if err != nil {
    return err
  }
  return nil
}

func main() {
  lambda.Start(signUp)
}
```

5. Implement a forgotten password flow for an unauthenticated user.

   Answer: A Go based Lambda function might be created to reset user password. The function's entry point is given as follows:

```go
package main

import (
  "os"

  "github.com/aws/aws-lambda-go/lambda"
  "github.com/aws/aws-sdk-go-v2/aws"
  "github.com/aws/aws-sdk-go-v2/aws/external"
  "github.com/aws/aws-sdk-go-
v2/service/cognitoidentityprovider"
)

type Account struct {
  Username string `json:"username"`
}

func forgotPassword(account Account) error {
  cfg, err := external.LoadDefaultAWSConfig()
  if err != nil {
    return err
  }

  cognito := cognitoidentityprovider.New(cfg)
  req :=
cognito.ForgotPasswordRequest(&cognitoidentityprovider.ForgotPa
sswordInput{
    ClientId: aws.String(os.Getenv("COGNITO_CLIENT_ID")),
    Username: aws.String(account.Username),
  })
  _, err = req.Send()
  if err != nil {
    return err
  }

  return nil
}

func main() {
  lambda.Start(forgotPassword)
}
```

Chapter 14:

1. Write a Terraform template to create the `InsertMovie` Lambda function resources.

   Answer: Setup execution role for the Lambda function:

```
resource "aws_iam_role" "role" {
  name = "InsertMovieRole"
  assume_role_policy = "${file("assume-role-policy.json")}"
}

resource "aws_iam_policy" "cloudwatch_policy" {
  name = "PushCloudWatchLogsPolicy"
  policy = "${file("cloudwatch-policy.json")}"
}

resource "aws_iam_policy" "dynamodb_policy" {
  name = "ScanDynamoDBPolicy"
  policy = "${file("dynamodb-policy.json")}"
}

resource "aws_iam_policy_attachment" "cloudwatch-attachment" {
  name = "cloudwatch-lambda-attchment"
  roles = ["${aws_iam_role.role.name}"]
  policy_arn = "${aws_iam_policy.cloudwatch_policy.arn}"
}

resource "aws_iam_policy_attachment" "dynamodb-attachment" {
  name = "dynamodb-lambda-attchment"
  roles = ["${aws_iam_role.role.name}"]
  policy_arn = "${aws_iam_policy.dynamodb_policy.arn}"
}
```

   Next, create the Lambda function:

```
resource "aws_lambda_function" "insert" {
  function_name = "InsertMovie"
  handler = "main"
  filename = "function/deployment.zip"
  runtime = "go1.x"
  role = "${aws_iam_role.role.arn}"

  environment {
    variables {
      TABLE_NAME = "movies"
    }
```

```
    }
  }
```

Expose a `POST` method on `/movies` resources in the REST API:

```
resource "aws_api_gateway_method" "proxy" {
  rest_api_id   = "${var.rest_api_id}"
  resource_id   = "${var.resource_id}"
  http_method   = "POST"
  authorization = "NONE"
}

resource "aws_api_gateway_integration" "lambda" {
  rest_api_id   = "${var.rest_api_id}"
  resource_id   = "${var.resource_id}"
  http_method   = "${aws_api_gateway_method.proxy.http_method}"

  integration_http_method = "POST"
  type = "AWS_PROXY"
  uri = "${aws_lambda_function.insert.invoke_arn}"
}

resource "aws_lambda_permission" "apigw" {
  statement_id  = "AllowAPIGatewayInvoke"
  action        = "lambda:InvokeFunction"
  function_name = "${aws_lambda_function.insert.arn}"
  principal     = "apigateway.amazonaws.com"

  source_arn = "${var.execution_arn}/*/*"
}
```

2. Update the CloudFormation template to trigger the defined Lambda function with API Gateway in response to incoming HTTP request.

Answer: Add the following properties to the `Resources` section:

```
API:
    Type: 'AWS::ApiGateway::RestApi'
    Properties:
        Name: API
        FailOnWarnings: 'true'
DemoResource:
    Type: 'AWS::ApiGateway::Resource'
    Properties:
        ParentId:
            'Fn::GetAtt': [API, RootResourceId]
        PathPart: demo
        RestApiId:
```

```
                Ref: API
DisplayMessageMethod:
    Type: 'AWS::ApiGateway::Method'
    Properties:
        HttpMethod: GET
        AuthorizationType: NONE
        ResourceId:
            Ref: DemoResource
        RestApiId:
            Ref: API
        Integration:
            Type: AWS
            Uri: {'Fn::Join': ["", "-
\"arn:aws:apigateway:\"\n- !Ref \"AWS::Region\"\n-
\":lambda:path/\"\n- \"/2015-03-31/functions/\"\n-
Fn::GetAtt:\n - HelloWorldFunction\n - Arn\n-
\"/invocations\""]}
            IntegrationHttpMethod: GET
```

3. Write a SAM file to model and defines all the resources needed to build the
   Serverless API we built through this book.
   Answer:

```
Resources:
  FindAllMovies:
    Type: AWS::Serverless::Function
    Properties:
      Handler: main
      Runtime: go1.x
      Role: !GetAtt FindAllMoviesRole.Arn
      CodeUri: ./findall/deployment.zip
      Environment:
        Variables:
          TABLE_NAME: !Ref MoviesTable
      Events:
        AnyRequest:
          Type: Api
          Properties:
            Path: /movies
            Method: GET
            RestApiId:
              Ref: MoviesAPI

  InsertMovie:
    Type: AWS::Serverless::Function
    Properties:
      Handler: main
      Runtime: go1.x
```

```
              Role: !GetAtt InsertMovieRole.Arn
              CodeUri: ./insert/deployment.zip
              Environment:
                Variables:
                  TABLE_NAME: !Ref MoviesTable
              Events:
                AnyRequest:
                  Type: Api
                  Properties:
                    Path: /movies
                    Method: POST
                    RestApiId:
                      Ref: MoviesAPI

          DeleteMovie:
            Type: AWS::Serverless::Function
            Properties:
              Handler: main
              Runtime: go1.x
              Role: !GetAtt DeleteMovieRole.Arn
              CodeUri: ./delete/deployment.zip
              Environment:
                Variables:
                  TABLE_NAME: !Ref MoviesTable
              Events:
                AnyRequest:
                  Type: Api
                  Properties:
                    Path: /movies
                    Method: DELETE
                    RestApiId:
                      Ref: MoviesAPI

          UpdateMovie:
            Type: AWS::Serverless::Function
            Properties:
              Handler: main
              Runtime: go1.x
              Role: !GetAtt UpdateMovieRole.Arn
              CodeUri: ./update/deployment.zip
              Environment:
                Variables:
                  TABLE_NAME: !Ref MoviesTable
              Events:
                AnyRequest:
                  Type: Api
                  Properties:
                    Path: /movies
```

```
Method: PUT
RestApiId:
  Ref: MoviesAPI
```

3. Configure Terraform to store the generated state file in a remote S3 backend.

   Answer: Create an S3 bucket with the following AWS CLI command:

   ```
   aws s3 mb s3://terraform-state-files --region us-east-1
   ```

   Enable server side encryption on the bucket:

   ```
   aws s3api put-bucket-encryption --bucket terraform-state-files
   \
       --server-side-encryption-configuration file://config.json
   ```

   The encryption mechanism is set to AES-256:

   ```
   {
     "Rules": [
       {
         "ApplyServerSideEncryptionByDefault": {
           "SSEAlgorithm": "AES256"
         }
       }
     ]
   }
   ```

   Configure Terraform to use the bucket defined earlier:

   ```
   terraform {
     backend "s3" {
       bucket = "terraform-state-files"
       key = "KEY_NAME"
       region = "us-east-1"
     }
   }
   ```

3. Create a CloudFormation template for the Serverless API we built through this book.
   Answer:

   ```
   AWSTemplateFormatVersion: "2010-09-09"
   Description: "Simple Lambda Function"
   Parameters:
     BucketName:
       Description: "S3 Bucket name"
       Type: "String"
   ```

```yaml
  TableName:
    Description: "DynamoDB Table Name"
    Type: "String"
    Default: "movies"
Resources:
  FindAllMoviesRole:
    Type: "AWS::IAM::Role"
    Properties:
      AssumeRolePolicyDocument:
        Version: "2012-10-17"
        Statement:
          -
            Effect: "Allow"
            Principal:
              Service:
                - "lambda.amazonaws.com"
            Action:
              - "sts:AssumeRole"
      Policies:
        -
          PolicyName: "PushCloudWatchLogsPolicy"
          PolicyDocument:
            Version: "2012-10-17"
            Statement:
              - Effect: Allow
                Action:
                - logs:CreateLogGroup
                - logs:CreateLogStream
                - logs:PutLogEvents
                Resource: "*"
        -
          PolicyName: "ScanDynamoDBTablePolicy"
          PolicyDocument:
            Version: "2012-10-17"
            Statement:
              - Effect: Allow
                Action:
                - dynamodb:Scan
                Resource: "*"
  FindAllMovies:
    Type: "AWS::Lambda::Function"
    Properties:
      Code:
        S3Bucket: !Ref BucketName
        S3Key: findall-deployment.zip
      FunctionName: "FindAllMovies"
      Handler: "main"
      Runtime: "go1.x"
```

```
      Role: !GetAtt FindAllMoviesRole.Arn
    Environment:
      Variables:
        TABLE_NAME: !Ref TableName

InsertMovieRole:
  Type: "AWS::IAM::Role"
  Properties:
    AssumeRolePolicyDocument:
      Version: "2012-10-17"
      Statement:
        -
          Effect: "Allow"
          Principal:
            Service:
              - "lambda.amazonaws.com"
          Action:
            - "sts:AssumeRole"
    Policies:
      -
        PolicyName: "PushCloudWatchLogsPolicy"
        PolicyDocument:
          Version: "2012-10-17"
          Statement:
            - Effect: Allow
              Action:
              - logs:CreateLogGroup
              - logs:CreateLogStream
              - logs:PutLogEvents
              Resource: "*"

      -
        PolicyName: "PutItemDynamoDBTablePolicy"
        PolicyDocument:
          Version: "2012-10-17"
          Statement:
            - Effect: Allow
              Action:
              - dynamodb:PutItem
              Resource: "*"
InsertMovie:
  Type: "AWS::Lambda::Function"
  Properties:
    Code:
      S3Bucket: !Ref BucketName
      S3Key: insert-deployment.zip
    FunctionName: "InsertMovie"
    Handler: "main"
    Runtime: "go1.x"
```

```
            Role: !GetAtt InsertMovieRole.Arn
          Environment:
            Variables:
              TABLE_NAME: !Ref TableName

  UpdateMovieRole:
    Type: "AWS::IAM::Role"
    Properties:
      AssumeRolePolicyDocument:
        Version: "2012-10-17"
        Statement:
          -
            Effect: "Allow"
            Principal:
              Service:
                - "lambda.amazonaws.com"
            Action:
              - "sts:AssumeRole"
      Policies:
        -
          PolicyName: "PushCloudWatchLogsPolicy"
          PolicyDocument:
            Version: "2012-10-17"
            Statement:
              - Effect: Allow
                Action:
                - logs:CreateLogGroup
                - logs:CreateLogStream
                - logs:PutLogEvents
                Resource: "*"

        -
          PolicyName: "PutItemDynamoDBTablePolicy"
          PolicyDocument:
            Version: "2012-10-17"
            Statement:
              - Effect: Allow
                Action:
                - dynamodb:PutItem
                Resource: "*"
  UpdateMovie:
    Type: "AWS::Lambda::Function"
    Properties:
      Code:
        S3Bucket: !Ref BucketName
        S3Key: update-deployment.zip
      FunctionName: "UpdateMovie"
      Handler: "main"
      Runtime: "go1.x"
```

```
      Role: !GetAtt UpdateMovieRole.Arn
    Environment:
      Variables:
        TABLE_NAME: !Ref TableName


DeleteMovieRole:
  Type: "AWS::IAM::Role"
  Properties:
    AssumeRolePolicyDocument:
      Version: "2012-10-17"
      Statement:
        -
          Effect: "Allow"
          Principal:
            Service:
              - "lambda.amazonaws.com"
          Action:
            - "sts:AssumeRole"
    Policies:
      -
        PolicyName: "PushCloudWatchLogsPolicy"
        PolicyDocument:
          Version: "2012-10-17"
          Statement:
            - Effect: Allow
              Action:
              - logs:CreateLogGroup
              - logs:CreateLogStream
              - logs:PutLogEvents
              Resource: "*"

      -
        PolicyName: "DeleteItemDynamoDBTablePolicy"
        PolicyDocument:
          Version: "2012-10-17"
          Statement:
            - Effect: Allow
              Action:
              - dynamodb:DeleteItem
              Resource: "*"
DeleteMovie:
  Type: "AWS::Lambda::Function"
  Properties:
    Code:
      S3Bucket: !Ref BucketName
      S3Key: update-deployment.zip
    FunctionName: "DeleteMovie"
    Handler: "main"
```

```
        Runtime: "go1.x"
        Role: !GetAtt DeleteMovieRole.Arn
        Environment:
          Variables:
            TABLE_NAME: !Ref TableName

  MoviesApi:
    Type: "AWS::ApiGateway::RestApi"
    Properties:
      Name: "MoviesApi"
      FailOnWarnings: "true"
  MoviesResource:
    Type: "AWS::ApiGateway::Resource"
    Properties:
      ParentId:
        Fn::GetAtt:
          - "MoviesApi"
          - "RootResourceId"
      PathPart: "movies"
      RestApiId:
        Ref: MoviesApi
  CreateMovieMethod:
    Type: "AWS::ApiGateway::Method"
    Properties:
      HttpMethod: "POST"
      AuthorizationType: "NONE"
      ResourceId:
        Ref: MoviesResource
      RestApiId:
        Ref: MoviesApi
      Integration:
        Type: "AWS"
        Uri:
          Fn::Join:
            - ""
            - - "arn:aws:apigateway:"
              - !Ref "AWS::Region"
              - ":lambda:path/"
              - "/2015-03-31/functions/"
              - Fn::GetAtt:
                - InsertMovie
                - Arn
              - "/invocations"
        IntegrationHttpMethod: "POST"
  DeleteMovieMethod:
    Type: "AWS::ApiGateway::Method"
    Properties:
      HttpMethod: "DELETE"
```

```
        AuthorizationType: "NONE"
        ResourceId:
          Ref: MoviesResource
        RestApiId:
          Ref: MoviesApi
        Integration:
          Type: "AWS"
          Uri:
            Fn::Join:
              - ""
              - - "arn:aws:apigateway:"
                - !Ref "AWS::Region"
                - ":lambda:path/"
                - "/2015-03-31/functions/"
                - Fn::GetAtt:
                  - DeleteMovie
                  - Arn
                - "/invocations"
          IntegrationHttpMethod: "DELETE"
  UpdateMovieMethod:
    Type: "AWS::ApiGateway::Method"
    Properties:
      HttpMethod: "PUT"
      AuthorizationType: "NONE"
      ResourceId:
        Ref: MoviesResource
      RestApiId:
        Ref: MoviesApi
      Integration:
        Type: "AWS"
        Uri:
          Fn::Join:
            - ""
            - - "arn:aws:apigateway:"
              - !Ref "AWS::Region"
              - ":lambda:path/"
              - "/2015-03-31/functions/"
              - Fn::GetAtt:
                - UpdateMovie
                - Arn
              - "/invocations"
        IntegrationHttpMethod: "PUT"
  ListMoviesMethod:
    Type: "AWS::ApiGateway::Method"
    Properties:
      HttpMethod: "GET"
      AuthorizationType: "NONE"
      ResourceId:
```

```
      Ref: MoviesResource
    RestApiId:
      Ref: MoviesApi
    Integration:
      Type: "AWS"
      Uri:
        Fn::Join:
          - ""
          - - "arn:aws:apigateway:"
            - !Ref "AWS::Region"
            - ":lambda:path/"
            - "/2015-03-31/functions/"
            - Fn::GetAtt:
              - FindAllMovies
              - Arn
            - "/invocations"
      IntegrationHttpMethod: "GET"

DynamoDBTable:
  Type: "AWS::DynamoDB::Table"
  Properties:
    TableName: !Ref TableName
    AttributeDefinitions:
      -
        AttributeName: "ID"
        AttributeType: "S"
    KeySchema:
      -
        AttributeName: "ID"
        KeyType: "HASH"
    ProvisionedThroughput:
      ReadCapacityUnits: 5
      WriteCapacityUnits: 5
```

6. Create a Terraform template for the Serverless API we built through this book.

   Answer: In order to avoid duplication of code and keep the template file clean and easy to follow and maintain, Loops, conditions, maps and list can be used to create the IAM roles for the defined Lambda functions:

```
resource "aws_iam_role" "roles" {
  count = "${length(var.functions)}"
  name = "${element(var.functions, count.index)}Role"
  assume_role_policy = "${file("policies/assume-role-
policy.json")}"
}

resource "aws_iam_policy" "policies" {
```

```
  count = "${length(var.functions)}"
  name = "${element(var.functions, count.index)}Policy"
  policy = "${file("policies/${element(var.functions,
count.index)}-policy.json")}"
}

resource "aws_iam_policy_attachment" "policy-attachments" {
  count = "${length(var.functions)}"
  name = "${element(var.functions, count.index)}Attachment"
  roles = ["${element(aws_iam_role.roles.*.name,
count.index)}"]
  policy_arn = "${element(aws_iam_policy.policies.*.arn,
count.index)}"
}
```

Same can be applied to create the required Lambda functions:

```
resource "aws_lambda_function" "functions" {
  count = "${length(var.functions)}"
  function_name = "${element(var.functions, count.index)}"
  handler = "main"
  filename = "functions/${element(var.functions,
count.index)}.zip"
  runtime = "go1.x"
  role = "${element(aws_iam_role.roles.*.arn, count.index)}"

  environment {
    variables {
      TABLE_NAME = "${var.table_name}"
    }
  }
}
```

Finally, the RESTful API can be created as follows:

```
resource "aws_api_gateway_rest_api" "api" {
  name = "MoviesAPI"
}

resource "aws_api_gateway_resource" "proxy" {
  rest_api_id = "${aws_api_gateway_rest_api.api.id}"
  parent_id =
"${aws_api_gateway_rest_api.api.root_resource_id}"
  path_part = "movies"
}

resource "aws_api_gateway_deployment" "staging" {
  depends_on = ["aws_api_gateway_integration.integrations"]
```

```
      rest_api_id = "${aws_api_gateway_rest_api.api.id}"
      stage_name = "staging"
    }

resource "aws_api_gateway_method" "proxies" {
  count = "${length(var.functions)}"
  rest_api_id = "${aws_api_gateway_rest_api.api.id}"
  resource_id = "${aws_api_gateway_resource.proxy.id}"
  http_method = "${lookup(var.methods, element(var.functions,
count.index))}"
  authorization = "NONE"
}

resource "aws_api_gateway_integration" "integrations" {
  count = "${length(var.functions)}"
  rest_api_id = "${aws_api_gateway_rest_api.api.id}"
  resource_id =
"${element(aws_api_gateway_method.proxies.*.resource_id,
count.index)}"
  http_method =
"${element(aws_api_gateway_method.proxies.*.http_method,
count.index)}"

  integration_http_method = "POST"
  type = "AWS_PROXY"
  uri = "${element(aws_lambda_function.functions.*.invoke_arn,
count.index)}"
}

resource "aws_lambda_permission" "permissions" {
  count = "${length(var.functions)}"
  statement_id = "AllowAPIGatewayInvoke"
  action = "lambda:InvokeFunction"
  function_name =
"${element(aws_lambda_function.functions.*.arn, count.index)}"
  principal = "apigateway.amazonaws.com"

  source_arn =
"${aws_api_gateway_deployment.staging.execution_arn}/*/*"
}
```

Other Books You May Enjoy

If you enjoyed this book, you may be interested in these other books by Packt:

Cloud Native programming with Golang
Mina Andrawos, Martin Helmich

ISBN: 978-1-78712-598-8

- Understand modern software applications architectures
- Build secure microservices that can effectively communicate with other services
- Get to know about event-driven architectures by diving into message queues such as Kafka, Rabbitmq, and AWS SQS.
- Understand key modern database technologies such as MongoDB, and Amazon's DynamoDB
- Leverage the power of containers
- Explore Amazon cloud services fundamentals
- Know how to utilize the power of the Go language to access key services in the Amazon cloud such as S3, SQS, DynamoDB and more.
- Build front-end applications using ReactJS with Go
- Implement CD for modern applications

Go Standard Library Cookbook
Radomir Sohlich

ISBN: 978-1-78847-527-3

- Access environmental variables
- Execute and work with child processes
- Manipulate strings by performing operations such as search, concatenate, and so on
- Parse and format the output of date/time information
- Operate on complex numbers and effective conversions between different number formats and bases
- Work with standard input and output
- Handle filesystem operations and file permissions
- Create TCP and HTTP servers, and access those servers with a client
- Utilize synchronization primitives
- Test your code

Leave a review - let other readers know what you think

Please share your thoughts on this book with others by leaving a review on the site that you bought it from. If you purchased the book from Amazon, please leave us an honest review on this book's Amazon page. This is vital so that other potential readers can see and use your unbiased opinion to make purchasing decisions, we can understand what our customers think about our products, and our authors can see your feedback on the title that they have worked with Packt to create. It will only take a few minutes of your time, but is valuable to other potential customers, our authors, and Packt. Thank you!

Index

Twelve Factor App methodology
  about 287
  reference 287

U

unit testing 227, 230, 232
use cases, AWS Lambda
  chatbots 17
  data ingestion 16
  IoT 15
  mobile 15
  tasks, scheduling 17
  voice assistants 17
  web applications 15
user control access
  with Amazon Cognito 270, 271, 272, 273
user management
  with AWS Cognito 277
user pool 270

V

version, Lambda function
  FindAllMovies v1.0.0 135
  FindAllMovies v1.1.0 135
vulnerability scanning
  for dependencies 296

W

web applications
  developing, with Angular 187, 189

Printed in Great Britain
by Amazon

76669896R00237